No Idea

No Idea

Control, Liberation and the Social Imagination

scottish left
review press

Published by Scottish Left Review Press
46 High Street, Biggar, ML12 6BJ, Scotland

Scottish Left Review Press is a trading name of Left Review Scotland Ltd.,
741 Shields Road, Pollokshields, Glasgow G41 4PL

www.slrpress.org

First published 2005

British Library Cataloguing-in-Publication Data are available

ISBN 0-9550362-0-8

Printed and bound in Great Britain by
Digisource, Unit 12, Dunlop Square, SW Deans Industrial Estate,
Livingston EH54 8SB, Scotland, UK

Contents

Section Four
Recapturing the Social Imagination

"Write! Write as if you are writing in the early days of a better world!"

Alastair Gray

With special thanks to Peter Callan, Joanna Cockburn, Jane Denholm, Isobel Lindsay, Jill Powlett-Brown, Kirsty Rimmer, Bob Thomson, Helen Wyllie and Imogen Wyllie

Robin McAlpine is the Editor of the Scottish Left Review

Section One

The Social Imagination

Nabokov's ape

Vladimir Nabokov, author of Lolita, became obsessed by a story he heard about an experiment in animal intelligence. Animals could be observed to calculate, to communicate, to negotiate and to learn, but they had never been observed to create beauty for its own sake – what we might call art. In 1940 in Paris he read about an experiment which was undertaken to see if it were possible to change this; to see if it was possible to teach an animal to create a work of art, to seek signs of an animal imagination. The subject was an ape in the Jardin des Plantes and the process long and difficult. Lack of dexterity, difficulty in recognising and replicating geometric shapes, the complexity of transforming three-dimensional objects into two-dimensional representation; these and many other problems had to be overcome. Above all, it was essential that the ape should have some understanding of what it was doing and why – if the experiment resulted in nothing more than a learned repetitive movement it would prove nothing. However, in time the experiment seemed to achieve its aim. Using a piece of charcoal and a piece of paper the ape eventually managed to create a piece of art. And yet, in this victory the scientist must have found an unpleasant hollowness.

With its charcoal and its paper, the ape drew the bars of the cage in which it had been held captive.

Where are all the ideas?

We have to stop deluding ourselves about the nature of our world. The last 100 years have been among the most violent in the history of the world – Vlad the Impaler could barely dream of an act of violence to compare with Hiroshima. We now live in a world that is possibly more unequal than in any other time – in Western Europe this often seems counterintuitive, but that is precisely because most of us are in the top five per cent of the world's richest. The lives of the many are remote from us.

So what is so new about this? Well, a few things. Firstly, we have the opportunity to know better; telecommunications mean that we as a society have to try quite hard to be unaware of poverty or to see what it does to people. Secondly, we are currently in the most productive phase of human existence and have the ability to do something about it. But thirdly, and most curiously, we have a remarkably ambivalent response to it. From the philosophers of ancient Greece through heretics such as Jesus; from people trying to build alternatives such as the reformers of the Church of Rome in the 16th century right up to dissenters such as the Levellers and conscious revolutionaries such as the Bolsheviks; always there have always been people who drove change. Of course, there still are – but something is missing. Change begins with small numbers of people with a vision. As this vision becomes a set of ideas, more people begin to share them. Eventually, when enough people share an idea, change happens – sometimes gradually but often suddenly.

In the early 21st century you can find people with a vision of a better world – peace, justice, tolerance, equality – but you will struggle to find much by way of concrete plans for achieving it. Put simply, when it comes to changing society for the better we have no ideas. This is an unusual situation. If there is a constant thread through human history it is a plethora of schemes for changing that very history. That we now have only people asking for more of the same or for some of what is currently happening to be stopped is an aberration. This book is an attempt to find out why this has happened.

It will argue that social change comes from a collective vision shared by people in a community or a society – the social imagination. It will argue that vested interests throughout history have opposed and repressed social imagination, but that with widespread education and telecommunication the means by which this is done have evolved. It will explore the ways in which we have been made to believe that change is impossible, but in doing that it will also seek to show how the social imagination can be quickly and effectively recaptured and reinvigorated.

Drawing the bars of our cage

The case of Nabokov's ape seems to be a pretty good analogy of where political debate has reached in the early 21st century. The things that make us think the way we think have become not only enormously powerful, but enormously confining. It has always been difficult to think 'out of the box' (as today's management consultants would refer to it). Those who *really* think out of the box are few and far between and are noted by history – Copernicus, Newton, Marx, Freud, Einstein. Many others are at least willing to try to imagine life outside the box and to discuss and debate what it might look like and how we might get there.

But it isn't a box. A box implies temporary containment; something in which to store your cornflakes until you want to eat them, something to keep the ring safe until you propose, a container for your toys when not playing with them. It is implicit that the box is not intended to be there indefinitely, that the box is not the *purpose*. For the management consultant (a group who will be used repeatedly in this book to demonstrate the vacuity of the pseudo-science that so constrains us) thinking outside the box means precisely to be the first to pour out the cornflakes, to take out the ring, to fetch out the toys. To think out of the box only means to be the first to notice the way it was *meant* to be all along. To talk of a box is to suggest that it is only cardboard, temporary, nothing to be worried about.

We are not living in a box, we are living in a cage. From Plato to Marx and beyond, social thinkers have always thought of the ideologies, philosophies, religions, discourses, myths and sciences which structure our thought in terms of manacles, chains and cages. They are not intended to hold us temporarily until we find a better solution; to rip apart easily under eager hands and release us for the use for which we were destined. They are not a stop-gap, a holding answer to help us along until someone figures out the real answer. They are, by their very nature, a universal truth, a divine insight, the one transcendent answer. The Romans weren't larking around while waiting for Christianity (bear in mind that they crucified Christ). The flat-earthers were not just filling in time until someone discovered that the earth is round. The Roman Catholic Church, Newtonian physics, feudalism, plutocracy; none of these gave up their hegemony lightly. But equally, part of the trick is to make that which preceded them look as obviously wrong as possible. How the medieval cosmologists must have laughed at the flat-earthers when they first realised that all of the heavenly bodies were actually set in seven giant spheres of jelly which rotate around an axis at the centre of the earth.

None of this is news; the charting of our changing epistemology is extensive, the theories and analyses of ideology numerous. What is important right now is to consider the shape and nature of our current cage. Over the last hundred years something slightly different has happened. In the post-Enlightenment world there has been – notionally at least – a democratisation of the social imagination. In theory, anyone can challenge the way things are generally perceived. In theory, we have stopped burning heretics. Of course, the merest glance at, say, McCarthy-era America (or, indeed, any political discussion in the US from abortion to religious observance) or the portrayal of even mild dissent in the tabloid press would disabuse you of that notion. But, slow as it might seem in comparison to technological change, social change – and even more so the debate on social change – has been consistently and significantly more rapid than in any other era. Or right up until the last three decades at least.

Let us consider where we have reached. In Britain we have a government elected with a powerful mandate to deliver social change, and yet there is little to show for it. Ask a Labour MP having served at any point under the Blair era what the Government has actually done and they will, morally offended (this is part of the training), reel off a list of things which have actually been done (this, too, is part of the training). Minimum wage, devolution, tax subsidies to support working families; the list is believed to be impressive. So allow me to disabuse you of that notion. A minimum wage is an accepted piece of social welfare law the world over – even America has one. It is so consensual in most developed economies that it by no twist of the imagination represents radical politics. The introduction of a minimum wage is a very welcome development, but precisely because it was an incomprehensible anomaly that we didn't have one. It was, in a very real sense, the least we could do. So too devolution, something which is common the world over, an integral part of even conservative nation states and which has had demonstrable support of a majority of the Scottish people since the late 1970s. Devolution, enormously important as it will be to the future of the UK and the countries which make it up, is not radical because it is, by definition, consensual. It was the least that could be expected from a democratic government. And subsidising low wage families through tax credits to both legitimise and perpetuate low levels of pay by hugely profitable corporations as radical politics? Proof only of a sense of humour among elected politicians, surely?

More worryingly for those who would like to believe (as we all once did) that the Blair Government was going to make a difference, none of these policies emerged from the Blair 'project' (Working Family Tax Credits being little more than an extension of existing tax exemptions for the poor which were put in place decades ago). Even media commentators who are sympathetic (sometimes verging on sycophantic) to Blair and New Labour are displaying disillusionment at the paucity of ideas in the Blair agenda in his second (never mind third) term in office. If they were being more honest, they would admit that after the first two years of Blair nothing meaningful was done. And once they had admitted this they would come to realise that almost all of the achievements of 'New Labour' were in fact nothing more than the long-standing policy commitments of Old Labour which the new guard couldn't ditch (proper reform of the House of Lords wasn't so lucky, a ban on foxhunting had to be forced through by backbenchers). For anyone interested in social change in Britain, Blairism has implemented some scraps but generated no positive thinking – and even their own free-market-driven initiatives such as partially privatised hospitals and 'faith schools' are old (right wing) ideas.

There is nothing in political debate in Britain which would have been unfamiliar to the political classes of the 1960s or 1970s (other than the ominous international trade agreements and issues such as cloning or genetically-modified food which have been driven by technological advance). The only unfair thing in this analysis is to pick on Blair and Britain; the same things can be seen not happening in almost the entire developed world. (The developing world is another question, giving reason for both optimism and pessimism.) Equally, it is unfair to pick only on the political classes. Academia spent the 1990s discussing irrelevancies, the media ignores anything which does not include a smirking celebrity, campaigners have either failed to produce alternative thinking or thought that they should keep their thinking well inside the boundaries of the cage and the public just switched off. The (sometimes misdirected) belief of the enlightenment and post-enlightenment thinkers that with the application of human will power anything could be achieved was all but abandoned in the social and economic sphere (retaining currency only in the scientific and artistic spheres). Fatalism ensued. We are all complicit in the 'endarkened' decades in which, by failing to shine a torch on our society, we happily left it to dwell in shadow.

This is how the intelligent, committed left came to a place where they can imagine space travel, instant global communication, the modification of the building blocks of organic life, the perfect replication of an individual human lifeform, but are unable to imagine even the most simple of social transformations. (As we shall see in the next section a properly working home delivery system for groceries is beyond the imagination even of some of those who would genuinely like to see a different society). It is the systematic repression of social imagination, the undermining of belief in a better world.

Every era has its cage, its set of ideas and beliefs that constrain its thinking. What is different now is that we have all the intellectual tools to escape many of those constraints, yet we seem unwilling to use them. We are not caged apes, bashing and shaking the bars of our cage hoping in vain for something else. We are Nabokov's Ape. We have been trained in the ability to imagine an alternative picture and to draw it for others to see so they can believe in its possibility. And yet, all we do over and over is draw the bars of our own cage.

The Social Imagination

Loaded trade agreements, broken treaties, war; in the last five years the neo-conservative, free-market ideologues have gone too far. Too far because, after almost three decades in which the active policy of the free-market governments of the West has been to disengage ordinary people from politics lest 1968 ever happens again, 1968 is beginning to happen again. In the '70s the political process of dismantling the post-1945 political consensus was started and the oil crisis was used to make us feel vulnerable and at risk. The '80s saw a concerted backlash against the liberal revolutions of the '60s, and consumerism and individuality were pressed into action as replacements for any other form of collective identity. The 'softer' '90s were about telling us that it was OK to be who we wanted to be so long as we worked hard during the day to achieve it, and that snowboarding (or whatever off-the-peg lifestyle we chose) was more important than politics. All this was an intentional distraction. The liberal chattering classes in the West are much preoccupied at the moment with 'voter apathy' and the disengagement of ordinary people from civic life. They seem unable to recognise that this has been a key aim and necessary goal of the neoconservative movement for at least three decades.

But this is all turning and there are signs of citizens re-engaging. While the anti-globalisation protests in Seattle or Genoa were not particularly representative of ordinary people (although more so than the media would have us believe), when something like more than one in 50 of the British population came out on February 15 2003 to march against the war in Iraq (and for many of them this was a proxy for a more generalised unease with the drift of international politics) something is changing. In Scotland the 2003 election returned a block of socialists, greens and left wing independents which represents virtually the third biggest grouping in the Parliament (this is a very big development in UK politics). Trade unions in France run political and cultural learning events in the summer which attract hundreds of thousands of people. Activists are emerging right across the globe, and they are more informed than ever before.

And yet this movement is still tagged as an 'anti' movement, a protest, a 'travelling circus' in the words of Downing Street. It has been successfully portrayed as having no 'big ideas'. Is this fair? Well, not entirely. Events such as the World and European Social Forums have seen many different kinds of organisation come forward with many different kinds of ideas. But there are two problems with what is happening. The first is that many of the ideas are of the form 'stop...'. So we have 'stop subsidising Western agriculture and dumping it on developing countries', 'stop granting patents on biological organisms', 'stop the international trade in arms' and so on. Every one of these is entirely necessary and unless action of this sort is taken change will not happen. But they do not have the psychological effect of suggesting to us that we have an alternative. They do not look like 'big ideas', like alternative suggestions for how to organise our society and our economy. They are too easily portrayed as a negative agenda, and in the West they do not speak loudly enough to people to explain how the injustices in their lives will be addressed. This is not the kind of agenda which on its own will generate a mass public support, and we all have to recognise that mass public support is necessary if there is to be change.

The second problem is one of momentum and critical mass. There *are* ideas out there which give the promise of a different and fairer way of organising things. Radical economic think-tank ATTAC in France has a well developed manifesto for economic reform with well understood proposals such as the introduction of the Tobin Tax. Radical moves affecting people's lives such as changes in working hours and pay ratio legislation (in which the best paid employee of a company, including the chief executive, can only be paid a limited multiple of the salary of the least well paid employee, including the cleaner) have been proposed. And there are many examples of innovative and transferable practice in social provision, law and education (among other things) which could form the basis of a radical alternative social agenda. Together, these do indeed give the impression that - in the catchphrase of the World Social Forum - another world is possible. But the social justice movement has so far failed to generate the momentum behind these ideas which would put them on the table as a matter for political discussion, to bring them into mainstream political debate in such a manner that Tony Blair and his myopic counterparts around the world can no longer claim that they have no case to answer in their unswerving and uncritical support for the unrestrained market.

So what is preventing visions of change taking a greater hold in public debate? Why is there no *Communist Manifesto* for the 21st century (a period every much in need of one as the mid-19th century)? Well, despite the ideologies of rampant individualism, imagining is more of a social act than an individual act. Our imagination is not a light-as-air emanation from our eternal souls but an act of rearranging the jigsaw pieces of what we know. When the Victorians dreamed of travelling to the moon, they imagined doing it in hot air balloons and petticoats. Before Galileo people did not dream of going to the moon. The problem we face is that new worlds emerge from the imagining of them and our imaginations have been ensnared by the socially-defeatist ideology of the free market. One of the consistent threads in imagination, from the Bible to the counterculture '60s movements, has been Utopia. But it is difficult to find a dream of a Utopia in the last 30 years, a period dominated by the dystopia. The uses of language, ownership and power in the last 30 years have been a specific attempt to end the hope of a utopia. The powerful and the vested interests realised that when people imagine a better world, they do not imagine it with the massive inequalities of wealth that we have now. They do not imagine it with the misuse of power, with the suffering and selfishness, with the blatant injustices which typify free market capitalism. Since 1968 (at least) the free market project has been as much about the contraction of hope as about the expansion of the economy. They didn't want to defeat the Labour movement, they wanted to defeat the belief that there could be a Labour movement.

So how has it been achieved? The control and management of the social imagination is as old as society itself. It starts with the myths of wisdom and age. The earliest communities would structure themselves around kinship, family groupings which were hierarchical on the basis of 'elders' who are to be listened to on the basis of their greater experience and wisdom. People had an intuitive understanding of what their place in these communities was, the structures being fairly simple and stratified on simple bases such as gender and age. Religion emerges for a number of reasons – not least of which an inherent desire in humankind to understand where we came from, where we go to and what we ought to do between these times – but it also has an important role in controlling the social imagination. We are encouraged to believe utterly and completely in a better world (or a transcendental existence beyond suffering, or a better existence in the existing reality, depending on the nature of the religion in question), but it can only be reached by a process of obedience in the world we have – you achieve a new world, you don't change this one. Religion also provides a sophisticated justification of the world we have as the result of the unfathomable decisions made by a superior being, something not to be argued with. The more sophisticated the society, the more sophisticated becomes the religious narrative – it becomes a complex theology with equally complicated structures of social hierarchy.

When large communities start to interact with each other there is a need for even more structuring – kings or emperors become anointed purveyors of divine will, societies need more complicated sets of rules. Trade and war need to be brought within the framework of understanding, and this begins to push at the boundaries of what religion can explain on its own. We start to see science and philosophies (particularly sociology, psychology and economics) exerting pressure on the general narrative which explains our world to us. The Western world goes through an 'enlightenment' when rationality and calculation become the bases for understanding. By the 19th century, however, there is a tension between these various ideas, and we start to plunge into modernity and a different way of seeing the world. Then a couple of crucial things happen. The first is the spread of education. As we teach people the basics of how to think and how to understand so they begin to be able to order their world for themselves. Next we have significant change in social relationships which starts to raise questions about the long-ossified structures which had previously contained the social imagination. On top of this is a much better understanding of a world of diversity (and the Soviet experience is important here as for the first time people become widely aware of different social orders working *at the same time*). And finally there is the phenomenal shock of two world wars which begin to raise questions about our understanding of everything. Then we end up in Paris in 1968 where these trends all come together. An educated, active, engaged and organised workers' movement meets up with a mass student movement and the social imagination pushes French society to the edge of real and significant change.

And that is the last time that it ever happens (in the developed West). From that point on the political and media establishment begins a process of disengagement. We still live in a world which is structured to benefit a tiny minority. The last thing that that powerful minority wants is a powerful and informed majority challenging it, or at least holding it to account. There is much gnashing of teeth over the continual drop in participation in elections among the general population in the West. We are supposed to believe that this is a crisis that worries those in power. Nonsense; it is the desired outcome of a process which has been underway for at least three decades. We are being trained to *not* engage or participate, and that is how the powerful like it. So we no longer imagine a different world but rather busy ourselves with our place in this world. One choice; live with it.

The problem for the left is that this has been the constant state of affairs from the point at which many of us began to learn how to think. The extent to which this elevation of one choice as the only choice has been internalised by the West (this is a process needed primarily in democracies) means that even the left has a nagging doubt that alternatives are possible, and everyone has been trained in the means of discrediting hope ('socialism will never work - look at Russia' as almost any taxi driver will tell you, detailed knowledge of the development of state communism in the Soviet Union or not).

So it is a hopeless case? Not at all. To return where this chapter began, the right has gone too far. The world is getting to a point not of There Is No Alternative but of There Is No Alternative But To Change. It is up to the left to ensure that the change is the right change. A positive agenda for a better world has to be developed and it has to be shared. If a critical mass of people and organisations collectively get behind a number of strong proposals those proposals will begin to look possible. At the very least the right will have to start to engage with them. It is up to the left to paint a picture of a better world and to let as many people as possible see that picture. In this way is social imagination created, and from that comes real change.

This book attempts to look at some of the first steps in achieving that. It will argue that the only way to regain the social imagination is to become aware of what is constraining it and, collectively and individually, to become aware of what is beyond those constraints. That is where we will once again find a vision of a different, better world and the ideas which will take us there.

This first section has provided an introduction to the idea. The next will take a case study of a debate and look at how it has defined its own terms in a self-serving way. The third section will then break down all the means and techniques used to control the social imagination and explore how each works. And the last section will finish with a few thoughts on how we can start to fight back against these constraints.

Section Two

Stuck in Traffic - a case study

Congested thinking

In the summer of 2003 I was having a discussion with a friend about Edinburgh's traffic congestion problems – a discussion which was being repeated thousands of times over in different parts of the city every day. Edinburgh is a historic city of winding streets with few boulevard-style roads to provide traffic arteries. It also has a very compact city centre and the traffic problems that result are compounded by a lack of transport infrastructure – there is little by way of intra-city rail track and no tram or underground system (although the reintroduction of a limited tram service is planned). What Edinburgh really needs is a proper underground system but, in a politico-economic climate which deems public investment of the scale needed to develop an Edinburgh Metro system not even fit for discussion, the debate about transport in Edinburgh now takes place in a depressingly narrow channel.

The question of the future of transport in Edinburgh found itself crawling along a circular one-way system with only one perceivable exit. For two years a major debate raged about the possibility of a charge for bringing cars into the city centre – so-called 'congestion charges'. It reached the point where the controversy was so great that the City Council felt that it had no option but to seek public support for the proposal in a referendum before implementing it. It pulled out the stops, campaigning hard, adjusting the policy to provide opt-outs and perks for anyone who was going to get a vote (but ignoring commuters from neighbouring areas), even – it was alleged – clogging the city with road works in the months leading up to the poll to really make people angry about congestion. The referendum was held in early 2005 and the policy was rejected on an enormous three-to-one basis. But throughout, not a single group – supporter or opponent – put an alternative proposal forward for consideration.

The build-up to the launch of the policy was instructive. If the supply of an effective transport system is denied entry into the debate, the only remaining option for discussion is how to reduce the demand. If the sensibilities of a car-loving nation are not to be offended, managing demand has to be done in a way which doesn't stop people bringing their cars into the city. This only leaves one option; drivers have to be made not to want to bring their cars into Edinburgh. This is going to mean making something about bringing cars into Edinburgh unattractive. What might this be? Traffic wardens with water pistols soaking drivers when they get out of their cars on George Street? Local authority-sponsored tearaways scratching your paintwork while you are in Marks and Spencers? Of course not – it just has to be made more expensive to bring a car into Edinburgh.

How do you introduce the transport policy equivalent of speed bumps? The first attempt was to tax car parking spaces, but this made the simple mistake of trying to pass too much of the cost onto business, something its powerful lobby was never going to allow. So we ended up with a simple choice – congestion charging or congestion. Either we would have a boundary around city-centre Edinburgh which it would cost you something in the order of £2 to cross or we will all die of respiratory disease while stuck in an interminable jam in a smog-filled hell. Frankly, who could argue?

Well, me. My left-leaning, environmentally-aware friend told me that we need congestion charging because we have to end our 'love-affair with the car' (note the dismissive ridicule). There is a characteristic of modern political debate which has puzzled me, and that is the regularity with which I find myself in complete agreement with one half of a sentence while disagreeing completely with the other half. Yes we have to end our dependence on the car, but that does not necessarily lead us to the inevitable conclusion that we have to introduce congestion charges.

I have two specific problems with congestion charging, one practical, one ethical. My practical problem is that, in the long run, it simply won't achieve its aim. The day after charges are introduced, the absolute volume of traffic might indeed decline (as it has in London where charges were recently introduced at a much higher level), but I would expect a readjustment over time. Pay claims would begin to take congestion charging into account and people would gradually return to the roads, like crows tentatively perching on a scarecrow. The cost of housing in London ought to have such a deterrent effect that we should be witnessing a mass exodus, but we aren't. I suspect that this process would have been even more rapid in Edinburgh where there is much less of an alternative – we simply don't have a London Underground and barring the introduction of a proper city-wide park-and-ride system I can't see an obvious alternative for someone like me (I commute into Edinburgh daily from a semi-rural area with little public transport). And even if traffic flows did decrease and stay lower, the problem wouldn't have been solved at all. So long as we have significant amounts of traffic in city centres, most of the associated problems will remain – it only takes one car to run your child down and 80 per cent (as opposed to 100 per cent) of a lung full of particulate matter still isn't good for you.

But it is the ethical problem that bothers me more (after all, a partial solution is better than no solution). Many who have genuine environmental concerns have been too quick to find an accommodation with free-market capitalism. 'If the markets are the cause of the problem', they argue, 'let's use markets to solve those problems'. This is where 'pricing mechanism environmentalism' has emerged from, with an emphasis on changing behaviour by pricing it differently. The problems with this are two-fold. Firstly, pricing mechanisms are far too clumsy for the purpose. Put a tax on dumping waste in landfill sites and fly-tipping increases. Increase the tax on cigarettes and the poorest people skimp on the grocery bill to pay for it.

Pricing does change behaviour, but often in ways other than the one sought. Secondly, pricing does not impact equitably. Pricing mechanisms affect the ability to pay. This might be fine if everyone started from the same base, but they very clearly don't. No rock-star ever smoked so much as one cigarette less because of the tobacco tax, and no aristocrat reconsidered their skiing holiday because of an airport tax. Pricing is wrong because it affects those most sensitive to price – the poor. The high-fliers of Edinburgh's financial district would not be leaving their Audis at home for the sake of two quid. It would be their secretaries who would have had to change busses three times to get from the only homes they can afford on the outskirts of town into the office, a much harder start to the morning than when they used to take their rusting old Nova to a place where they can get a single bus to work. (The night cleaners, like the CEO, would probably be unaffected, having been unlikely to be able to afford a car in the first place.)

Congestion charging in Edinburgh wouldn't have been fair and probably wouldn't have worked all that well anyway. But that does not mean that the rejection of the policy means we are stuck back in our one-way system with no exit, because there were always other approaches. Altering behaviour can be done by pricing it to make it less attractive. It is a perfectly reasonable approach to a problem. We could discourage theft by charging burglars an 80 per cent tax on everything they steal in the financial year, taking the profit motive out and thus making theft a much less attractive career option. Alternatively, we could of course just regulate against it, make it illegal. And just as it is possible to apply the logic of markets to areas we assume will be regulated, equally we can apply the logic of regulation to areas where the market is the sole focus for discussion.

The aim has to be a significant and permanent reduction in the amount of traffic on the streets of Edinburgh, so why don't we just regulate to prevent people bringing cars in? Glasgow city centre is dominated by a pedestrianised 'Z' in the middle of its shopping district. The main parts of Sauchiehall and Argyll Street and all of Buchanan Street are closed to traffic. It makes for a much more pleasant shopping environment and does not appear to have had any adverse affect on the economic performance of the area; quite the opposite in fact – Glasgow has become the biggest shopping destination in Britain outside London since the pedestrianisation development. Indeed, there would be a public outcry if the move were to be reversed and the elegant paving stones ripped up for tarmacadam. There is no reason to believe that a similar (if more ambitious) approach wouldn't work in Edinburgh.

A combination of mass pedestrianisation and the development of a widespread tram network on the now car-free streets would return the centre of Edinburgh to people. People would find their air quality improving immeasurably, they would sleep in peace and quiet, the varicose veins of asphalt we assume afflict all urban spaces could be replaced with land-scaped pedestrian boulevards, trams would take you quickly and efficiently to wherever you wanted to go without the expense of running a car. Perhaps above all the low-level yet constant subconscious stress that living with dangerous fast moving objects create would be gone. The peace people find in rural life might be imported into our cities. Systems of park-and-ride centres, peripheral garages for those who live in a city but need a car for regular travel outside the city, mass subsidised car rental schemes for those who want an occasional trip to other towns or villages, a home delivery network for those who don't fancy lugging their weekly shopping home on a tram. In short, it isn't actually that hard to imagine an alternative to the current traffic problems of Edinburgh which does not put a further burden on those on the lower end of the economic spectrum while failing to solve the problem but rather which safeguards the environment, improves economic performance, protects the health of the population and transforms people's lives for the better.

None of this was discussed. Nobody considered such an alternative. Like children being told not to move away from the swings, we voluntarily populated the narrowest of debates. A host of intelligent media commentators applied their considerable intellectual talents to the question and came out either in favour of or opposed to congestion charges. Academics in our fine universities considered the likely impacts of congestion charging in a sincere attempt to help us come to a decision. The future of life in Scotland's beautiful and historic capital city was reduced to the most facile of questions – £2 or £3?

So I made an impassioned plea to my friend; there is an alternative, and it looks pretty good to me. Her response? "It'll never work. They'd keep delivering your groceries to the wrong place."

Ending where we're supposed to

The case of the debate over Edinburgh's transport system tells us quite a bit. One of the things which defines much modern political discourse is that it is designed from the outset to end at a predestined conclusion. (The tautologies, leaps of logic, false axioms and substitutions involved in the preordained debate are not new; in fact, they mirror closely the twisting logic of much theology.) Let us consider the separate stages through which we ended up in a narrow and unhelpful debate on 'to congestion charge or not to congestion charge'.

The first step in this ideological game of *One Man and His Dog* (our imaginations being the sheep) is to define the question in such a way as to steer the debate away from undesired conclusions. The question grows out of the assumed end-point, not the other way round. Traffic causes many difficulties for urban life. The most significant can be found along the environment/health axis. Even when using unleaded fuel, the emissions from internal combustion engines are (quite literally) lethal. They kill people. As well as the effects of carbon monoxide and excessive nitrogen – both released in large amounts – exhaust fumes contain very large amounts of tiny particulate matter. These microscopic particles of sooty carbon (and worse) are harmful when breathed. They can harm the development of lungs in young children, they can bring on asthma and other respiratory diseases in adults and can be lethal for people who already suffer respiratory diseases. The Institute of Occupational Medicine has said that air pollution kills more than 600 people a year in the central belt of Scotland. And this deadly tide of pollution flows through our cities in very specific currents. You can map their flows – depending on the prevailing wind and the eddy currents caused by buildings, one specific street, one particular alleyway, one town square can have many times the city's average concentrations of particulate pollution. This could be your street. Pollution also affects a city in other ways. It erodes historic buildings, it can affect weather and, simply, it doesn't smell nice. On a wider scale it damages biodiversity and harms water supplies. On a global scale it affects global warming. The emissions from motor vehicles are a bad thing.

In 2000, in the United Kingdom as a whole, 3,409 people were killed, 38,000 people seriously injured and 278,000 people were slightly injured in road accidents. Cars are dangerous and deadly. They make us afraid to allow our children out to play or to walk to school, so we drive them. A less obvious effect, though I would argue every bit as important one, is the psychological impact of this on all of us. The danger of imminent death by motor vehicle surrounds all city dwellers on a virtually 24-hours-a-day basis. Sure, we are perfectly capable of crossing the road safely, but only because we are at all times attuned to the ambient radiation of risk (look left, look right, don't step off the pavement to avoid the woman with the mountain of shopping, I'm five minutes late can I make it across this road?, it's a green man but has that van noticed the stop sign?). Life in cities is inherently stressful, and the constant flow of heavy metal objects is a big factor in the constant chipping away of our peace, serenity and tranquillity.

And then there is the structure of our cities. We seem more and more to be building and adapting cities not for people but for cars. The Reclaim the Streets movement has, in small and isolated ways, shown what it might be like if your neighbourhood was designed with you in mind and not your Vauxhall Astra. Stunts like closing streets off for impromptu parties, even turfing over suburban streets to turn them into gardens help people to see what things might be like otherwise. Compare shopping on Buchanan Street to Union Street next to it (if you don't know Glasgow pick any pedestrianised and any non-pedestrianised streets). Think of the pleasure of lying in Princes Street Gardens during a summer lunch hour (if you don't know Edinburgh, pick your own leafy haven). Have you ever planned a small part of a city in your head (wouldn't it be nice if they took that street and...)? Did this imaginary town planning ever increase the amount of space dedicated to cars? (Imaginary town planning undertaken while stuck in traffic or hunting for a parking space doesn't count...) Even the inhabitants of the most commercially-minded city in the world deep down secretly long for their space back – imagine telling a New Yorker that you were going to build over Central Park.

So let the debate begin. "The daily nightmares that commuters in our cities face must be ended", say our civic leaders. "We have to get the traffic in this city flowing again", say our business leaders. You will therefore allow me a double-take at this point. Forget the deaths, forget the stress, forget the constraining of our lives, forget the corrosion of our heritage, forget global warming, polluted water and threatened biodiversity, forget the theft of our cities by Ford, General Motors, Shell and Esso. This debate starts from the most illogically-skewed premise; that the outcome of the debate has to be a solution which gets traffic moving freely around our cities again. Let us be specific about the goals we are being pointed to. Our aim is to ensure that, for our children's generation and for their children's generation, a future of lungs full of soot, road deaths, stress and environmental and cultural degradation is secured. Is it any wonder that by asking such a stupid and unfair question that we arrived at such a stupid and unfair answer?

This is not just an anti-car diatribe, nor a dig at any specific decision-maker/policy-advisor/elected official. It is not even designed to lead to the answer hinted at above (indeed, it doesn't even formulate a question). It is just to point out the narrow fallacy of the starting point. In the case of discussing the future of Edinburgh's transport we should have started from somewhere other than the place we started. The correct approach would be to assess the impact of traffic (and travel) on Edinburgh, the surrounding area and the wider world. It would engage with the best scientific and social theory we have to test assumptions and inform not only the solutions but also the questions. It would position a debate firmly within the context of other debates taking place – on tackling poverty, on improving social infrastructure, on generating economic development, on reducing crime.

It means resolving conflicting goals (the litany above simplistically fails to consider that there are many communities in the Lothians which simply have to have access to Edinburgh). But above all it would integrate people fully and properly into the debate. People who live in Edinburgh, people who work in Edinburgh, people who work with Edinburgh, people who live outside Edinburgh but rely on its infrastructure, people who visit Edinburgh for social reasons, people who left Edinburgh. This doesn't mean a street survey on congestion charges (done one – ticked the box saying I was sick of traffic and only discovered a month later in the *Evening News* that this meant I was in favour of congestion charging). This means letting these people set the goals, create the question so that, if a successful answer can be found, it delivers what they want.

Why does this not happen? Because it would not deliver the right question and therefore would end in the wrong answer. What is the wrong answer? The wrong answer is any answer which contravenes the boundaries of the existing free-market ideology. Congestion charging is steeped in ideology. It stems from the same ideological heartland as the Poll Tax (it is funny that some of the opposition parties in Edinburgh have stumbled across this analogy although probably only for soundbite rather than analytical reasons). In fact – and this did trouble a few environmentalists and liberal commentators – is came from *precisely* the same source as the Poll Tax. Extreme right-wing think-tank the Adam Smith Institute came up with the Poll Tax, the privatisation of public utilities and congestion charging. It is about shifting cost away from any progressive system of taxation (which would be redistribution). It is about untempered individualism (it is stridently non-collectivist). It is about removing society from the equation (free market – pay it when you use it). It is, in every way, non-progressive. Road tolls, congestion charging and many other forms of needs- and means-blind charging have been enormously popular with the political right precisely because they systematically undermine the idea and ideals of welfare provision – from each according to ability to pay to each according to need.

But, if it is possible, congestion charging has aspects even more insidious than the Poll Tax. The Poll Tax was at least about paying for collective provision (minimal as it might be in its creators' conception). Congestion charging is first and foremost about stopping people doing something by making it prohibitively expensive. And by refusing to have any element of 'means testing' in it, it is specifically designed to stop poorer people doing something. As a sop, its creators say that proceeds will be used to invest in public transport; but, given the scheme's running costs, it is an inefficient way to fund investment. Congestion charging is just as much a part of the global right-wing, free market, every-man-for-themselves hegemony as loaded trade agreements, imposing doctrine through war or intellectual property rights abuses. Make absolutely no mistake, congestion charging is primarily ideological and that is why it had be arrived at as the correct answer (and why in turn the question had to be loaded to arrive at it).

This is the second trick of the debate; to pretend that ideology is finished. This must surely be the most absurd thing about the last decade of British politics for anyone with a passing familiarity with the social sciences – the idea that ideology is dead and that what is now being pursued is a pure, almost Platonic ideal of the pragmatic. "What counts is what works" cry the Blairites, having scrubbed themselves clean of any contaminating ideology that morning. It is of course barking mad – every human action is, by definition, imbued with some form of ideology and even pure maths is only an expression of our current cosmology (when creationism was the dominant ideology it was scientific fact that the Sun orbited the earth). Just as, to enjoy *Peter Pan* we have to believe that a boy can fly, to enjoy rabid free-marketeering we have to believe that it is the only practical option. It is not.

And yet there was something which doesn't seem to add up in this argument. In the Edinburgh debate the case for congestion charging was largely being driven by the left/green axis. Not those who claim left roots while openly and consciously advocating and pursuing a right-wing agenda; the actual left. This needs explaining, but to do so isn't difficult; indeed, in large part that is what this whole process is about. The first two steps explored above are the first two steps in bringing social progressives on board; make sure the question steers people along the right path (and never encourage questioning of the question) and reassure them that everyone is on the same side (there'll be no ideology here thanks – just the facts). So we have set off on a journey which has begun hundreds of miles from the starting point and we are allowing the person who chose this beginning to navigate. What this navigator has to deal with now is the travel sickness.

During the course of the debate, key stakeholders (voters, politicians, commentators, civic partners) were bound to become edgy or anxious about specific issues. Returning to the *One Man and His Dog* analogy, sheep are going to stray, or they are going to start meandering. They have to be returned to the flock and spurred along. What we need here is distraction and motivation, and that's where the environment made its way back in to the debate. Getting traffic flowing again wasn't enough of a motivation to keep all the stakeholders on board, and there was a real risk that people might start asking 'why?'. Distract and loop back, distract and loop back – another characteristic of this debate. When those driving the policy had to defend it in public, they naturally chose the defence that was going to be most palatable to the given audience. When talking to business it was all about economic development and getting the city moving again. 'Frankly, we all like the environment but, in the end, we wouldn't be doing any of this if it were bad for your businesses.' When talking to the population (usually through the local newspapers) it was all about quality of life. 'You will breathe more freely, sleep better and traverse your city with ease.' (Only here is the city conceived as something belonging to the people who live in it.) When talking to members of the political class (Edinburgh is Labour-controlled and the local political structures retain a good number of activists with left or green sympathies) it became about environmental protection. 'We have a responsibility to our planet and to do nothing would be a betrayal of our children.' There were many subtle transformations of each of these arguments (often feeble ones, such as when the social justice question is raised and it is then argued that the move is inherently socially just because the poor usually face the worst consequences of pollution).

Of course, none stands up to much scrutiny. Certainly transport has an economic impact, but it is only one of a number of often contradictory factors. For example, widespread pedestrianisation might have some marginal impact on the cost of deliveries, but it is reasonable to expect that the improvement in shopping environment it would bring about would be likely to increase consumer spending in the area. So much business is now conducted electronically that delivery of goods is the most important economic factor of transport to an area (assuming there is good commuter access); this is seldom done during rush hour so surely isn't affected by the congestion problems. What exactly are the economic problems? Do they make Glasgow, with its significantly better transport infrastructure, inherently more competitive than Edinburgh? Apparently not. The economic case for congestion charging seems weak. But then, a lot of business doesn't really need to be persuaded – congestion charging is right up its street.

There was much more of a difficulty in persuading Edinburgh residents of the need for charging (although, given that there will be a fairly small minority who take their cars out of the city on anything other than an occasional basis, perhaps not as much as might be expected). That is what the 'lifestyle' argument was for but, again, it is hard to see how it stands up. People get annoyed by traffic late at night, and yet how much of this would be reduced by congestion charges designed to target the rush hour and which wouldn't apply after seven at night? People get annoyed by poor air quality, and yet congestion charging would have the specific effect of ensuring a steady stream of emissions-producing traffic through the centre of the city for the foreseeable future. People get annoyed by the risks their children face walking to and from school, but again congestion charging would perpetuate the problem without significantly reducing it (remembering that much of the traffic round schools at this time of the day is the local 'school run' traffic which wouldn't be affected by charging). And anyway, less traffic means faster traffic. People get annoyed by not being able to find a parking place near their homes because of commuters leaving their cars, and yet it is likely to do no more than shift much of the problem to another neighbourhood (presumably the one just outside the charging boundary). Any claims that congestion charging would change the experience of living in a city in any significant way need to be challenged; how does ensuring traffic remains an ever-present in that city change anything fundamental?

And then there was the green argument for those who might have political concerns. Yet they face exactly the same problems as the lifestyle arguments. This move was not designed to result in any significant change in behaviour (only a moderation in it) and would therefore barely have begun to scratch the surface of the problem. There might have been some shift towards the use of public transport, although it is hard to see how many people have not already shifted to that option where it is a reasonable alternative (remember, Edinburgh is not a sprawling metropolis like London and has much less internal commuting). It is likely there would have been fairly minimal changes in the emissions produced at best, and existing behaviour would largely have been embedded (it is hard to see how any of this would have affected levels of car ownership).

These arguments in favour of congestion charging disintegrate at the merest examination. That is because none of them are the actual reasons charges were proposed. They are designed to subdue various constituencies which might have made trouble but wouldn't delve deeply into answers. None of these arguments stand up, but none were going to be rigorously challenged. They were not designed to inform the debate, they were designed to control the direction of the debate. If anything looks like steering it from its chosen path, one of these arguments would be deployed to cut off the counter-debates at the pass. It is argument as distraction (or often confusion because not everyone has the knowledge or commitment to assess them for themselves). A box of arguments, none particularly convincing in itself but which, if used collectively for short bursts each, appear to be sufficiently convincing. If the public consciousness were a whale, thirty harpoons can kill it where one would never be enough.

Even so, you'd think that eventually people would begin to have doubts – or at least might think that, given the alternative, the status quo might be easier and simpler. Frankly, there were lots of the elected classes who stood to lose more than they gained out of congestion charging, electorally speaking. Equally, setting the scheme up was going to be expensive in the short term and there were many more popular things that might be done with the money. This is where we hit one of *the* big lies of current political debate – 'doing nothing is not an option'. What makes this one of the biggest lies is that it is so patently untrue; doing nothing is very much an option. It may not be a sensible option, we may regret it in time, it might even be harder to do nothing than to do something, but it has to be possible – by definition. The imperative contained in this statement is surely objectionable, especially because it is not the imperative of people who want to get *something* done, it is the imperative of people who want to get *their thing* done. Consider your reaction to this command; does it feel empowering or rather does it feel you are being told to step aside. Compare it even to the command that 'we have to do something'. Does this not at least feel that you might be involved in deciding what that something was? These differing reactions are not coincidental. You are not supposed to react to the command 'doing nothing is not an option' in any other way than by submitting, acquiescing. Never trust someone who tells you that doing nothing is not an option.

And then the sucker punch – There Is No Alternative. TINA is the patron saint of the caged mind, of contemporary political debate. TINA is, in barely a breath, the essence of everything that is wrong with our society. There is no alternative to congestion charging, not even the correct ones such as investing more in public transport, taking steps to reduce the need for travel (such as by offering incentives to distribute employment opportunities more evenly), banning traffic from areas of the city, putting in proper park-and-ride facilities, creating affordable social housing in areas suitably connected to employment centres. There is *always* an alternative. Edinburgh is a central city in a global society and economy which has created wonders greater than a park-and-ride scheme. Make no mistake, it is perfectly feasible to create a complex underground rail network in Edinburgh. There may be arguments against doing it – it would certainly be expensive and might not be justified by demand – but we have the riches, the materials and the know-how to do it if we want to. It absolutely *is* an alternative.

If we had had the debate properly we would not have allowed so many possibilities to be ruled out before they were even discussed. The fact is that, from a multitude of options, all bar one were never considered or were ruled out before the debate started. We were given a *fait accompli*, a done deal. Now all it took was to convince us that doing nothing wasn't an option, that better people than us had thought it through and had come up with a solution ('you want reasons, we got loads of reasons') and it was then our job only to realise that There Is No Alternative.

So we can see how one choice became the only choice, and we can see how many in the political classes were co-opted in and many others were (for a while at least) neutralised. But this still leaves behind an important question. We know from where the policy originated. But the Adam Smith Institute (as far as I can gather) did not come to Edinburgh to push or lobby for the city to adopt this policy. The policy itself was first implemented in London, but by a notably left-wing mayor. Those who were most vocal supporters in Edinburgh were the Green Party, along with the more environmentally-minded members of the local Labour Party. It was supported by liberal commentators who were worried about pollution, but it was also supported by some less than liberal commentators who were sick of the Edinburgh traffic. Some businesses wanted it while others did not. Exactly whose agenda was this? It is owned by the environmental left as much as by the ideologues of the far (in economic terms) right. Is this really the end of class politics?

Well, no it isn't the end of class politics. At the risk of sounding outdated (note the pressure to defend oneself in advance from the ridicule of those who despise ideas which are contrary to their dominant ideological viewpoint), congestion charging is a blatant class-based attempt to control our physical public space. It could only be those from an income bracket which would benefit who could favour such an idea – you either have to be pretty unconcerned about a £50 a month hit on your expendable cash (on top of the cost of running a car) or you have to be able to afford a house in central Edinburgh. Or probably both. Even if congestion charging managed a 30 per cent reduction in traffic it would make a barely perceptible difference for those without cars (you'd barely notice it from the pavement). The benefit is to those with cars and who can afford charging. It is an upper-middle-class trick to get the roads back from the poorer.

So how does it end up being the policy of important constituencies of the left? It is not that their core principled beliefs have changed. It is because the horizons of what is considered possible have been internalised by everyone, irrespective of political standpoint. We have all been subconsciously taught to find our solutions from within the parameters of free-market-liberalism. It is epistemology and ideology, a rearranging of the furniture we already have. Our minds have been so colonised by the ideas of one group that this shapes the thinking of all of us, even when we oppose the views of that group. That group is the group with control and power. It is the interplay of the mindset of this group, the power that it holds and its self-interest, which gives birth to ideas such as congestion charging, and it always has. The people who, in their various ways, thought up, promoted, supported and would have implemented congestion charging did not need to get together to talk it through. It is simply the expression of the will of the powerful (even left politicians are the powerful), a will which stems from a largely similar experience of the society they inhabit. Their goals might be different (none of this is to suggest for a second that the Greens didn't want to make a difference to the environment), but because we are all now forced to look from the same perspective, we see things only from a certain angle.

It is one of the difficulties that the new global left is facing. People want to know who the enemy is. People want to know what building they have to storm to bring the revolution. Whose head to cut off? The answer is, first of all, our own. Who forced Nabokov's ape to draw the bars of his cage? No-one did. So it was drawn of its own free will? No. How can both these things be true? Because the enemy within is our own imagination, which makes the left want Adam Smith Institute ideas. The anti-globalisation movement has created its own Winter Palaces to storm; the World Trade Organisation, big corporations, the White House, Fox News. And all of these are institutions which need massive reform. But it isn't enough. We have also to reform the narratives, the ideologies, the discourses; or, in plainer language, we have to start to describe the world in a different way.

But in Edinburgh the congestion charges were defeated, and defeated resoundingly. How did it happen and is it a good thing? Well, there is a final and enormously important process which is necessary to complete a project of this sort. When a policy is bad for a lot of people and where there are lots of good arguments against it, it is simply not safe to let it out on its own. The public space for debate must be controlled. The people who are allowed to write in the newspapers have to be the right people, the stories selected for broadcast news have to be the right stories, the politicians who might throw a spanner in the works must be controlled, the public voice must only be heard when it says the 'right thing', the ability to formulate alternative policies has to be restricted. The control of these things failed in Edinburgh, as did the final underpinning strategy – encouraging people not to get involved at all and to leave it to the 'experts'.

Firstly, the main evening newspaper in the town was fairly sceptical about congestion charging from the beginning and came out strongly against a 'Yes' vote in the referendum. The crucial media space was lost. Politicians are controlled through party whips, but in this case a number of the political parties eventually came out in opposition to the policy (the balance of whether this was principled or cynical is for debate). So the political space was lost. Finally, by calling a referendum the public space was also lost because the public was provided space for a clear and decisive 'Yes ' or 'No', which meant only the space actually owned by the City Council was still fully in the control of those who wanted a 'Yes' vote – which is why the city was covered in lamp-post banners. You simply can't control people's imagination if you can't control the space.

So is this a good thing? Well, it shows that democracy can certainly have a decisive effect, and it shows that if you can democratise space then a diversity of views emerges. On the other hand, it shows that you still need power and money to make those views heard. It would be pushing things to describe the outcome as a triumph of democracy. All in all, for many people in the political classes the whole Edinburgh debacle has been a dispiriting and disheartening experience. But, if nothing else, it shows us what is wrong.

The substance of the bars

The case of Edinburgh's congestion charging is a pretty good example of how our social imagination is failing us, or rather how it has been emasculated through the manipulations inherent in the debate. In some ways it is not the best example of how the process of altering and constraining communal views works. The issue of congestion charging actually isn't as consensual among the middle classes as it could be. Quite a large part of the iconography of middle class life is centred around the car – ownership, status, empowerment, delineation. When we are presented an aspirational picture of middle class life a car almost always features. Anything which has a negative effect on the car has an associated negative effect on the mindset of the middle classes. They see increased petrol duty or higher MOT specifications or more speed restrictions as a direct attack on their lifestyles.

For that reason, not all those who would usually form the constituency of support for congestion charging actually support it. Equally, much as congestion charging conforms to the free market and individualistic view of the world dominant in the current political discourse, there is a strong strand in that discourse which sees any attempt to distort the 'natural' flow of capital as being interfering and wrong-headed; the ability to move your expensively-purchased car around the city as you see fit being an example of that natural order. For these reasons, the debate about congestion charging is not consensual (although these are such bad reasons that the debate is only prolonged rather than enlightened).

There are much better, more ideal-type examples of how the nature of public debate is controlled and shaped to specific ends. Indeed, the way in which the 2003 Gulf War was justified by Tony Blair and George W. Bush in the months preceding it is almost an object lesson on how unhinged we have allowed political debate to become. What is particularly interesting about the congestion charging debate is the opposite effect to the war debate. The techniques of confusion, obfuscation and misdirection used in the justification of that particular war were so blatant and so obvious that everyone noticed them, and for that reason they failed to work (well, everywhere apart from America that is). It was clumsy and made people far too aware of the bars of the cage behind which the debate was taking place. They rebelled against that captivity and that is what brought millions onto the streets of the world in protest.

No, the run up to war in Iraq was an example of a failure to contain people's thoughts sufficiently, despite every attempt being made to do so. It is precisely because people aren't aware of the same things being done in the congestion charging debate and because they haven't taken apart the questions which are being asked that makes it interesting. It is precisely because even those who ought to know better have been persuaded that There Is No Alternative that we should look and ask what is happening.

So, on a wider scale, what is happening? The current anti-capitalism or anti-globalisation debate has highlighted an awful lot of what is happening. The gap between the richest and the poorest in the world has now accelerated to such an extent that we are probably witnessing greater disparity in the concentration of wealth than we have ever seen in the history of human society. Most of us in the developed West can probably count ourselves in the top five or ten per cent of the world's most privileged (is it any surprise that we think the system is pretty effective?) and even we don't feel ourselves to be wealthy in comparison to the really wealthy among us. Poverty and starvation is more widespread than in many pre-modern times. War, terrorism and torture are probably more widespread than in medieval times. We are witnessing the end of the pretence that there is anything approaching an international system of justice.

Frankly, international law only means anything when it is applied to the weak; it is meaningless when applied to the powerful. America has not engaged in a single military adventure in the last sixty years without breaking a significant amount of international law. The extent to which it is overlooked will surprise many. For example, America's preferred method of attack – aerial bombing – is illegal because it fails to make any distinction between combatants and non-combatants. Yet almost no-one is seriously willing to discuss this fact because international law is so far outside the realm of the debate.

The post-enlightenment ideals which we in the West are supposed to hold dear above all are equally meaningless in the real world. We hold the ideal of democracy above all others as a principle beyond debate, and yet well we know that our governments happily prevent or destabilise democracy at our will. Venezuela is only the most recent example of American power being used to destabilise a democratically-elected government because it is doing things America doesn't like. Meanwhile we spend our time replacing international law based on human rights with an international law based on corporate rights. You can be fairly sure that no American president in the foreseeable future has to take account of the possibility of facing a war crimes court when making a decision which infringes international human rights. In contrast, you can be absolutely sure that any government which infringes international trade or intellectual property rights agreements will be prosecuted swiftly and successfully, even if they just want to be able to provide medicines to a dying population.

At the same time we are facing a belligerent attack on the minds and imaginations of a generation. The market has become so powerful that we are now virtually all told what to watch, what to listen to, what to read, what to buy and – by extension – what to think. We have an education system which no longer considers art, culture, creative thinking, self expression or scepticism as central or important. We are expected to accept, to consume passively. Other than passivity, the only other collective emotion we are encouraged to experience is fear; fear of crime, fear of terrorism, fear of asylum seekers, fear of paedophiles, fear of black rap music, fear of gun culture. The fact that cool-headed analysis tells us either that there is little to fear or that there is much less to fear from these things than there was in the past shouldn't get in the way. You are supposed to retreat indoors because engaging with the real world is dangerous. (The panic of a suburban middle class housewife at the rise in inner-city gun crime could be addressed if someone could just explain that unless she wakes up tomorrow as an unemployed black man in her twenties or a low-level drug dealer living in a crumbling housing scheme she is fairly safe).

Meanwhile, we have stripped away most of the moral or ethical route maps which people rely on. We have endless choices and unprecedented power to make them (if we are in that top five or ten per cent), but we no longer have much to tell us how to make those choices. Religion is in decline, moral politics is unfashionable, ideology is decried, families are consumer units rather than support networks. We are floating along in the chilly waters of anomie. We do not have any clear sense of how we would decide which way is up. We are alone. Perhaps one of the most disturbing things I have read over recent times was an examination of what kills young men in Scotland. I would have confidently put the largest killer of young men down as car accidents. If I was told that this wasn't the cause I would have guessed drug- or alcohol-related death. It was therefore something of a shock to discover that the biggest single killer of Scottish men in their twenties was suicide. Surely this ought to shake our belief in our society pretty deeply? Surely we ought to be asking some fundamental questions about this damaged generation? Or perhaps we just set up an emergency hotline...

We have drifted into the 21st century persuaded that, because we have mobile phones, we have achieved civilisation. In actual fact, the plunge into this new century has been characterised almost entirely by dehumanisation and the right of the powerful to impose their will. This does not look like a period of civility, it looks like a period of barbarity. What we seem to be experiencing is the relapse back into the 'rule of power' ethos which the shock of the Second World War made us turn away from.

The three godfathers of 19th century social analysis seem more relevant now than for decades. Durkheim, often the most overlooked of the three, seems to be of prime importance right now. His analysis of suicide, of collapsing moral frameworks, of anomie and alienation, of disorientation seem to drive right at the heart of our current domestic problems. No less so Weber and his analysis of power and influence structures and the extent to which they create and perpetuate our situations. And, of course, Marx's analysis of our entire social and economic edifice as a dehumanising trick to manufacture profit and create the fetishism of commodities keeps proving to be accurate anew for each successive generation. We have a pretty good basis for understanding what is happening.

And there is more to be optimistic about. We seem to be heading towards one of those periods in history where the elastic snaps back. The re-emergence of protest and a surge in interest in political alternatives is a symptom of the experience of oppression by the powerful. Global communication networks mean that it is possible to learn much more quickly what is being done around the world in our names. There is even some hope that political parties in the West are going to start to migrate back to the left (if only because it is hard to see how much further right they could go). And we are perhaps beginning to see one of the most fundamental shifts in world governance to have been experienced for a while – the dispossessed regions are beginning to make their voice heard. It seems much less likely that we will be able to go on ignoring Africa and Asia.

This, give or take significant room for emphasis, is what life inside the cage currently looks like. It is very hard to imagine that we would choose it if we had the choice. And yet we do, of course, have the choice. It is only the bars of the cage, our self-imposed limitations, which are preventing us from moving on and imagining a preferable alternative. As with the analysis of society, we have the framework and means to understand the forces and processes which are constraining our social imagination. They are built only of ideology, discourse and the use of power. Ideology: the way we interpret and understand the things we observe by building them into some sort of cosmology or 'science of our existence'. What is subjective, temporary and optional solidifies into a set of rules which we then believe to be objective, permanent and beyond debate. Be it religion or free-market doctrine, we convince ourselves that what we see is a result of a natural order. Discourse: the ordering of the words and other signifiers we possess to shore up and protect the ideology and the means of perpetrating its will; the use of language and meaning to begin to shape our thought before we have them. The use of power: implementing the actions which grow out of the discourse and ensuring that the ideology and the discourse are not challenged.

These are, naturally, pretty sketchy definitions of concepts which have filled books-worth of philosophical thought. In particular, it may be a mistake to differentiate between discourse and ideology (ideology being perhaps no more than a function of discourse). However, given their regular and distinctive use as popular terms it is helpful to consider them separately. It is also possible (perhaps necessary) to think of the use of power as part of discourse and not independent of it. This is of course true, but it can make it harder to understand when we have crossed over from debate to action. In actual fact, a detailed knowledge of any of these concepts is not necessary to an understanding of what is happening – they describe it rather than define it.

The only mistake which makes it impossible to get to grips with where we are is to try to think in terms of solid or discreet things. There is no single ideology which describes any way of thinking adequately. The whole point of discourse theory is that society is characterised by an endless number of discourses running through, around and into each other. They contradict each other, alter each other and evolve. There are some discourses which are dominant and others which are minority pursuits, and only in an observation of this interplay do we see the wider picture. If this seems too abstract, just think of the difference of view between a libertarian free-marketeer (who will have no qualms about someone's sexuality so long as they are making him/her money) and the religious-right (who believe no less strongly in markets but because they are God's will, while gays clearly aren't). The outcomes are support for free markets and a debate about whether there is any place for morality in them. Either way, we get free markets.

So if we are to attempt to identify the bars of our cage we will need something more sophisticated than charcoal. The substance of the bars is dynamic, endlessly moving and changing, the interplay of power, ideology and discourse suggested above. It makes them more difficult to see (and is the reason we are so quick to redraw the bars whenever we try to imagine something new), but it also makes them possible to change and move. This is how we can get out of the cage we are in, or more accurately, this is how we build ourselves a better cage.

This has all been a rather complicated way of saying, if we want to understand and change the nature of the political debate that hems us in, we need to begin by understanding the techniques that characterise that debate.

Section Three

A Toolkit for Control

The means of control

When one is aware of being controlled, it is much less likely that one has actually been controlled. The subtlety of product placement, for example, can be significantly more effective in making someone desire an object than direct advertising. When we see a movie star drinking a certain brand of whisky in a movie, we are not being told what that whisky tastes like (the thing which ought to be more or less the sole factor in our choice of a drink). In fact, we learn not much about the product but a lot about the associations that product has. When the product is advertised, we know immediately that someone is trying to sell us something and we are much more resistant to the message.

This is the dichotomy at the heart of shaping the modern mind. On the one hand, we are probably more media literate and generally suspicious than any previous generation, and yet we seem more susceptible to persuasion than ever before. That is because the web of influencing has become even more complex than our complex response to it. It is perhaps precisely because we now believe ourselves to have the measure of the salesmen and their techniques that it becomes so possible for them to overcome our scepticism. We think we know when we are being 'sold' and we put our guard up, so when we think we know that we aren't being sold our guard is dropped even further. The truth is that people do have a rudimentary understanding of what has become known either as 'spin' or the sales pitch – an awareness that previous generations perhaps didn't. But it is a very rudimentary understanding. Frankly, few of those who believe themselves to be on the cutting edge of analysis of the world and its affairs have a particularly good understanding of what is shaping their thoughts. The most politically aware, best informed and most intelligent of political commentators simply aren't properly aware of the processes through which their views were formed.

The 2003 war with Iraq highlighted the problem clearly – the vast majority of journalists and commentators simply weren't up to the task of decoding what they were being told, what they weren't being told, what appeared to be happening and indeed what they were actually seeing. They seemed incapable of not being used (in many cases I do not believe they were being used willingly, Fox 'News' aside). The webs of control which shape political debate are too strong for the experts to escape; the general public doesn't have a chance.

And yet, they are far from impossible to see. The techniques which control discussion and debate to lead us to think in a certain way are not beyond the understanding of everyday people. Once you understand and are aware of them, you can recognise them. Once you can recognise them, you have much more control over whether you let them influence you or not. And once you decide what you will allow to influence you, then you are in a position to start to push back the bars of the cage. These techniques are not black magic, they are surprisingly mundane. In fact, it is not so difficult to write them down, and the following chapters are an attempt to do just that.

There is no ideology

There is *always* ideology. Ideology is the set of core assumptions which un-underpin any viewpoint, the series of 'stories' which link together what we see around us and convert them in turn into a coherent narrative. As soon as humans attempt to make sense of the world around them they immediately and automatically create an ideology. Belief in God is an ideology. Believing in the divine right of a king to govern is an ideology. The concept of the nation state is an ideological concept. Belief in government of the people, by the people, for the people is an ideology. Socialism and its many strands and off-shoots are ideologies. And total faith in free markets is certainly an ideology.

We all now accept that the feudal world order with its God-given hi-erarchies is a 'primitive' ideology. We would accept that because we have developed much more convincing ways of describing our relationships to each other and have discovered better ways to organise society (well, we certainly think we have). But it is the nature of every ideology to believe that it isn't an ideology though all the preceding or alternative ways of seeing the world are. Without some giant leap forward in evolution, humans will never have complete knowledge of our cosmos, so everything we think we know will always be nothing more than a best guess, and the gaps will be filled in with ideology. There is no serious thinker who will challenge this, though some would have us believe that through a process of trial and error we have finally arrived at the 'correct' ideology (we will encounter the End of History and the Natural Order below). Ideology is, quite simply, ever-present in human society.

And yet, there is a breed of modern politicians who tell us that their programme for government has nothing to do with ideology. In fact, it is very much the political fashion to stress that whatever your policies are they are not ideological. Blair and New Labour are the leading proponents of ideology-free politics (for American politics ideology is more acceptable so long as it is the right ideology). We have heard the explicit statement that ideology has had its day and we are now only interested in what works best, but even when not explicit this argument underpins everything the New Labour government does. The mantra is 'what counts is what works'. In every policy announcement we are deliberately and specifically led to believe that ideology was a silly argument that only preoccupied the political classes and which was confined to the 1960s, 1970s and 1980s. We are asked to believe that each of these policies are the result only of a calm, dispassionate and objective assessment of what is best for us and the country and has nothing to do with an underlying political doctrine. In this vision of modern politics we have set aside the toy guns, the dressing up clothes, the crayons and all the other playthings which require us to make a creative choice and now we are working solely with the Meccano and we are building only things we need. Blair wants us to believe that, in actual fact, he and his fellow Government Ministers are not really *politicians* but are a new breed of *pragmaticians*. Utter nonsense, of course.

Anyone who has a basic understanding of any social analysis should know immediately that the idea of escaping ideology is not only impossible but is an ideology in itself. No sensible political commentator should accept such a claim. That it is not more firmly challenged is in large part down to the fact that nobody actually believes that Blair is using the term ideology in its proper sense. What he is talking about is the imprecise use of the word 'ideology' to mean doctrine. An ideology and a doctrine are different things. Where an ideology is a way of seeing, a framework for interpreting the world, a doctrine is a set of prescriptions, a programme of action, a manifesto, which is shaped by that ideology. It isn't that the realms of political commentators have become so beguiled by Tony Blair that they actually believe that he has succeeded in seeing the world with the clarity which previously only God could (although to read some you might occasionally think it). What has been widely accepted is that, other than in the most general ways, Blair does not work to a standard political doctrine. Many seem genuinely to believe that in most of what Blair has tried to do he has been driven by a pragmatic managerialism underpinned by a deep personal morality. A politician who is, in fact, outside and above politics. This, too, is of course utter nonsense.

The end of ideology has been trumpeted in a number of different forms. On the intellectual front we have seen Francis Fukuyama and his thesis on the End of History. Under this model we are to believe that we have reached a crucial turning point in social evolution. Much as Blair saw politics ending somewhere in the mid-1980s, Fukuyama has seen history end somewhere around the development of late international capitalism. The thesis is essentially the same – the old games have played themselves out, the opposing forces have clashed and the outcome is not an overall conquering success by one but their mutation into a single consensual belief. And when we all live under one consensual belief, the forces which drive social, political and economic change (that is change in direction rather than development down a single path) no longer exist.

Thus, by reaching a point of consensus which provides an almost perfect understanding of the way humans will live together, we will no longer see the great upheavals of history. It is a view which, in various forms, has permeated itself round the middle-brow thinking classes with some success. Of course, this imagining of a history-free, ideology-free world is open to some serious questioning from the outset. It talks from and to a small proportion of the world and generally describes only their existence. We have to believe that conflict-torn and forcibly impoverished Africa is party to this consensus, that the starving victims of Congo's civil war believe that the Washington model will deliver for them if they are patient. We also have to assume that aberrations such as the rise of Islam and the middle-eastern resistance to much of this consensus is an aberration which will die off as one of the last vestiges of Old History. The usual Western approach applies here – we just assume that if they had televisions they would see the Truth and come round to our way of thinking. (Incidentally, one of the surprises for Westerners of the second Gulf War was the discovery that quite a few Arabs actually *do* have televisions. However, the discovery that all these people see on their TVs is jaundiced propaganda viewed only from one side of the argument explains in large parts the root of the problem. If they had our television, they would think like us – Fox News is the End of History.)

We also have to ignore the many contradictions in this proposal which might otherwise challenge it at home in the West – the growing inequality gap, the widespread resistance to much of this 'consensus', its patent failures. The rule of the Exception Which Doesn't Disprove the Rule will be considered below. Suffice to say that there ought to be enough of simple observational concern to raise significant doubts about this thesis without even having to delve into the conceptual. When we begin to do that, the thesis falls apart even more quickly.

Some simple thought experiments prove problematic for the End-of-Historians. Are there any of these arguments which could not have been applied to feudalism? Would it not be possible to re-write *The End of History* from the viewpoint of a 15th century Scottish nobleman and come to the same conclusion. After all, there was probably a much stronger and more deeply rooted consensus of belief in medieval theological cosmology than there is in advanced capitalism. It is perfectly possible to construct a theory in the terms of this debate which would conclusively prove that feudalism, slavery or any other form of socioeconomic order is in fact the final order and that history has come to an end. If you start to consider the argument in relation to the wealth of intellectual thinking on ideology (in its meaningful, non-Blairite sense) it becomes even more difficult to sustain. Of course we (the dominant 'we' of those who have the power to make their thoughts heard) conceive the world in terms which make our existing order seem 'right'. That is what ideology is. It is difficult not to find examples which demonstrate that history is in action as we speak and that geo-political order has certainly not ossified into one final form for all eternity.

Another example of disappearing ideology is the world of management economics. A fad of Rubik's Cube proportions which lasted for the whole of the nineties, management gurus were falling over each other to demonstrate that running the economy, the markets, the labour force and by extension the world had nothing to do with ideology (here again meaning doctrine). The time spent trying to frame economic and political decisions in terms of an understanding of the relationships of people with people, countries with countries, interest group with interest group, was time wasted. All this did was to result in endless abstract debates about the meaning of life. What we should have been doing was to apply the simple and verifiable effective practices of private sector management. Stop defining actions in terms of the big picture and just do the little things by the unchallenged methods of the market and we'll all get along just fine. By getting rid of ideology we can make the world a more efficient place.

The extent to which this nonsense gripped America in particular over that decade began to feel quaint and dated within a year or two of its peak – surely a failure of the argument so rapid and comprehensive that you might have thought it would end the nonsense for quite a while to come. Not so of course; there are plenty ways to shore up a sinking ideology. Nonetheless, the 'scientifically proven' claims that the stock market would never again fall in value that were taken seriously on a widespread basis, only to be proved wrong by a stock-market crash a matter of months later required some squirming by the free-marketeers. The argument which seemed almost unchallengable in the late nineties – that corporations were by nature responsible and therefore needed to be regulated on a lighter and lighter basis – is impossible to justify after the Enron accounting scandal of 2002. It is possible to list dozens of accepted facts from the nineties management gurus which it is almost impossible to sustain now. And yet what hasn't been challenged is that these were always non-ideological, the mistakes just a misreading of the fact.

It is possible to follow this trail almost anywhere which is within the spheres of government or industry. The content of the school curriculum is now accepted to be a matter of best practice, the funding of hospitals is nothing more than the matter of value for money, the management regime in a prison is purely a matter of delivering a few key aims, downsizing a workforce to increase shareholder profit is simply following the rules. The outcomes are that industry gets workers educated in the way most conducive to its interests (rather than the interests of the pupil), private companies start to make big profits out of owning hospitals, prison management is run on a profit-making basis and poverty pays for shareholder dividends only proves how right the process is. You see, the private sector does things more efficiently – that is why we adopt their working practices – so the fact that the outcomes hand responsibility for things back to the private sector proves that the process is working. We needn't worry about the bleeding-off of private profit because this is nothing more than the fuel which makes this super-efficient machine work. And the fact that it is all so obviously and verifiably 'right' just proves that it has nothing to do with ideology.

Perhaps this need to make ideology disappear is a function of the modern world. In previous world-orders there was no need to hide an ideology because it was so firmly embedded in the consciousness and because the information and conceptual tools to challenge it were not widely available. Now we have a mass of available knowledge which might make us doubt what we are being told about the world. While our media generally continues to act to shore up our world view, it will still show us evidence of the failure of that world view. If a 15th century lord was involved in corruption there would be little chance of it becoming widely known and no opportunity to challenge it anyway. The Enron scandal can't be hidden so easily. Ideology has to be smarter now.

The problem for the free-marketeers is that the dominant ideology is, by its nature, supposed to be invisible. It is supposed to be our way of seeing the world and we are supposed to agree with it so instinctively that we don't even consider it to be 'there'. The problem is that we have access to so much information that we keep seeing things which question our view of the world and this brings our beliefs about world order into vision. Our ideologies are too prone to becoming visible, and when they do they are at risk. For this precise reason ways have to be found of making it disappear again. The management diatribes of the nineties are of the same order as the convoluted attempts of 13th century theologians to tie up some of the confusing loose ends of the Bible (such as how can we find evidence – beyond what we have been told – of the existence of God). They are simply a way of both reinforcing and resisting dissent from the accepted norm.

(Incidentally, it is in fact a mistake to assume the passivity of people in pre-modernity. Actually, the dominant ideologies of the pre-modern world were often challenged by brilliant and intelligent people. Equally, even the lowest orders of feudal society had a much better understanding of what was going on than we are often led to believe. The use of force was regularly used to shore up social order; many of the battles which took place around the reformation and counter-reformation of the Church of Rome in the late 15th and 16th centuries were as much about redistribution of wealth as about theology. Drawing a category difference between resistance to the dominant ideology in the modern and pre-modern worlds may be falling into the very 'End of History' trap which sees Us as of a different order from Them. It may simply be a matter of the pace of social change in combination with access to democratic means of change which is the prime difference.)

If someone ever tells you that there is no ideology behind what they are doing, it is time to start being distrustful. What they think they mean is that they are not following a set doctrine, but what they are in fact saying is that their actions are somehow outside the realm in which they can be challenged on anything other than pragmatic and practical terms. This is never the case. Everything we do is informed to some extent by some world view, by some way of seeing things, by some set of beliefs; in short by some ideology. Therefore when assessing the content and implications of any political debate it is essential to explore its ideological underpinnings. Tony Blair is an unashamed believer in the healing powers of the free market. He is explicit on this, championing international trade agreements which favour only big business, reforming social services in such a way as to hand power and profit to big business, intervening in world events in such a way as the outcome always seems to have significant benefits for big business. He doesn't even deny this. What he says is that it is only an assessment of the most practical approach which brings the greatest benefit to the largest number of people possible. He is driven not by ideology but by personal morality. That he is being dishonest in saying this is not the problem – we do not expect our politicians to be open and honest at this level.

The problem is that this statement is not challenged and assessed on a case by case basis. If it is your morality which is driving you to war, Mr Blair, why choose Iraq when human rights abuses in Uzbekistan were probably worse by the start of the second Gulf War. (Uzbekistan has been a close ally in providing America important military access to the region while Iraq wasn't playing ball with its oil is, of course, the answer). And why after that did Blair urge the world to turn its attention to the atrocities in the Darfur region of Sudan (where between 10,000 and 30,00 people had died in inter-ethnic violence) rather than the Congo (where over two million people had died in inter-ethnic violence)? Might it be because there is oil in Darfur and none in the Congo?

If handing public contracts to the private sector demonstrates genuine public benefit, why are all the contracts so highly secretive (commercial confidentiality simply doesn't wash)? And then we would have to assess the administration as a whole by considering the cumulative implications of each of these cases. This is what we should be doing; we should be looking closely and building up a clear picture of the ideological outlook of the government and making our decision on that basis. We should decide if the hidden doctrine which is being enacted in Britain is in our best interest. Blair purports to have no ideology because if he did he would have to be held account for it. But, just like everyone else, he does, and it is entirely right that he should be held to account for it.

In fact, the problem was summed up in a single sentence spoken by a more-thoughtful-than-average (but basically Thatcherite) former Tory MP at a seminar in Edinburgh. He said "it's not that there is no ideology anymore, it's just that our ideology won". This is rule number one in controlling the political debate; keep the politics out.

There Is No Alternative

Once we are well and truly into the world of ideology-free politics it is never long before we meet the Patron Saint of the cause – TINA. There Is No Alternative is the big lie which keeps the debate and thus any programme for government on track. It is part of the 'pragmatisation' of politics that we ought to assume that anything which can be done has (or will) be done and anything which hasn't can't. Once you have taken ideology out of government you find yourself in the righteous pursuit of the 'best way to do things'. And there only is one best way, because the alternatives don't work. That is what makes them the worst ways and the chosen way the best way. So if you are choosing only between a number of theoretical options it becomes easy to work out which one will work. Once there, you know that the others don't work (or don't work well enough to be considered). That is why we choose the path we do. Because by definition There Is No Alternative.

Let us consider what this means. It means that we can stop worrying about where we are going, because we just have to identify the actions to which There Is No Alternative and follow them. It means that alternative ways of ordering things can quickly be dismissed because they would imply that there is an alternative. It means that we can be comfortable with the entrenchment in perpetuity of what we have got. It means that we have reached the End of History.

Of course, on a case-by-case basis this argument is harder to sustain. It requires that certain assumptions are accepted and certain questions aren't asked. It requires that debate is limited and that those who oppose that to which There Is No Alternative are marginalised by demonisation, ridicule or simply by ignoring them. Thankfully, all of these things are taken care of in the process of controlling debate as we will see. That is why it is possible to accept statements of the type "it is inevitable in this world of mass transit and communication that trade will be international and it is therefore inevitable that we have international trade rules. There is therefore no alternative to continuing to make progress on the General Agreement on Trade in Services".

Well, actually, no. Firstly, there are many alternative forms of international trade and not all of them require trade to be put solely in the hands of multinational corporations. The GATS rules start from the basis that the freedom of companies to trade is the key to international trade. This is not necessarily the case. The freedom of individual countries to sustain a viable local economy from which to export and import might seem to be a significantly better starting point. Restraining multinationals could easily be argued to be the best way to ensure safe, balanced and 'free' trade (where free refers to people and not corporations). There are also many alternative types of trade rule that could be implemented. If your aim is to ensure a global economy of strong and diverse linked national or regional economies you do not codify rules which give multinational corporations precedent over everything else. In short, there are alternatives to GATS. Every free-market messiah who points out the inevitability of the way international markets are developing is being dishonest. The speeches of politicians and business leaders which bamboozle us with the striking changes that technology/cheap transport/communications has brought about in the world to justify the One True Way which has No Alternative are nothing more than sophistry.

On a local level the debate is even more rigid. There are a number of precepts which make this so. So for example there is no denying that people don't like to pay taxes and the freedom of individuals to make choices for themselves is unchallengable. Both of these statements require rigorous scrutiny and in fact they don't stand up as the consistent edifices that common perception would have us believe (to be discussed below). But so long as we accept them they do indeed limit our choices. A state-owned media removes the right of citizens to choose where they get their news from and is therefore wrong (the fallacy of 'free speech' will be considered below). For this reason There Is No Alternative to the current state of affairs. To provide universal high-quality childcare for all would be unaffordable. There is No Alternative to means-tested and targeted benefits and for the same reason we will always have to rely largely on private provision.

Well, no. The BBC is a state-owned media outlet so we already have an existing alternative. What if daily newspapers were converted into a franchise and the number of titles was increased ten-fold. They could be state-funded but the franchises distributed to a large number of different non-profit trusts chosen through a public process to ensure that all strands of political opinion had a fair and representative forum for news and discussion.

You don't need to agree with such a vision to accept that this is at the very least an alternative. It is even easier to imagine alternatives to means-tested childcare benefits to be spent in the private sector. As well as direct state provision it would be easy to impose a requirement on employers to provide childcare for any member of staff who wished to take it up. Public provision would require investment and perhaps a slight increase in taxation, but it is certainly an option. Imposing an additional cost on industry might have a marginal impact on profits, but it is an option. We as individuals sometimes find ourselves in situations where we appear to have no alternative, but even this is a fallacy. We have to earn money to buy our children clothes? Sure, but that broad claim encompasses many possibilities. The amount of work required could be greatly reduced if we take measures to reduce the cost of our children's clothes. We can buy only unbranded goods, we can return to making more of our own clothes, we can recycle. So when you get to the level of government with all its power (and remember that governments have not *lost* their powers in recent years, they have chosen to give them away) you always have an alternative. This is hard for modern governments to accept; if it is true we actually have to hold them to account for their actions rather than shrug our shoulders and assume that There Was No Alternative.

A brief aside at this point. If we are to begin to recapture the public imagination in a way that enables change and can free us to shape our world as we want it, we need to look all the way up. The current system of international market capitalism is only one of a number of models of capitalism. There are alternatives. Beyond even that, as a species with the ability to conceptualise and realise things of an incomprehensible complexity – DNA, satellite communication, space travel – it is possible to imagine a world ordered on a basis other than financial transaction. Even if there are no alternatives currently on the table, it should not be impossible to imagine that there are alternatives to our current economic system. Capitalism itself is optional.

Our natural order

The nature/nurture debate has taken a swing in favour of the former. The question of whether who we are is determined by our genetic makeup from the day we are born or whether we learn to become who we are from our social surroundings has swung back and forward for decades and more. The political right preferred the nature argument; this justified much of the wrongs of society and largely let society and its institutions off the hook. If intelligence is genetic and inherited, no wonder we have poverty and no wonder social mobility is so limited. If it is down to the genes we can stop worrying about education or social welfare. The left, on the other hand, favours the nurture argument. It frees people of personal (albeit genetic) responsibility and condemns the failure of the capitalist system. It is not a cop-out to sit somewhere in the middle on this one (nor does it necessarily weaken any of the left's arguments). The decoding of DNA is a giant leap forward in the human understanding of life on earth, but we are still a very large distance away from concluding that our fates are genetically programmed. That our skulls are lumpy in shape is not in dispute; this does not make phrenology a credible science.

Serious geneticists do not claim to have found the 'shyness' gene. This is a construct of the popular ideologies of our times. Few of us are competent to assess the scientific significance of recent discoveries or their application to public policy. But that does not mean we cannot see the context in which they have developed. Remember, science is a way of seeing the universe, a sort of cosmic ideology. Scientific models tell us as much about the age which generated them as the cosmos they describe. The medieval cosmology which saw the universe as seven planet-encrusted rotating jelly spheres circling round the axis point of earth was a decent shot at describing the observable night sky given the astronomical tools of the time. But what it actually told us about was the intensely hierarchical system of government and social order out of which these cosmologists peered. They were recording the social order as much as the physical order. The spheres were a reflection of the hierarchies of feudal society.

We of course believe that we have evolved beyond such crudity. Well, our tools have improved, our data is significantly better and our models are certainly more sophisticated, but it is arrogance to assume that we have hit on objective certainty. We are still making best guesses and no more than that. The science we have tells us about our priorities. The cost of unlocking DNA has been conservatively estimated in the billions of dollars. This will be a very great underestimation of how much it really cost – after all, the education of all the bioscientists who *didn't* cut the mustard is just as much a part of the final expense as is the education of those who did (which wouldn't have been factored into these calculations anyway). And in the sense of 'standing on the shoulders of giants', the years of expenditure prior to that is also a necessary cost. Suffice to say, the money spent to unlock human DNA is significant. There is little doubt that this will prove to be money well spent in the long run, but it has been a political decision to spend it in this way. If a fraction of this money had been spent researching the social issues which affect health there is every reason to believe that as many lives might have been saved.

The emphasis on DNA also reflects the priorities of a post-enlightenment society which believes that a lengthy formula based on four letters could unlock the secret of everything human. It may very well do so, but equally it may turn out to be of more limited use, telling us only what to do when the genetic order goes wrong. It is simply far too early to tell. Just try to bear in mind the cosmologists of the spheres. Think how certain they must have been that they'd cracked it. Think how they must have congratulated themselves when they unlocked the secrets of the universe. Now consider how the cosmologists of a millennium from now will consider our new certainties.

What the tale of the unlocking of DNA points us to is the resurgent belief in a 'natural order'. For most of the twentieth century Western civilisation concerned itself with dismantling a belief in natural order, with the decaying of certainties, with existentialism and chaos. In the plastic arts the defining forms were cubism – the dismantling of form as we know it – and abstract expressionism – the abandoning of recognisable form altogether. In music we saw the dismantling of accepted tonality. In literature we found existentialism, stream of consciousness, unreliable narration, magical realism. In science we had relativity and chaos theory, changing forever Newtonian certainties. Where Newton from his 18th century enlightenment viewpoint saw two objects colliding in certainty, Einstein saw from his relativist century some partial observer watching two objects collide. The collision we can only know from one viewpoint at a time, not absolutely.

But the social mind has fought back, and it may be dragging the rest with it. The relativist world probably reached its peak in the 1960s. Since then the social conservatives have fought back. They have demanded a natural order. They want a God back. They crave certainties. They need you to know your place. In many ways America provided more freedom for the human imagination than any other country. As of last year, 80 per cent of Americans said they would consider voting for a black president. Even around 60 per cent said they would consider voting for a homosexual president. But fewer than 50 per cent would consider handing the keys to the White House to an atheist. Belief in a natural order is rampant, and it is right at the heart of what is constraining the political imagination around the world.

You will find the resort to natural order all over the place. The free market is the natural way for humans to distribute commodities. Women staying at home is the natural way to raise children. Acquisition of property is the natural way for humans to exist. Physical love between two people of the same sex is not natural. The poor will always be with us. You can't change human nature. It is in a boy's nature to play war games. Greed is inevitable. The extent to which Joe Public is an expert on genetics, social conditioning, communal morality and trading relationships never fails to amaze. Why did three millennia of philosophers waste so much time considering the human existence?

However, to reject the rigid natural order put forward by the neo-conservatives is not to accept that the corollary is true. Things do fall, things do decay, people do die. There are indeed some certainties in which we can see order. Equally, there are a range of less tangible certainties; all humans are capable of compassion and cruelty. But neither compassion nor cruelty are part of a definite natural order. It is perfectly possible to imagine a world of almost total cruelty. If we didn't stop to look closer the last decade of life in the Balkans could look that way.

Equally it is possible to imagine a world dominated by compassion. We have an entire branch of literary imagination dedicated to it which we call utopianism. Therefore neither total cruelty nor total compassion is part of a natural order. We can choose. There is a simple test for what we should reasonably call 'natural' – it has always existed, it will always exist, it exists everywhere and it behaves consistently. Gravity (to the absolute extent of our knowledge) is part of an inescapable natural order among which we live. Money and greed are a choice.

Always beware of anyone who tells you that something is automatic or natural, that it will always be this way or that it is pointless trying to change something. Unless they are talking about the basic laws of chemistry, physics or biology, they are wittingly or unwittingly trying to stop you thinking of an alternative.

Controlling space

People whose eyes well up when they talk about freedom of speech better have had experience of living under a repressive dictatorship; if not they are really kidding themselves. In the modern Western world, freedom of speech may not have become entirely meaningless but it is far from meaningful. Firstly, speech isn't free in the sense that you can do it without fear of consequences. Secondly, speech isn't free in the sense that you can use it without having to pay. When it comes to self expression, free neither means liberated not without cost.

Why is this? Because to speak is only half of the equation. It is easy to speak almost indefinitely but unless someone is listening it can have no effect. After all, words are just words unless someone recognises the meaning behind them. And for words to be heard, they need a space, and that space is rigorously controlled. Study after study has shown that, during the Iraq war, your chances of being interviewed on television were enormously reduced if you took the majority position and opposed the war. Marches of tens, even hundreds, of thousands of people were given virtually no coverage – and yet pro-fox hunting marches of many fewer people garnered massive coverage. A tree falling in the woods only makes a noise if the media hears it.

There are many ways in which space is controlled, but they fall into two main categories. The first is controlling access; controlling who is able to be heard in the first place and controlling which voices will be called upon to comment on any issue. The second is tone and presentation, controlling the terms and context in which an issue is discussed and therefore how it is perceived and understood. Indeed, this type of control regularly goes much further and actually consciously chooses and defines what is accepted as fact and what fiction.

In all discussion of the issue of controlling space it is important to guard against the view that people are now smart enough to recognise that they are being controlled and therefore choose not to be controlled by it. This is a myth. Cynicism may very well have increased over the last couple of decades, but that does not mean that throughout history ordinary people were not actively aware of being manipulated. In fact, when people refer to the new powers of immunity to manipulation by media and government, they are usually doing so by reference to the period between 1940 and 1970. During this thirty-year period the shattering effects of two wars had generated something which was approaching a much more consensual Western viewpoint. People wanted to believe that civilisation had been saved and that was where they were living. In this regard that period was probably an anomaly – the exception rather than the rule.

During the twenties and thirties there was real social unrest in Britain and the working class uprisings or the suffragette movement probably lead to a much more intelligently sceptical understanding of the control exerted by the powerful and a much more realistic assessment of the power of the ruling classes to shape the world in their image. The same is probably true of the Victorian era when ordinary people would be perfectly well aware that the rules were both set and interpreted by a small elite. This pattern probably extends back indefinitely – feudal peasants who knew perfectly well that the feus raised by local lords were not being used to glory God or to protect the kingdom but to provide a life of luxury for the aristocracy and so on. No, we are no smarter or more sophisticated in our understanding and analysis of the means of control now than in previous eras. We just think we are.

Let us first consider the disappeared. In times of war the application of control is always more blatant. What appears on our screens and in our daily papers is filtered more consciously than ever. As soon as the second war on Iraq was launched, anti-war sentiment largely disappeared from view. The anti-war Daily Mirror did at least maintain some muted criticism of what was going on and, along with the anti-war Independent and Guardian, was the only source of even partially balanced information on what was going on. But even here balance was not really typical of most news reporting. In the run up to the war, opinion polls generally reported opposition to war at between the mid-60 to mid-70 per cent mark. Then, when war began, the polls shifted to show support for the war running at between the high 40s and high 50s per cent mark.

With one voice the media reported this as a big swing in support for war. In actual fact, this shows something more like a swing of only 15 per cent which, at a time of war, is remarkable. Indeed, the most interesting thing in this was that this was the least popular war in which Britain had ever been involved, with barely half the population supporting it. However, that is the problem of presentation which will be discussed below. What represents a problem of access here is that no representative of that approximately 50 per cent of the population who did not support war (it would be wrong to describe 'don't knows' as opposing the war but in this context it represents a specific lack of support) was given any air time and very little by way of column inches. The three main UK political parties either supported the war with gusto or were afraid to speak out against 'our boys'. Individual politicians who opposed the war either chose to be silent or were only news when being vilified. And because we have a news system which considers the views of any individual who is not an elected politician or any organisation which is not a political party to be something other than mainstream news, all other voices disappeared.

People will point out that the Guardian (or in Scotland the Herald) printed lots of anti-war letters and gave space to many anti-war columnists, but the news element of the paper (i.e. the bit which people believe to be 'true' rather than just an opinion) was substantially the same. There is a little reason to be sympathetic to news editors in this. It is difficult to know what is a legitimate voice. An elected politician has, by definition, some legitimacy for what he or she says, whereas the chief executive of a pressure group has no clear mandate. This is, nonetheless, a very great failure of space, both political and media.

During more normal times, things are little better. Unless a politician (and it really has to be a senior politician) holds a view it is unlikely to become news. The hundreds of thousands of protesters who have been conveniently wrapped up in the banner of 'anti-globalisation' have been granted almost no voice. In fact, they have almost no face. We are only shown a couple of hundred of them rioting, never tens of thousands of them making legitimate protest. Tony Blair memorably informed the nation that "these people have no arguments, and where they do they are totally and utterly wrong". This is hard for most people to challenge because most of us are given no opportunity to hear what those arguments might be. Most people will probably believe that anti-capitalist protesters are just rioters, a gross and unacceptable distortion.

There are more subtle forms of access-denial. Listen to your evening news broadcasts and consider the accents you hear. Skip over the anchors and commentators – no-one expects them to be representative. Skip over much of what someone has decided is news (what constitutes news will be considered below) such as money markets and the trivial concerns of the business classes. Listen to the rest. Even here the accents are the same. In Scotland you will only hear a broad dialect accent in one of three occasions. The most common incidence of dialect is crime stories – neighbours commenting on someone from their street who killed their children despite having seemed 'quite a nice guy', poor people caught up in scams, stories on vandalism, petty theft and so on.

The second is when a story stumbles into an area where the interests are primarily working-class interests – closure of a factory, increasing debt burdens, local authority policy making. The third is where big politics meets small politics – the devastation of the fishing industry, the fire strike. When you start listening like this you will notice some odd things. For example, when the broadcasters want to put together a package on how debt is affecting people it is more often than not that they will interview a middle class family who is about to lose their house and be forced into the indignity of living in a council house and scrapping their foreign holiday this year. That is not to dismiss the fear of the family, but it is to say that next to a family where the mother has been beaten up by debt collectors, had their possessions sold and is about to be evicted from the very council house that the middle class family is petrified of being given, their concerns are less alarming.

Yet for some reason the television producers assume that the middle class family is more like 'us' (again, 'we' and 'you' will be considered below). Another thing you will notice if you keep listening is that these voices are rarely asked the question 'why?' and only occasionally the question 'how?'. All that television reporters want to know from someone who speaks in dialect is when, where, what and who. The assumption is that a middle class middle manager has something to tell us about what the mass redundancies caused by 'downsizing' in his company means for the state of the economy but that we have nothing to learn about this subject from one of those made redundant. The poor have no power of analysis in our media. They are not analytical beings ('why did this happen?'), they are purely sensory and emotional beings ('did you see this happen?', 'what did it feel like when it happened to you?'). They are also victims and suffer fates which make us want to turn our heads. There is no space for the intelligent working class in our media.

It is not just these political issues which are largely controlled by limiting the access to space. We have an entire generation which thinks it chose that Celine Dion album when in fact it was chosen for them. The songs that get played on the radio are selected by a combination of senior programmers and big business (which bribes and bullies the programmers). The CDs which get advertised are the ones which big business chooses to advertise. Record shops run promotions on these same albums. Other shops play the same tunes in the background. If your song is not one of these predestined few, you can almost forget mass sales. In fact, the most common way for smaller acts to get cross over is for them to be placed in some other mass-market product such as a film or an advert. But this is not particularly liberating, given that all the adverts are owned by big business and the movies we have the opportunity to see are controlled much more rigorously than the music we can hear.

We can listen to music anywhere but movies need a cinema (there is DVD and video, but to raise enough awareness to make an impact films need a theatre release first). And given that the number of cinema screens is limited, and given that most of them are owned by big business, it isn't exactly difficult to see what chance a small independent film has. Sure, some break through, but not many. And most of those which we think have made a breakthrough are not actually independent films at all but are small projects from big studios which catch them unawares. It is possible to do this indefinitely.

Consider everything you have bought recently (much of which you undoubtedly like) and consider how much of a choice you made. Your clothes probably came from one of a dozen shops which are actually owned by fewer than half a dozen parent companies. Your car came from a giant manufacturer with enormous power over dealerships. Your furniture probably looks surprisingly similar to your neighbour's furniture. Your microwave oven, manufactured by one of a single-figure number of white good producers and sold in one of a handful of retailers, is microwaving a pre-packaged meal sold by one of the big-five supermarkets which dictated to the farmers who produced the food what size each vegetable had to be and exactly how much it had to be sold for. The spaces where you buy things are ones over which you have minimal control. If you doubt it, try to buy a non-sweatshop produced T-shirt or a copy of Noahjohn's excellent 2001 album *Had a Burning*. These are not out-there, kooky or esoteric choices. Nevertheless you will find it difficult. And that assumes that you have ever had a chance to hear (or hear of) Noahjohn or can find out how your clothes were manufactured.

This is another consequence of the control of space; the myth of Freedom of Choice. We are told that you always have a choice. Even if someone is about to kill you you still have the choice to go out quietly or go out putting up a fight. This is true, and gets right to the point of the problem. It is more a freedom of selection than a freedom of choice. If the soon-to-be-deceased in this parable *actually* had a *free* choice they would presumably choose not to die. This is not a choice open to them, so they select between two ways of dying. Yes, we can choose to fight back against the colonised space, but consider how difficult that is. Like the T-shirt/CD example above, it can be done but it is difficult. Set yourself three very reasonable ethical guidelines for how you interact with the social space around you. Let me give you three simple ones: don't listen to second-rate corporate music which is forcing aspiring young musicians to give up; don't eat food which is excessively processed; don't buy any products the manufacture of which significant affected a person's human rights.

None of these ethical guidelines seems to be unreasonable. Indeed, *not* having ethical guidelines of this sort seems entirely wrong. And yet stop and think how much effort you would have to go to follow them. You couldn't even enter most shops or shopping centres, almost all pre-prepared food would be off-limits, you would be unable to own the standard range of white goods, clothes would be very difficult to find, the radio and televisions would be a problem, in fact it is barely worth documenting just how restricted your life would be if you chose to live by these guidelines. Choose your own and try the same thought experiment before talking about free choice. And, in any case, free choice requires open access to information and an empowering education. After all, a choice which is not informed by these things isn't really a choice, it is a guess. Sure, people can avoid mainstream music (actually more of a puddle than a stream) but how would they know what to buy instead? Without the information it is difficult to know where to begin. You could buy specialist music magazines and try to establish what you think you might like and take a chance. You could get to specialist music shops with listening posts (although even this is more difficult than you might think). And you could get into the habit of having to order all your CDs in because they are not held in stock. But it is hard. In any case, far from being encouraged and enabled to do these things we are discouraged and hampered. Through all the techniques discussed in this chapter, we are brainwashed into thinking that, because the thing we have is not objectionable, it would be foolish to look round the corner.

So access to space of all sorts is controlled in all kinds of ways. But it is not just the control of access which is the problem but the control of content. The question of what constitutes legitimate news will be discussed below

– this is such a big issue it needs to be considered separately – but irrespective of the news selected, its presentation is crucial.

This is another area about which masses has been written. There is no way to know world leaders personally, so we can only know them through the media. George W Bush is so obviously intellectually limited that anyone who has heard him speak unscripted becomes aware of it, and yet the right-wing newspapers in the UK have desperately been trying to paint a different picture of him as a misunderestimated (to use his own mangled phraseology) moralist. Meanwhile, erstwhile Labour MP George Galloway asks perfectly legitimate questions about the Iraq war and is called a cowardly traitor (and as a result is expelled from the party). Israel is a victim of unprovoked terrorism, big business corruption is the fault of individuals and not of regulatory frameworks, the abolition of foxhunting will cost thousands of Scottish rural jobs, privately-educated children are more intelligent than state-educated children, there is doubt over whether global warming exists, the British Empire was warmly welcomed by the nations it conquered. None of these are true, and yet they have all been reported as fact in recent years.

When it comes to perception, the distortions become even more ridiculous, with moderates being called extremists and extremist being called mainstream, liar called honest and the honest called liars, the patient called impatient and the impatient called patient and so on. In the run up to the second Iraq war President Chirac of France said he would refuse to support a United Nations Security Council resolution authorising war. In almost all of Europe this has been viewed as a wise, sensible and (at least partially) moral stance. It was met with widespread support across the continent. Except in Britain where the media colluded with the politicians to present it as arrogant and unreasonable, childish and short-sighted, and (for The Sun editor Rebecca Wade the ultimate insult) 'typically French'. The British public seem to agree. So are the people of Britain somehow different from the other peoples of Europe? If they are so sophisticated in their ability to avoid being hoodwinked by media distortions, how come they have followed the views of the media in the opposite direction to their closest counterparts? Where exactly are they getting these aberrant views from if they are too smart to be influenced by the Sun?

In the British tabloids the distance between editorialising and reporting is almost indistinguishable. Meanwhile the broadsheets do little to move in the other direction. The right-wingers (Times, Telegraph) do much the same thing but with more sophisticated editorialising, the left-wingers (Independent, Guardian) still allow the debate to be shaped in the same way. *They* didn't say that the French were being extraordinarily reckless in threatening to use their veto, but they did report Foreign Secretary Jack Straw saying this very thing and failed to balance it by giving any prominence to the views of the representatives of the large majority of the other countries of the United

Nations which would have pointed out that it was Britain and not France which was reckless and out of step. The choice to not know something when the opportunity to know it is readily available has been called 'knowledgeable ignorance'. This kind of reporting is not factually incorrect, nor is it deliberately biased, but it is knowledgably ignorant, and the effect is much the same.

A final example from the Iraq war. The world saw the pictures of the Statue of Saddam Hussein being toppled in Firdos Square in heavy rotation – the iconic image of the fall of the Ba'ath regime that the Americans and British so longed for. I asked a number of friends for an estimate of the numbers of Iraqis celebrating in that square. Sensing that by the nature of the question it wasn't as big as they thought they offered modest estimates of about 5,000. In actual fact, this tallied with my own first reaction. It wasn't until I was sent a wide-angled photo of the toppling two days later that I discovered that there were fewer than 50 Iraqis in the square, and that they had been escorted in by the American soldiers. This was a clear set-up, and by use of close cropped camera angles the world had been fooled. It was followed up with lots of shots of Iraqis with posters of George W Bush (no-one seems interested in where these posters might have come from) and playful children. I guess that in the weeks after the war I saw in total a few hundred cheering Iraqis in a city of six million and a country of 50 million. Yet the whole of Britain believed that there was overwhelming gratitude towards the invaders. We know better since, and yet even then we were not seeing it in realtime. It would take a number of days before the media would finally decide that it couldn't ignore events any longer. The siege of a city would only emerge (in the mainstream media) days after it began. Oil pipelines were regularly bombed and still 'threats' of pipeline bombing were being reported as if they weren't happening.

Or how about Venezuela? A country in which a mass strike by the people has brought the government to the verge of collapse. What is not reported is that this mass strike is run by and involves not the people but the corporations, determined to overthrow the government precisely because its policies were providing a decent welfare state for the people and funding it through progressive taxation. How could this confusion arise? Well, for one thing all of the television stations are owned by people who are prime movers in organising the 'strike'. It will probably not surprise you to discover that these televisions stations fail to cover the massive pro-government demonstrations – unless something illegal happens, in which case it leads the news.

By way of an *aide memoir*, Hugo Chavez was democratically elected with an enormous majority and still maintains extremely high levels of support among the poor (which in Venezuela is a significant majority). It may also be helpful to remember that when an attempted coup by some military

54

generals was reversed by ordinary members of the armed forces who remained loyal to Chavez it was American military helicopters which flew out the conspirators, and a British Foreign Office Minister was quoted as saying that he hoped Chavez had learned his lesson.

Almost none of this was reported in Britain. This partial telling of the story continued. The opposition eventually amassed enough signatures (although there were serious doubts about their authenticity) to invoke a recall election which Chavez himself had written into the constitution as a check on the abuse of power. Throughout the campaign there was media reporting in Venezuela and around the world suggesting that the contest was too close to call. In *The Independent* newspaper on the morning of the result there was a story claiming that Chavez had been heavily defeated. He won by a landslide. The media reporting of this story would have made you believe something approaching the opposite of the truth, simply because the vested interests of much of the media ownership wanted it to be so (and because of extensive US investment in disinformation about the country).

The funeral of the Queen Mother in 2002 was reported in terms of millions of grief-stricken and grateful subjects thronging the streets to pay their respects to her cortege. I have looked at a lot of the close-cropped pictures and can see no part of the route where the crowds are more than a few deep. If so (and we can be sure that there are no more convincing pictures which the royalist press chose not to use) the reports of how many turned out would seem to be well wide of the mark. Everyone ought by now to be aware of how footage and pictures of the 1984 Miner's Strike were selected – every picture showing what appeared to be angry and threatening miners, no pictures showing the widespread police brutality which had caused much of it. But few of the smart, sophisticated media generation *do* know it. It would be no difficulty to fill a book much larger than this with nothing other than thousands of examples similar to these.

Freedom of speech? A member of the middle-of-the-road pop-country band The Dixie Chicks said that George W Bush made her ashamed to be from Texas. American radio stations – most owned by a conglomerate called the Clear Corporation which had funded and organised pro-war rallies during the Iraq war – refused to play their records. The pro-war rallies (which, in spite of the money and power behind the organisers were poorly attended, certainly in comparison to the 500,000-plus people who marched against war in New York) organised ritual destruction of their albums. Remember, this is the same corporation banning their records and organising their public destruction.

Freedom of speech? See what happens if, as a public figure in America, you take a pro-abortion stance. Freedom of speech? As an ordinary citizen try and make your voice heard on any issue deemed left-wing by the mainstream media. Free choice? Try to make a choice other than those big business would like you to make and judge how free you were to make it. Space is fundamental – it is where we live, it is where our minds are created, it is where we shape the world. But it is almost wholly owned and controlled by a minuscule minority of the world's population. The depths of the penetration of the control over us and our lives which this engenders cannot be underestimated. Yet it almost always is.

Deciding what is news

Among the porn and the Viagra salesmen, the worldwide web has given us access to information we could never have dreamed of getting access to before. Take a look at a website like www.newseaum.org and you will discover things that you couldn't discover by reading every line of every newspaper published in this country. Newseaum provides a copy of the front pages of the day's papers from right round the world. OK, you will need to be pretty multilingual to absorb it all, but it will quickly demonstrate that in the scheme of things gossip about the stars of soap operas is not actually all that important. If you were to explore you would discover that Africa is full of countries with different governments doing both good and bad things on a daily basis. You would discover that there are artists and writers working in Latin America. To your possible shock you might find that there are scientists in the Middle East working on renewable energy or diabetes and not just weapons of mass destruction. Asia may have bird flu (well, at the time of writing the front page headlines in Britain reveal that a total of sixteen people have caught bird flu in the last six months) but it also has a thriving airline industry. Or how about the 'Japanese play football' shock?

We live at the very bottom of an enormous inverted pyramid of information. At the top of this upside down triangle is what we will call, for the sake of a manageable phrase, 'the real world'. Here you will find almost 200 nation states with a similar number of governments each making a vast number of decisions every day affecting the six billion people living in them. These people meanwhile are doing things too – protesting and writing, cooking and inventing, shopping and murdering. Add to that the forces of nature and there is a phenomenal amount of interesting and important things happening on any one day.

The next layer of bricks down our upside down pyramid is the global media, a world of newspapers, news-sheets, pamphlets, radio and television shows, the internet and academic journals and papers. These will cover everything from the effects of global warming to the announcement of the marriage of two young people in the remotest part of northern Pakistan. There will be lots of things which go missing between 'the world' and 'the global media' – generally things which could condemn the most powerful – but there is at least enough general information to put together a fairly good picture of a lot of what is actually happening. We probably won't hear much about the work of the covert security services but we could get a pretty good picture of the state of human rights around the world (for example).

Unfortunately, even with the internet we don't in practice have access to the global media so we have to make do with 'our media'. Suddenly we find ourselves plunging down the sides of our pyramid to a much narrower segment close to the bottom. The first thing that we lose is almost all of the information about things which happens outside our country. We get quite a bit of information about the United States of America and it is perfectly possible to keep up to speed with the ins and outs of what is happening in the White House or who is being executed for what in which US state. We get a basic rundown on what is happening in Europe, but only if it has implications for more than one country or if it happens to be an issue which by coincidence is also high on the news agenda in Britain. So we suddenly learn about how the French healthcare system works but mainly because we happen to be having some problems of our own in this area. And yes we know the outcome of the referendum on the Euro in Sweden but that is of collective interest. Beyond that we will only hear about the exceptional or things which have a direct impact on us. A particularly bad air accident in Asia or a worse-than-usual famine in Africa will worm its way into our media. A much smaller air accident will also get into our papers if there are British passengers. War is always of some interest, but even this is sporadic – you can run a civil war for quite a few years before a UK-based news editor discovers that children as young as eight or nine are fighting in it and suddenly this becomes something worth showing, at least once or twice. But beyond this we have virtually no knowledge of what is happening in the world.

And while this amount of knowledge is a possibility offered by 'our media', it is mainly notional because by the time we hit the bottom of the pyramid we have left behind the theoretical and we come face to face with the reality. It is not 'our media' which we get our information from but 'the things we read/watch'. So we can find out a bit about the various civil wars ravaging central Africa if you regularly read the Guardian or the Independent's international news pages. But unfortunately we don't. The minority of us who read broadsheets do not read every bit of the broadsheets, and the sections most likely to be browsed or skipped altogether are the international pages; that is why they always come at the end of the news sections. Meanwhile if you read a mid-market tabloid (the so-called blue tops) you are going to have to work much harder to find out this kind of information, and if your daily read is a red top tabloid you might as well forget it. When it comes to the bottom of our inverted pyramid, the place where you find most people, there is little on offer worth knowing.

This has effects on many levels. On the most obvious level it means that we simply can't form opinions or views on the world because we are totally ignorant about it. Should we have bombed Afghanistan? Why are you asking us– we read the British press. How would you be equipped to assess the government's foreign policy when you know nothing about anything foreign? So in our glorious accountable democracy how do we hold governments to account for the many world-changing foreign interventions we make? The simple and depressing answer is that we don't. Until it tips over into a situation where our armed forces are at risk of being deployed we simply don't know it is happening. Then, when we discover it is happening, we have no basis for deciding whether it is right or wrong. So we frankly don't bother and we let the government of the day get on with it in a virtually unaccountable way.

On a deeper level it continually reinforces a particular kind of world view. If you never show the people of the Middle East curing cancer and instead you mainly show them blowing other people up, it is inevitable that you begin to develop a certain worldview of the region. If nine out of ten images of Africa are of desolate rural areas and not of their bustling modern cities, is it any surprise that we generally believe that they are a primitive 'race' either in need of our help or beyond helping? If we skip over the massacre of hundreds of thousands of dark-skinned people while dwelling indefinitely over the murder of two blond girls no wonder we have such a partial view of the value of life. We are trained how to think as much by what we are not shown as by what we are shown.

And don't for a second think that there is anyone in power who is worried about this state of affairs. It is not for them a case of unavoidable reality, it is a case of the utterly desirable. The manipulation of news sources on foreign affairs by government is extensive. Through a continual system of releasing and withholding information according to the interests of our leaders we are encouraged not to know. This will not be much of a surprise to anyone. We know all the justifications – we're only giving our readers what they want, if we put it in they wouldn't read it anyway, this isn't relevant to our readership and so on. Which by the rules of our corporate media is fair enough. Just don't pretend we live in a functioning democracy.

Nor does this limit itself to geography; we are denied access to information on a subject basis as well. If you were to try to work out what the biggest problems facing Britain were by assessing the content of the media you would conclude that we were all dropping dead of mad cow disease but that poverty was pretty rare. You would conclude that the merger of large corporations was quite a few times more important than low pay. And you would certainly conclude that football and soap operas were of infinitely greater significance than the virtual extinction of many of our native species of plants. If our media reflects the place we live in then we must be experiencing mass hallucination.

It really is unnecessary to dwell on this. We know we are ignorant and we know that we don't know much about things outside our daily ambit. In fact, a lot of us make quite a virtue of this, almost bragging about the 'inconsequential' things happening to foreigners about which we have no interest. What is less obvious is what is done with the news we do get. The way news is reported is a complicated process of filtering, assessing and presenting which is absolutely laden with value-based assumptions. The news media has decided that we're going to skip most foreign coverage altogether. It has then decided what of the rest of what's left is 'important' or 'interesting'. There is at least a crude measure of 'interesting' in circulation figures, but even this is misleading. Yes, the news-lite of the tabloids appears to be popular, but does that therefore mean that people are uninterested in anything which isn't in these papers? If news of monumental corruption and American collusion in Peru was squeezed in among the semi-naked women would people just skip it? The case of Vladimir Montesinos is pretty riveting; a handsome and charismatic secret service leader who secretly films himself offering bribes to hundreds of leading figures while all the time being backed by the CIA? This man embezzled billions of dollars and lived the life. Surely this might be of passing interest to people who are titillated by scandal and wealth? It seems that we will never know.

So if the definition of interesting is a troubled one the definition of important is even more troubling. Recently the BBC national news led with the story that an American cable television corporation which no-one in Britain had heard of was launching a hostile takeover bid for Disney. Now this is certainly a piece of news which would be categorised as interesting purely on the basis of the iconography of The Mouse. It would also produce the world's biggest media conglomerate which is certainly of some importance. But to whom exactly? What makes this so earth shattering (it hadn't actually happened at the time it was reported and later fell through) that the British public *en masse* are required to believe that it is of overriding importance to them? Frankly it simply isn't. Unless you are dealing in the stocks and shares involved or you are keenly interested in media ownership patterns and their implications it is simply of no more than a passing interest. Fat cat tries to buy out fat cat – not exactly the thing most people are going to lose sleep over. Business news is repeatedly given more priority than, say, employment news. Given that the vast majority of us are employed but few of us are businessmen in any meaningful sense, the balance should be the other way round.

Why isn't it? Well, partly it is a conscious choice to define what is important. It is always useful to look to the tabloids for crude examples. Asylum seekers posed and pose no threat to Britain or to levels of unemployment here – the numbers are too small. But a group of tabloids decided that this was to become a major news story which was to be of interest to all of us, and they single-handedly made it so. In the same way there are plenty forces who would wish us to consider the profiteering of business as of great importance and so they stretch and strain to make it a high-profile matter. The number of business-orientated newspapers which have been launched in Britain only quickly to fail shows the imbalance between the desire for people to care about business and the reality. In almost any other sphere a single failure of that sort would be the death knell of that kind of niche marketing.

But it is not all conscious. The news editors who are the key arbiters of what we are going to read or hear have to produce a lot of papers in a year. They, just as much as anyone else, get drawn into an automatic response to whatever it is they see on a daily basis. When we get to our front door in the morning we can, without thinking, identify which letters are ones we want to read and which aren't. We may very well get it wrong and if we are putting aside bills which we really should pay it may not end well for us. But we do not need to think to make this quick filter. In exactly the same way news editors know fairly instinctively what has proved to be a popular or effective story in the past – things which ran, things which caught the public imagination and so on. It is painful to say, but as soon as the news editors saw the photographs of Holly Wells and Jessica Chapman, the two young girls murdered in a small English village in 2002, they knew what they had. The picture was simply so powerful that they would know without having to think that people would want to read about it. They were two pretty girls wearing a football top of the country's most popular team with the name of the English football captain on the back. They were smiling and it was difficult to imagine how they could have looked more wholesome. The priority it was going to receive over the following year was clear immediately.

The same things happen in a much more subtle way with the lower profile stories. News editors on most of the popular press dismiss immediately things they consider to be 'for the chattering classes', 'the usual do-gooder stuff' or 'for the bleeding hearts only'. This could mean two children of a similar age to Holly and Jessica who died for reasons of poverty – tuberculosis brought on from substandard housing will get some coverage, but the prejudices and assumptions which come into it will relegate it well down the agenda. Tuberculosis is not photogenic, it isn't sudden enough, there is no identifiable perpetrator and there is an assumption that poor people die while middle class people don't which makes the deaths of the poor inherently less important. Similarly in the other direction; this is about a business deal so it must be important even if I can't immediately get personally excited about it. A church leader has got excited about something and while it is hard to see what exactly is bothering him there are presumably lots of his followers who want to hear this stuff. And then the very same editors note continually what their peers are putting in and leaving out and they learn.

However it isn't just what gets in but how it is presented that matters. The deliberate editorialising of tabloid news 'reporting' can actually have less effect than people believe. While the drip-drip of stories such as the asylum story have an alarming cumulative effect, the more apparent the editorialising the more people are likely to be suspicious. There is a more subtle and every bit as damaging process of deciding what kind of news a piece of news is. There are certain types of story which are considered to be 'good news' and certain types of story which are considered to be 'bad news' and quite why they ended up in these respective categories is not immediately clear. Take for example the matter of house prices. It doesn't matter where you look in the media the vast majority of reports of house prices consider rises to be good and falls to be bad.

Now, what house price rises mean in reality is that people are going to have to outlay an ever-growing multiple of their salary if they wish to live in a house. People are being forced into increasingly less affordable debt (especially first-time buyers) and given that prices are rising equally for buyers and sellers hardly anyone (other than dealers, property agents, developers etc.) experience any financial benefit. So why exactly is it considered good news? Rapidly falling house prices are certainly bad news for a lot of people; if the value of a house falls rapidly people can end up with an asset which is worth less than the current borrowing on it. But it is an entirely illogical deduction that because falling house prices are bad then rising house prices are good. Virtually the only reason that house prices fall is because they have previously risen too fast and the market is correcting itself. If there hadn't been the unrestrained inflation in house prices there wouldn't be the crash.

There is another reason that house price rises might be considered to be bad news. In almost every other area of life we refer to increasing price as inflation and inflation in any other circumstance is considered by almost everyone to be bad. So what is different about house prices? Well, they act as an important buffer to the economy. Over the first half of the first decade of this new millennium we have seen a massive crash in the value of the stock market. Throughout the '90s currency and economic stability had been underwritten by the illogical promissory note that was share prices which were worth more than the security to which they were nominally tied. People had speculated wildly not on the value of things which could be measured (real estate, capital) but on things that couldn't (brand value, 'coolness'). So when things collapsed something else had to be found to anchor a global economy which was overpriced. Something was needed which was solid and steady, which didn't collapse or disappear and which was capable of absorbing all that unsecured capital. The thing about property is that its value is defined more by price than by cost; that is to say that the value of a house is not in its bricks and mortar but in its desirability. It is worth precisely what someone is willing to pay for it so collectively the housing stock can absorb a lot of the imaginary money which would have brought the global economy down if it didn't have a home to go to.

This is an acute example of why house price rises are good news; they are not good news for people who live in houses but they are good news for an abstract economy the functioning of which is so illogical that it needs sumps and buffers to absorb the shocks of the speculation (i.e. gambling) which now fuels it. So we all cheer when the latest house price index shows a rise even if it means that few of us really gain and many of us end up less secure or worse. Similarly praise the Lord for giant corporate mergers; yes we might all lose our jobs but look what it does for the stock market. And let us be grateful for productivity increases. It would be churlish to complain that they are often achieved by depressing wages, worsening working conditions and lengthening working hours when some corporate manager gets his profit margins up. Good news all of it. So there is a deeply embedded value system which consciously and subconsciously defines what is news or not news and what is good news and what is bad news.

Above we saw how the selection of voices used in our news broadcasts is heavily skewed away from the working classes. What does this mean for the wider 'voice' of what constitutes 'important' news. Perhaps someone would attempt to argue that lower levels of education or interest in politics means that the working class genuinely have nothing to say. This is utter nonsense. One of the defining features of much of life on the margins is paradoxically that people tend to become entwined with the political process; welfare systems, anti-poverty projects, the caricatured subjects of political debate. A project was run in an area of Scotland which had been designated as a 'Social Inclusion Partnership', that is to say an area of multiple deprivation which is targeted for social development activity. The project interviewed people in the community about their views on what was being done, how effective it was and what they would do differently.

The transcripts of the interviews are fascinating. Certainly the language is not that of the standard political commentator. It uses dialect, slang and metaphors and similes which would not usually be used by an academic, say. However, there were two things that struck me when I read them. The first was that while the language might not be the one we have become familiar with in politics, that was often because the lazy use of cliché was replaced with a living description of the matters being discussed. The second thing I became aware of was that much of the analysis of the problem was infinitely more sophisticated than that which passed for debate on the subject in the Scottish Parliament. This is not patronising; rather quite the opposite. What politicians don't recognise about the project-focussed approach to relieving poverty is that most of the cost is associated with wages and the wages are invariably paid to people – 'experts' – who live outside the community. The approach can have benefits but in the end it is trying to tackle lack of money in a poor community by filtering money into wealthy communities. A number of the respondents to the survey were not only very well aware of this policy inversion but had both a detailed critique of it and alternative suggestions.

So there is really no justification for excluding working class voices from any position of power or insight in the media. What about the corollary? Who is news when they speak? Well, the main answer to that is businessmen. If you run a business of almost any sort virtually anything you say turns out to be of news. "Chief executive of company says anti-English sentiment is harming Scottish economy" has been known to be the front page lead in a major broadsheet newspaper. But what exactly qualifies this businessman to make such a comment? His social science degree? His broad-base research on the subject? Something new and important to say? Of course not. He is just considered to be important and happens to have an anecdote. Business leaders are one of the most biased and least balanced commentators in the world. It is a simple fact that they have a degree of self-interest which stretches round everything they do. If you listen carefully and for long enough you will find that every problem in the world can be traced back to business taxes which are too high and employment legislation which protects workers too much. Profiteering and mutilation of workers is the key to all good things, apparently. And your argument need only be backed by an anecdote. Recently the higher education sector in Scotland was attacked twice by businessmen. These happened within six months and both caused consternation among politicians who Wanted Something Done About It. The first was a chief executive who complained that he couldn't get graduates with the skills he needed, which included both a background in engineering and foreign language skills. The second was a chief executive who complained that he couldn't get the bioscientists he needed because all the graduates he came across had diluted their scientific studies by wasting their time learning foreign languages. Both of these things constituted news. Neither was backed by any evidence. Can you imagine the leader of even a big charity making the front page by throwing out an opinion on something he or she was neither qualified to comment on nor could back up with any evidence? No, because that isn't news.

As a species we defer to the leaders of our pack just as much as any other animal. The things which are presented as important by people or institutions we consider to be important (and for all the scepticism about them our newspapers are still considered important) is internalised by us as something important. We learn, like any other creature learns, by what we see. Africans are poor and helpless. Arabs are bloodthirsty nutters. The environment isn't important but corporate mergers are. Unemployment ('downsizing') can be good news. The poor have nothing to say for themselves but business leaders are a fount of wisdom. The selectivity of information we are provided and the way it is assessed creates both ignorance and false knowledge. It makes us believe things that aren't true, makes us celebrate things which are bad for us and hides from us things that ought to make us furious. None of this is random; all of it points us in the same direction, and all of it reinforces the same narrow political programme which is propped up again and again for reasons we don't understand.

Read all about it indeed.

Just the facts

Thankfully, among all the selectivity and ideology there are clear and identifiable facts upon which we can make decisions. Except it isn't as straightforward as that. Our unerring faith in science leads us to believe that we can at least partially live among definites, that while interpretations may vary we still have the ability to identify what is always so. So while it is up to policymakers to decide what the tensile strength of the crash barriers at the side of a road bridge should be, the scientists can absolutely agree that if a car breaks through the barriers gravity will cause it to fall. Yes, there are some scientific assertions which we can take to be almost unchallengeable such as the existence of gravity or the chemical reaction which combines hydrogen and oxygen to create water. But that doesn't actually tell us much. 'Scientific facts' tell us that action X will result in reaction Y (or more specifically that in all observable cases this proved to be true). It is just that there is far too much complexity in everyday life to be able to conclude much based only on observations of this sort. Almost no decision is made on the basis of this sort of 'fact' alone, because there is always complicating contexts. No treatment is given the go ahead to be provided by the NHS purely on the basis of whether it works or not. There is a mass of other considerations which have to be taken into account and these include cost and infrastructure. Science only provides us with a guide.

Equally, science itself is often contradictory or can lead to alternative conclusions. In the past month there have been news stories about research which shows either that cannabis consumption can be more damaging to the lungs than had been previously thought or that cannabis may actually prevent degenerative brain diseases such as Parkinson's or Alzheimer's. How does this enable us to draw conclusions about the 'safeness' of cannabis and whether it should be decriminalised or not? How do policy-makers balance this against the many other pieces of research into cannabis use? Science does not tell us what to do, it only tells us what was observed to have happened in certain circumstances. And then there is the selectivity of how research findings are used. On the non-conspiratorial end of the scale there is the selectivity in the way the media adopts some pieces of research and not others purely on the basis of whether an editor considers it to be 'news' or not or whether it is suitably quirky to prove interesting to readers. And then there is the presentation – newspapers want to deal in absolutes, so in the pages of the tabloid newspapers 'cures for cancers' are regularly discovered but the identification of certain types of gene which may have a role in finding and identifying cancerous cells doesn't appear to happen much. That this is because the latter is usually reported as the former doesn't usually register in the public consciousness. On the more sinister end of the scale, research is specifically manipulated to produce a pre-defined and politically-motivated outcome. And yet, even though we know this happens (or should at least have the ability to know that this happens), we want to believe in the infallibility of science.

The ways in which the use of 'objective statistics and evidence' can be used to manipulate the public imagination is startling. Perhaps the most blatant and widely-known use of this kind of distortion relates to the global warming debate. Right now the human race is engaging in activities which are both depleting the earth of resources which it is impossible to renew and which are producing outcomes which our ecosystem is unable to absorb. The level of atmospheric nitric acid production which takes place for reasons other than human activities (mainly as a result of lightning) is part of a balanced ecosystem. The additional nitric acid created by the internal combustion engine is not. That is why we need to worry about acid rain.

This is even more apparent when it comes to carbon dioxide production. Through a combination of the destruction of the means of converting carbon dioxide back into oxygen (especially deforestation) and the very sharp increase in the carbon dioxide generated by the burning of fossil fuels, we have a higher preponderance of this gas in the atmosphere. The scientific models of our atmosphere we possess lead us to believe that this causes heat to be trapped beneath the outer layers of the atmosphere, resulting in global warming (the so-called greenhouse effect). This is supported by data which shows that there has been a steady increase in the global temperature since the industrial revolution began the greenhouse gas-producing phenomenon. That doesn't tell us everything, however. There have been all kinds of climactic changes in the global ecosystem over the millennia and we do not always fully understand the causes. The death of the dinosaurs and the ice age may be the results of external agents – such as asteroid impacts – but they may also be part of a general pattern in our ecosystem which produces occasional periods of rapid and extreme weather changes. So perhaps we are living through a period during which our weather systems are undergoing a flux which is not entirely due to the activities of mankind. Even so, that should not get us off the hook because it is still within the best guess of our existing knowledge that the lifestyles we are pursuing are very likely to contribute to the problem. And in any case, there are many other good reasons to moderate our behaviour – not least the fact that we are destroying irreplaceable resources (who knows, perhaps the future will reveal that the elusive cure for cancer will turn out to require a chemical only found in the oil supplies which we have just exhausted) and producing all sorts of pollutants.

So we have a world of science which points to one conclusion – we have to wean ourselves off of our reliance on fossil fuels. But that creates a political problem for the US whose entire existence is currently built on the ability to burn fossil fuels. The American economy is an oil economy and the American way of life is fuelled by oil. Changing this will involve not only real effort, it will mean facing down some very big financial interests. It does not take an expert in geopolitics to know that facing down big financial interests is not on the agenda of the George W Bush administration – quite the opposite in fact. So ways need to be found to create an escape route from the scientific consensus which will enable America to persuade itself that it doesn't have any scientific obligation to change. It is around about this time that a small number of scientists start to produce highly-contested counter theories which now 'prove' that it isn't in fact hydrocarbons which are producing global warming. Suddenly certain things don't matter to those who like the science to prove their point for them. It doesn't matter that these quack scientists are discredited by the rest of the world's experts on global warming. It doesn't matter that the data on which their case is built is far from convincing. It doesn't matter that these scientists turn out to have been funded by the very oil industry that was desperate to prove its lack of culpability. What matters is that American Big Oil and its client government can now stand up and say 'your science says one thing, ours says something else, there is no consensus on global warming so it is pointless us trying to do anything about it'. End of debate. End of Kyoto Agreement on global warming.

The much-trumpeted cynicism with which people approach what they are being told about the modern world loses much of its efficacy when it comes to science. Sure, there have been so many food-related health scares recently that people have become relatively immune to being told that eating X is bad for you, but generally we are still suckers for anything someone in a white coat tells us. There is reason to be worried about this. There has been a creeping big business infiltration of academia of late. In Scotland almost half of the income of all of the universities put together comes from private sources. Some of this is entirely positive – the fees of overseas students, for example. But some ought to make us uncomfortable, because it is generated by co-opting academics for the use of global corporations. This would be a worry even if rigorous academic standards were always applied, because it progressively skews the interests of academia towards the interests of profit-making enterprise. But rigorous academic standards are not always maintained (this has not emerged as a major problem in Scotland yet, but that is no reason to be complacent).

The nature of some of the commercial research contracts signed by universities in the US is contrary to the academic standards of full disclosure and impartiality. Contracts have been signed which specifically prohibit the publication of any research outcomes which might prove detrimental to the commercial interests of the commissioning company. For example, universities are agreeing to suppress results from a drug trial which might prove that while the drug may help with the disease in question it can prove to be lethal for some patients. Science can never be purely objective – as discussed above it will always be shaped by the society and belief structure from which is emerges. But that does not justify it being overtly dishonest. Science is increasingly becoming a tool with which to make us believe whatever it is that the scientists' paymaster would have us believe.

What this should alert us to is that the one thing people think is objective and beyond question – the natural sciences – is no such thing. It should not take you long to conclude what this means for those 'sciences' which are not based on the observation of physical, chemical or biological processes. The social sciences are by nature much more interpretive, and very much more difficult to disprove. We saw above how business interests invariably equate to authority. The same is true of business interests in the social sciences. In actual fact, most of the body of academic work in the social sciences is sceptical about the agendas pursued by the free-market ideologues. The leading figures in this cannon (Marx, Freud, Mills, Hume) all warn us against believing in the simple assertion that what is good for business is good for people. Indeed, that is why the right-wing media are so consistently antagonistic to academia.

And yet the vast majority of social science research which seeps into public debate appears to point in the opposite direction. Any economic consultant who makes an assessment or a prediction is co-opted by one side or another to 'prove' their point. The fact that most of these assessments and predictions are laughable in terms of academic rigour is ignored. On the morning on which I am writing this one of Scotland's broadsheets has led on an assessment of the Scottish economy which would have us believe that we are all doomed, carried out by a consultant with a very strong personal interest in generating that sort of coverage (remember, consultants are by nature always looking for work). The report of this 'research' is patchy and gives little indication of the data on which the assessment is built. Nor does the report consider what assumptions have been made. What it does tell us is that the problem has been caused by business rates being too high in Scotland.

It is probably a reasonable assumption to make that this assessment is the stuff of ego-driven snake-oil-salesmanship, that it is based on no data which would justify the conclusions, that the assumptions which have been made would not stand up to any critical scrutiny and that the conclusions are of little value to anyone who is interested in anything other than seeing their business rates bill slashed. What is certain is that I am aware of alternative research which is much more soundly based which indicates that the level of corporate taxation has no simple relationship with economic performance and that there is a host of evidence that higher rates of business taxation can in fact strengthen economic performance. These pieces of research seldom make the front pages.

When it comes to telling us how our social world works the manipulation is even more startling than the manipulation of what we know about the physical world. There are two quick examples which neatly illustrate the point. I was involved in a project which sought to compare 'productivity' in the different public services to identify which was performing best. Productivity is an input-output measure which tells us whether things are being done efficiently. So we mapped inputs against outputs in a number of areas and graphed the conclusion. Higher education came out well because the number of students being educated per million pounds of investment just keeps rising. Health did badly because new medicines are expensive. But the best performing public service in our model was the railway network. This is of course insane – the rail network is falling to pieces and the service is an utter mess. But by failing to invest in things like trains that work or track that won't kill you and still stuffing the passengers on this creaking mess, the productivity looks impressive. So the 'science' disguises the fact that productivity is often a measure of failure.

Another is the bizarre turn of events in the Scottish economy. For a decade and more the economic performance of Scotland has been a matter of large-scale angst. Right wing commentators have been lining up to tell us that our misplaced obsession with society and its ills is foolish and that it is time we woke up and got profit into the country again. In recent years this has reached fever pitch. A small group of economic evangelists have made their name and reputation through the mantra of 'educating' us all to take the economy more seriously – indeed more seriously than anything else. Our economic growth has been lagging behind the rest of the UK for the most part of two decades and something major had to be done. Nothing else really mattered – we had to act.

A series of lectures was organised by the world's leading economists to tell us where we were going wrong. Political parties started falling over each other in the rush to present themselves as the businessman's friend. Then to a minimum of fanfare it was announced that in actual fact they had been calculating economic growth by the wrong method all this time and when the same methodology used by the rest of Europe was adopted, it turned out that Scotland had outperformed the rest of the UK in economic growth for all but two of the last ten years. We will truly believe anything someone with a calculator tells us.

The fetishising of the 'scientific analysis' of economic and social factors is a never ending source of humour. There are regular news stories informing us of things such as 'personal emails sent at work cost the British economy £4 billion a year'. OK, I made this number up, but so did the people who wrote the real story. No serious thinker would believe that it was possible to draw any conclusion of this sort. In fact, the statement is so ludicrous that it seems worthless to take it apart, but just consider two factors which need to be taken into account in arriving at such a conclusion: how much time *over and above the time that is spent on other personal matters* does emailing constitute in a day (i.e. take off £X for every email but offset it by adding £Y for every personal call or internal gossiping session or staring out of the window which would have happened otherwise) and how do you price it meaningfully?; and how do you assess the productivity increases which we know are gained by allowing people short breaks in which they are able to take a few minutes away from concentrating on a specific task? It ought to take you about thirty seconds to conclude that there is no way to generate the data which would be required to form such an assessment and that the complexities of the assumptions which would require to be made to convert that data into a number would be so complex and arbitrary that any figure would be meaningless anyway.

This is not science, this is childish alchemy. For fun, write yourself some press releases on 'research findings' on other costs to 'British industry' and fax them out to newspapers to see if they get taken up. I'm rather worried that one of 'sneezing costs British industry £1 billion every year', 'bright coloured ties helping to push Britain towards recession' or 'employee pet ownership reduces British productivity' would be eagerly reproduced.

We are surrounded by false science and the rate at which theories are adopted and disseminated is directly proportionate to their sympathy to the interests of big business. This is a fraught area. Policy really ought to be based in part on evidence, and the risks in discrediting 'science' are every bit as real as swallowing it whole. Even more difficulty arises in finding criteria on which to decide what to believe and what to disregard – the reasons I have given above for dismissing the business-friendly nonsense of the economic consultant will be the reasons the economic consultant dismissed research which (say) shows a link between corporate profit rates and incidence of child poverty within an economy. By nature, it is difficult to know what knowledge is trustworthy. What is not difficult to know is that it will always be twisted by those who wish to make a case for something. Unfortunately, our intermediaries (politicians, journalists, commentators) do not appear to be particularly good at differentiation between good science and bad science, and the bad science tends to have the money and power. So we believe a lot of things which aren't true.

A particular kind of question

OJ Simpson trying and failing to squeeze into those intimidating-looking black leather gloves during his murder trial was the outcome of one of the classic mistakes of our times. The prosecutors forgot the golden rule of public debate – never ask a question you don't know the answer to. They figured that the sight of Simpson with those threatening gloves on would influence the jurors. They were so sure of it that they forgot to consider whether they were actually Simpson's gloves. They weren't, and that more than any other event or piece of evidence during the trial probably got Simpson off. This is a mistake today's powers-that-be seldom make.

One of the key ways in which public debate is controlled is by ensuring that only the questions which deliver the right answers are asked in the first place. When the Labour Government was elected in 1997 one of the things it began to do was to consult. At the time it would have been quite easy for most organisations to employ at least a full-time member of staff to do nothing other than respond to government consultations in the areas of interest of that organisation. All areas of government policy were up for discussion (it seemed) and this fitted very neatly with the rhetoric of 'open government', 'bringing ordinary people into the debate', 'breaking down the barriers of dogma' and 'sweeping away secrecy'.

The whole process became incredibly routine, almost mechanical. It begins with a keynote speech on the importance of the issue up for 'discussion'. There would be an announcement that there was to be a consultation on the subject. Within a few weeks there would be a glossy document with an aspirational title which contained an extensive first section on why the thing being consulted on was important. This would always contain much to agree with, but that is because it would always be couched in such generalised terms that it was almost impossible to disagree. Then, without a second's hesitation, the consultation would start to dissect the issue in detail, breaking it down into a number of specific aspects and processes. It would then proceed to select a number of consensual statements about each of these aspects, finishing with a selection of questions offering the consultee the opportunity to voice an opinion. There would always be a deadline of between six weeks and three months. The consultation document would be sent out to all the key interested partners and would be placed on a website. The key organisations would respond. A few individuals (quite often fairly unrepresentative individuals) would also respond. Sometimes an interim summary of responses would be issued, in which the range of responses would be filed under broad categories of generalised standpoint. Then it would all disappear for a few months and then an official response would be issued. The official response will invariably look pretty bland and satisfy none of the consultees. And then it will end up in some sort of legislative, policy or budgetary move which looks almost exactly like the legislative policy or budgetary move which the government was planning in any case. So nothing changes, other than that the government can say it consulted and that its policy has been informed and supported by a broad range of stakeholders.

In some regards this seems perfectly reasonable; after all, it is good that governments ask but in the end they have to make the decisions. But it is not the asking but what is asked that is key. Let us imagine that the process of decorating the communal close of six flats was pursued in the same manner. The man in flat six wants a bright yellow gloss close but doesn't think the other five flats will go for it. He holds a public meeting for all the residents of the close at which he announces that he thinks the close ought to be done up because it is becoming a bit of a mess. He then announces that he will send a questionnaire round all the other residents to assess how it is going to be done up.

Later that week a questionnaire falls through the letter box of all the houses. The questionnaire begins with a page on why a clean, fresh and warm close is good for the quality of life. You feel better about bringing friends round. There is less chance of germs or rats. It brightens your mood in the morning. It is easier to see and get rid of dirt. Picking reasons why a lick of paint is good isn't so hard. Then the questionnaire divides up the decision-making process into three key issues to be addressed – mood, tone, practicalities. Each of these has its own section, beginning with a statement of the importance of each. "Choosing the mood in the close is essential to generating the environment which will make us feel good about our property. In selecting the colours we have to consider what the effect will be on the ambience of the entry point to our flats." It then asks a number of questions with multiple choice answers. "Do you want the close to feel: A – warm, B – lukewarm, C – cold?" "Do you want the close to feel: A – bright, B – dull, C – dark?". A couple more along the same lines and the section ends. Next section, tone. "Which of the following colour ranges do you think has the tone which corresponds most closely with warmness: A – blue-purple, B – brown-green, C – yellow-red." "Which one out of each of the following tone pairings do you think correlates most with brightness: blue or purple? Brown or green? Yellow or red?" Next section. "Practicalities. Which of the following is the most important consideration for you in selecting a paint type for an area of heavy use and which is exposed to dampness? Please select three. Durable/quick drying/washable/cheap/low odour/brand name." Questionnaires back by next Tuesday.

A couple of days after the deadline the man sticks a summary of responses through people's doors. It turns out that the close wants the following. It wants the mood of the close to be warm and bright. It prefers the blue/green/yellow shades for brightness. It prefers the yellow-red spectrum for warmth. And it wants a durable, inexpensive, washable paint which dries reasonably quickly and doesn't have an odour problem. It doesn't care whether it is by a brand name or not. Residents are thanked for their help. A week later they get back from work to discover the close is painted a bright yellow gloss. A few are horrified, but they can't really complain because it is undoubtedly what the majority of the close wants.

What the residents do not get asked at any point is *what colour would you like the close painted?* Every one of the questions in the occupier of flat number six's questionnaire is a particular type of question. They are either general enough that the answers can point anywhere (every paint is reasonably quick-drying and has no long-term odour problem), are so specific that you don't mind answering yes (of course yellow is a bright colour) or are so consensual that there is absolutely no risk in asking them (who wants to live in a cold, dark close?). Yet in the timeless technique of the confidence trickster you *feel* like you've been treated fairly and can't quite put your finger on how you were tricked. Oh well...

The consultation process works in a more subtle manner, but the basics are the same. You are never given the opportunity just to say what you think, you are directed towards specific questions. Each of these questions lead you to a general sort of answer, even if the consequences of that answer give you problems when they are applied to other parts of the debate. Once again you are not choosing, you are selecting. Do you want to be able to use your mobile phone? Well you're in favour of a radio mast at the end of your road. Do you want a better quality hospital? Then you're in favour of handing the running of your local hospital over to a profit-making company. Do you think dictators should be allowed to kill civilians? Then you support us invading their country. Do you want inexpensive foods that don't go rotten as quickly? Then you're a fan of genetic modification. Do you think competition should be open and fair? Then you don't mind if your local chemist closes down. And so on. We have an entire political culture which is based on leaps of logic which can only be negotiated by deploying questions which you waste your time answering but whose only purpose is to distract you and make you think that the leap was where you were going anyway.

A particular kind of question breaks the real questions down so they can be managed. A particular kind of question starts after a dozen assumptions have been made to cut off as many options as possible. A particular kind of question gets you to reaffirm things that aren't being disagreed with to make you feel included. A particular kind of question does nothing more than trick you into thinking that you agree with 'us'. Think of a number. Double it. Add eight. Half it. Subtract the number you first thought of. We think the answer is four. I'm glad you agree with us.

These don't even need to be subtle or clever to work. As long as the person asking the question has a reasonable degree of power it is possible to turn the whole thing into a farce. Glasgow City Council, under pressure from a chain of politicians leading back to the Treasury, decided that it wanted to hand all of its municipally-owned housing stock over to non-profit charities in the form of housing associations which would borrow private capital.

This has two political benefits. Firstly, it further dismantles that foolish notion which was actually briefly popular for almost all of the last century that communal provision of services for those who can't afford to buy them privately is a good thing. Secondly, by shifting ownership out of direct public ownership and control, it reduced public liability which simply makes life easier for every tier of government, from local authority debt to Public Sector Borrowing Requirement (well, every level apart from the officers on the ground who have to deal with the social consequences).

The problem was that Glasgow is a notoriously public sector-minded city where the municipal ethic is still strong (especially so given the mess that is being made of public delivery as investment is gradually whittled away). To have taken a substantial proportion of the city's population and unilaterally swapped their landlords would have caused far too many problems. To get away with it they needed to be able to claim consent. So how do you get to claim consent when there is none? The response was breathtaking in its brazenness. Glasgow City Council had a significant rent arrears problem. The city is, by most measures, one of the most deprived in Britain and poverty is a real problem. At the same time tinkering with the tax base, the continual directing of hidden subsidies to Edinburgh and the Scotland-wide process of squeezing local authority budgets reduced the money the Council had to invest in housing stock. The budget was in deficit, insufficient backlog maintenance was allowing much of the housing stock to fall into disuse while insufficient general maintenance was allowing inhabited housing stock to deteriorate. Money had to be spent. This was exacerbated by the fact that no organisation could have considered accepting the transfer of the Council stock in its current condition and with the existing budget deficit. The transfer would have to have giant sweeteners and guarantees attached to it if it were to be possible, and the Council simply couldn't afford them. But given that this was a move being pushed from further up the political tree it wasn't a problem to find the money to oil the wheels. The political problem was that if this money was simply given to the Council, the Council could quickly fix the problems itself and the entire transfer would become unnecessary. In fact, it could do even more if the expensive process of transfer didn't also have to be funded.

Much to the annoyance of politicians, the people of Glasgow aren't stupid. It might be possible to bamboozle them with economics and persuade them that the only way to improve the housing stock was to transfer it out of Council hands. But, if they were to see that that was only possible by investing more than the amount of money which the Council needed to fix the problem itself, they would smell a rat. And they did. Anti-stock transfer protests gained momentum and opposition to the proposal grew. To demonstrate legitimacy the Council promised a referendum. This referendum was repeatedly delayed because opinion polls showed that the Council was very likely to lose it. But a referendum was eventually held and the results were announced in March 2002. Postmen were blushing when they put the two-option ballot papers through the doors. The people living in Glasgow's council housing were given a stark choice – agree to let the housing stock be transferred and all the necessary investment to remove the budget deficit and fix up your house will be made; oppose the transfer and the houses will be left to deteriorate. Do as you're told and we'll keep you warm, cross us and it's just you and the mildew. It is a sign of the hostility that the Council faced that 42 per cent voted for mildew.

This is a particular kind of question indeed. There is no logical sense in which it could be considered fair. There is no logical sense in which it could convey legitimacy on the stock transfer. There is no logical sense in which a victorious Council could claim consent. Indeed, the Council received some pretty damaging press coverage of the whole debacle. But the question was answered in the only realistic way it could be, the Council got the 'consent' it was looking for, the story disappeared from the papers, the deal was done. The campaigners haven't given up, but now that no-one is looking it doesn't make any difference. Case after case of mismanagement, dishonesty and trickery has trickled out of the process but nothing like enough to stop it. The whole thing is currently bogged down and no-one seems to be able to get it to work. But none of this matters, because the people chose; no mildew for us! We want to pursue a neo-liberal, free-market, ideologically driven political stunt! A particular kind of question indeed.

These examples are examples where actual questions have been asked; but even that is not necessary. The same technique is endemic in any political or policy debate where a question is even implied. The national crusade to end the 'scourge of drugs' implies only one question – how do we defeat drug dealers? Everything else is outside the sphere of the debate because it is built on a certain kind of question. When it come to economics the situation becomes ridiculous. We are living in the most complex system of production and trading that the human species has ever known, and yet the entire economic debate revolves around such puerile questions as half a per cent on interest rates or one pence in the pound off business tax. There simply isn't the space in a book five times the size of this one to do nothing more than list the assumptions that have to be made and the perfectly reasonable questions which have to be skipped over to get to that point. Start with the question of what we as the human race want out of a system of production and distribution and take it from there. One of the reasons that we have had thirty years of politics with barely a single answer to a single problem being discovered is that the questions are deliberately not being asked. No wonder people have lost faith in politics. If science had gone for thirty years without making a single discovery we would be pretty sceptical too. But then, if we had seen thirty years of scientific endeavour in which questions were only asked to prove what was already believed, that is precisely the outcome we would have got.

Repetition, repetition, repetition, repetition

You do not need to be correct to be believed. Believing is about confidence, not accuracy. Being correct is not an essential part of being believed. If you want to be believed, don't waste your time being correct. Rather, if you want to be believed, be confident. Being correct does no harm, but being confident is better. Look them in the eye and tell them you are correct, they will believe you. You might not be correct, but be confident. In any case, correct is only a matter of opinion, being believed is a fact. Do you feel confident that what you believe to be correct actually is correct? But you believe it anyway, and you are confident enough not to worry. After all, being correct is not the key, believing is. And we all want to believe confident people. Why? Because they seem to be correct. And, after all, being correct is an opinion, so why worry if they aren't correct all the time? They seem confident enough and therefore someone must have believed them. And if enough people believed them surely they must have been correct. So to be believed you have to be confident. People will feel that you are correct, and if they don't it is just an opinion. Don't let it bother you. You do not need to be correct to be believed.

Do you believe me yet?

This simply shouldn't work. If something sounds dubious once it ought to sound equally dubious the second time. In fact, by the third time you ought to be going beyond dubiety and heading for firm resistance. But somewhere deep inside small parts of the thing which you rejected seem to get left behind. Then, over time, these build up into a sort of cognitive stalactite and in the end they sound plausible. Don't believe it? A case study. In October 2001 an opinion poll asked Americans if they thought that "most or all of the September 11 bombers were Iraqis or whether the attack was masterminded by Iraq?" Only four per cent of Americans agreed with this statement.

Over the next few months the evidence to demonstrate that this statement was indeed incorrect mounted. Quite simply, the identities of all of the pilots were revealed and none of them were Iraqi. No evidence was found to link the attack to Iraq in any way (despite the desperate attempts of key figures in the Bush administration to force the intelligence agencies to find one) and all those who understood the nature of Middle Eastern politics knew that there was nothing but animosity between the Iraqi regime of the time and likely organisers of the September 11 attack Al Quaeda. The opinion poll question was asked again about a year and a half later. This time more than half of those polled believed that most or all of the Manhattan Bombers were Iraqi or that Iraq masterminded it. This is extremely troubling. If the two polls are representative, almost exactly half of the population of America came to believe something which wasn't true and which they once knew to be untrue even over a period where all the evidence which emerged showed quite clearly that it wasn't true.

What is even more remarkable is that no-one with any credibility (and for humour value let's include the American government, its agencies, the country's politicians and its main media commentators in this category) ever said it was true. Nobody actually thinks or says that the Manhattan bombings had anything to do with Iraq. What they did say was "Iraq", "terrorists", "September 11" and "Al Quaeda" in the same sentences over and over again. It was formulated in manners such as "We will not turn a blind eye to regimes like Iraq which harbour and give succour to terrorist organisations such as Al Quaeda and allow them to mount another attack on our country like they did on September 11". And a year and a half of this was all it took to hypnotise America.

These techniques of mind control can be subtle and complex or blunt. It is perfectly possible to make someone think exactly the thing you want them to think using only the power of suggestion. This is not the place to consider the ways in which the interaction between the psychological, the emotional, the associative and the semiotic can alter perception. It is enough to accept that choice of language affects our mood, that there are complex sets of associations we all have which can be manipulated and that we are not always consciously aware of what our mind is absorbing.

Consider how quickly the connotations of words can be altered. The phrase 'asylum seeker' was not the phrase we associated with the immigrant population which played most on our inherited fear of 'the other' and our learned fear of 'the invader'. When we thought of people we didn't want to settle in our country (and these are generally of a different race) the word that formed in our heads used to be 'immigrant'. An immigrant was someone who wanted in. The reason for their wanting in was not necessarily implied by the phrase. An immigrant probably had the association of economic migrant, but it did not exclude refugee (for example). The word 'immigrant' did not generally have positive connotations but it often had negative ones. 'Asylum seeker', on the other hand, had a clear association with 'victim'.

Our natural reaction to being told that someone was an asylum seeker was, up until a couple of years ago, probably one of compassion. It had strong connotations with persecution, suffering and escape. If the association with 'immigrant' was 'selfish', the association with 'asylum seeker' was probably 'sanctuary'. These were people we had to protect. But that is not something the right-wing press was happy about. Make no mistake, the Daily Mail *hates* the idea of 'Pakis', 'Niggers', 'Peasants', 'Arabs' or any of the rest of them getting into 'Great' Britain. Sympathy with the black man simply wasn't on. Britain had to be taught that having electrodes attached to your genitalia, having your bones broken and your joints dislocated, watching your family be slaughtered were all nothing more than the price you have to pay for not being white enough. The plight of these people could no longer be allowed to be associated with 'sanctuary' because that would make people sympathetic to letting them in. They had to be associated with 'selfishness'.

The technique was simple. All that they had to do was to stick the word 'bogus' in front of 'asylum seekers'. You see, however much it was willed, people maintain compassion for the persecuted, so they had to be persuaded that 'these people' weren't really the victims of persecution at all. They were chancers, fly guys on the make taking advantage of our better nature. A subset of 'asylum seeker' was invented – the 'bogus asylum seeker'. But the trick of repetition and association is that there are no subsets. It only took a year or so of the chant of 'bogus asylum seeker' before the phrase 'asylum seeker' itself was indefinitely polluted. The aim was achieved and today in Britain the phrase 'asylum seeker' is no longer one which generates sympathy. Simply by saying 'bogus' over and over again we have all been taught to hate. Welcome to Britain.

Or meaningless and illogical catchphrases can turn into nuggets of wisdom just by their continual repetition (particularly in contexts such as set-piece speeches where they can't be challenged). Thus half of the country is now convinced that, in Blair's words, a 'one size fits all' health service no longer meets the needs of society. Eh? If ever there was an area in which one size very much does fit all it is surely health. Unless there are some regional or class differences in the way the heart, lungs and kidneys work. Sure, when we start getting patients through our hospital doors and the admitting doctor say "oooh, three spines – I don't know how to treat this one" we may need a variety of health services. Until then I think we're working along the right lines as things are. But Blair's silly catchphrase is taken seriously, purely because he has now said it repeatedly.

Again, it is unnecessary to go on giving examples because it is everywhere. One year there is no such thing as a 'weapon of mass destruction', the next they are everywhere. One month the people of Scotland want to ban fox hunting, the next they think that the Scottish Parliament 'is wasting its time on stupid things like fox hunting while hospitals are falling apart' or suddenly a deeply unpopular piece of discriminatory legislation becomes a bulwark against 'gay sex lessons'. Even I have started to worry about the 'pensions timebomb', because 'the pensions system we have is no longer sustainable'. My rational head tells me this is just one more smart-arsed phrase designed to scare me into abandoning public provision altogether. I know that it is not a 'timebomb' which is inevitably going to go off no matter what we do but is rather a political decision we are allowing to happen. But I also know that for the time being the people who keep saying 'pensions timebomb' are doing so because they fully intend to explode the state pensions system. So I am scared and I save privately, and so in a few years they will tell me that the state pension is no longer necessary because people like me have now put money away. Bomb detonated, and I helped. And just because someone thought up a worrying phrase and repeated it enough times.

Remember, you don't want to pay more income tax. You do not want to pay more income tax. *You do not want to pay more income tax.*

Boiling a toady

I have never been happy with an analogy which requires me to think of frogs being boiled alive. However, the analogy has become so established that it is hard to avoid its use. It runs like this. If you drop a frog into boiling water it will make desperate attempts to escape the excruciating, scalding pain. However, if you put a frog in cold water and slowly raise the temperature until it is boiling, the frog will allow itself to boil to death without so much as a struggle. I have no idea if this is true and hope never to find out. But there is no doubt that, when the same principle is applied to public policy, we are all very placid frogs and the water around us is simmering.

The effect of indistinct incremental change can be observed everywhere – meeting someone you haven't seen for years and noticing how they have aged while people who saw them regularly have no sense of them being so much older, a building which gets grimier and grimier until no-one is really aware that what is now black used to be a light sandstone. Thus if you could go back to 1995 and tell the supporters of New Labour that they would become cheerleaders for 'faith schools' run by the religious right which refused to teach evolution or that they would support 'foundation hospitals' in which every aspect of every service (clinical and otherwise) could be run by American healthcare corporations, or that they would mount an invasion of Iraq with no legal basis, they would simply reject what you were saying.

But New Labour did not drop its acolytes (toadies rather than froggies) directly into boiling water. First they were told that certain things had to be said if Labour was ever going to get back into power, but that that it would be different in power. Then once in power they were told that certain of the things they said would have to be actually done if power was to be kept. Then they were told that these things were actually a conviction and would make the difference they were looking for but in a radical new way. And then they were told that these weren't enough and that more had to be done. And then they sold off all of England's hospitals to American profiteers. By now the water was pretty scalding, but the toadies didn't flinch.

It is an assumed part of history that the Second World War's concentration camps were the horrific masterplan of a group of petrifyingly evil men who took control of Germany in the 1930s. In actual fact, concentration camps are what happens when people are willing to accept Jewish ghettos, which are in turn what happens when people are willing to accept giving Jews a different legal status which is in turn what happens when the state is willing to overlook illegal persecution of Jewish people. This technique got us into a war with Iraq (each stage on the road to slaughter only seemed like a small extra step) and this technique is about to lead us to the privatisation of the Post Office – something too hot for even the Tories ten years ago. We saw a group of backbench Labour MPs uneasy with foundation hospitals refuse to rebel on the basis that they can swallow quite a lot of what is in the legislation and will amend the rest at committee stage. And the temperature rises a bit more.

A value-free world

The Church is dead, the sales rep is our new priest; no need to run over old ground on the transition from moral belief systems (moral does not mean 'good', just based on codes of conduct) to consumerism. We have largely come to accept a world in which there is no recourse to a higher power to aid us in the big questions – what should I do? How should I live? However, we still expect a value-laden world. We do not expect to be told how to behave on the basis of an existential quest for meaning but we do expect to maintain a basic sense of right and wrong. It may have become the province of the chat show ('do tha right thang') or its close relative American Politics ('Axis of Evil' for crying out loud), but we still believe that some things are good and some things are bad. Not when it comes to public or corporate policy, however. Here we exist in an almost entirely value-free state.

Take for example the socio-economic strategy of the government in Scotland. In 2001 the Scottish Executive published a strategy paper entitled 'A Smart, Successful Scotland'. This outlined its basic economic strategy and how that linked with its wider social goals. There is much in the general approach of the strategy to agree with. The basic argument is that Scotland cannot compete with other parts of the world on the basis of low-paid labour, so it will have to find another way to compete. It is of course welcome that low pay is nominally no longer the policy underpinning Scottish economic strategy. It is less welcome that nothing in the strategy is actually designed to end low pay other than a rather hopeful shift in the structure of the Scottish economy. It is also less than encouraging that it is clearly not intended that this strategy should really apply to many workers, with the large number of low-pay service-sector workers omitted – the vision of the hi-tech office has a bit of a blind spot when it comes to who is going to clean it or work in the staff canteen or manage the childcare of well-paid employees. It is also disconcerting the ease with which we can write off low pay as a market advantage for the poorest countries in the world and seem to envisage that just being the way of things to come.

However, the thrust of the argument – that we should try and generate new employment which is high in knowledge content – is correct. The scope for knowledge and discovery is one of the greatest facets of human existence and in principle a curiosity-driven economy ought to be a good thing. (Again, we have to set aside the suspicion that those who conceived the strategy probably mean the discovery of new ways to kill people in our fine defence industry or new ways to steal intellectual property rights from nature in our biotech sector.) But beyond this we ought to have some concerns (and not just because there is little sense in the document of how this vision might be realised).

Let us consider for a second the title of the document, 'A Smart, Successful Scotland'. The creeping Americanisms might be the first thing to worry us – where I grew up in Scotland 'smart' was not a compliment but was usually followed with 'arse' or 'bastard'. In its language it is as foreign to Scotland as a health strategy entitled 'Getting Sneakers on the Sidewalk'. But what is striking is the absolute value-free nature of every word in the title. One indefinite article, one noun and two adjectives which can mean absolutely anything. Why do we want a smart and successful Scotland? We certainly get no idea from most of the language in the strategy.

Let us consider what a smart and successful nation looks like. What would you pick? America? It certainly owns most of the world's intellectual property and in gross terms spends more on research and development than any other nation so you could certainly call it smart. If we are going to measure success in the usual market-capitalist manner, its productivity is high, its GDP is quite stunning, its international reach is unsurpassed in all of history and its military might is almost impossible to conceive? So our strategy is to be America? Really? We want massive income disparity, endemic poverty and crime, gross inequality in healthcare for millions, two million in a brutalised penal system, *de facto* racial segregation all over the country, international fear and hatred and blatant corruption? I suspect the authors of the strategy do, but they certainly don't say it. Well they couldn't could they?

It would have to be called 'A Selfish, Unequal, Grasping, Hated Scotland'. Of course, America isn't the only smart and successful country. By many measures (particularly if you favour social indicators to economic ones) the Scandinavian countries look pretty successful and there is no doubting their smartness. But that is certainly not what is being conceived of here. Japan used to be smart and successful but is now just smart. Historically Egypt, Mesopotamia or the Ottoman Empire were pretty smart and successful, although these are probably not the models we ought to be following either. And then there is the one we all try to avoid, because there is little doubt that Nazi Germany was both smart and successful.

Now, of course Scottish policy-makers are not considering modelling the country on Nazi Germany, but they really aren't giving us much by way of clues of what they *are* modelling us after. The debate is conducted in value-free terms so we can have little idea if they are our values. It was put well by one of Scotland's university Principals who said he had no problem with a smart, successful Scotland so long as we could also have a compassionate, creative Scotland. But can you imagine a government strategy document in the current phase of political doctrine exploring ways to generate and encourage compassion? Simply, no, because that would ascribe value to their actions.

There are endless examples of this. Blair is famed for his verb-free sentences, but people don't seem to have noticed the extent of his value-free sentences. It is also a worry that they are not usually the same sentences. So when Blair talks of his values he never tells us anything about what he is going to do to realise them and when he tells us what he is going to do we can infer no value-set from his words. What exactly does 'modernisation' mean? It is his mantra but it means nothing. When applied to Firefighters it seems to mean work them harder so that there can be mass redundancies. When applied to schools it appears to mean converting them into profit-making opportunities for the private sector. Ditto hospitals. When applied to government it seems to mean ensuring that accountability is replaced with opportunities for endorsement (oh, and some computers).

When Blair uses the word 'modernisation' it could mean anything. He could apply it to apples and it could mean genetically modifying them or it could mean revamping the unjust system of growing and trading them. Of course, it would always mean the former. Yet if you listen to the amalgam of these value-free actions and these action-free values it sounds vaguely moral. There is no mainstream political commentator who seems willing to challenge the basis of Blair's value set. They may claim that he has been badly advised or that he has got it wrong, but they never seem to be willing to challenge the purity of his intentions. Nonsense. Blair's value-free policies are designed to be exactly what they are – anti-egalitarian, power-driven and glory-seeking. But he implements them with a self-righteous tear in his eye so we assume he must be well-meaning. By expunging morality or value from action while maintaining a personal faith Blair has become an almost exact facsimile of Hogg's Justified Sinner.

Of course, Bush is no better. 'No child left behind' he says as he cuts the federal and state education budget in real terms in pursuit of that holy grail of value-free policy – efficiency. We did briefly have a value-based policy in Britain – the much-vaunted 'ethical foreign policy' – but soon got rid of it when we realised that it would be a bit contrary to the economic interests of the defence industry and the strategic interests of our international relations. And try to find value in 'economic interests' or 'strategic interests'.

And this is the nature of the world's politics. We chase productivity without asking what it means. We pursue profit without considering what it is for or where it came from. We fight wars for security without considering what it is that we want to be secure from. We allow people to be exploited without asking if this is good for the sum of humanity. This is at the heart of the problem this book is looking at. We don't stop and ask why? Why do we want economic growth if it is doing nothing to end global poverty? Why do we want profit if the price is a dying planet? What is politics for if the sum total of all its actions appears to be to make more and more people suffer? Oh, for some values. Not values to disguise what was going to be done anyway. Real values. For people and for the planet.

There is no history

One of the most astute comments on the Blair Government came from Paul Flynn MP. He said "for New Labour the past is continually changing – only the future is certain". The use and abuse of history is one of the keys to constraining political debate. Either you distort history into a series of black and white lessons which in themselves cannot be argued against ('communism doesn't work', the first and last resort of the market capitalist when any sensible alteration to the terms of their looting charter is proposed) or you begin from a completely ahistorical stand point – day oneism. Let us look at an example of each.

Recently a rather pointless debate has been running – was Stalin worse than Hitler and if so does this prove that communism is of a moral equivalence with fascism? The answer to the first question is in many ways unimportant, although it does raise important questions. Unimportant because it is like asking of two serial killers which was the worst – the one that killed more people or the one who killed the 'nicer' people (15 dead prostitutes or seven dead children). It is a meaningless question. Both are absolutely abhorrent and there is no better or worse. But in the recent public spat over this (letters and articles around the 50th anniversary of Stalin's death was the forum) people who really ought to have known better spent ages trying to calculate a head count of the dead. Hitler, you scored six million, Stalin, you scored nine million. Congratulations Stalin, you are the evilest.

It is difficult to resist pointing out the giant flaws in this revisionism. The Stalin headcount usually included not only dissidents or ethnic groups he had executed but everyone who starved to death under his rule and everyone who died in a war he was involved in. Of course, if you were to use the same basis for assessing all world leaders on evilness you would find a mini-Hitler in every British Prime Minister of the Raj, but comparability here would be dismissed by the very headcounters who started it. So evilness is not scored out of ten million. But it seems that there is something emerging from this regarding how the killing was done. Nazi extermination chambers are of a different order to allowing people to starve to death, not least because of the ideological targeting of a single ethnic group. (Stalin of course had his Gulags but again their operation in ideological terms appears different.)

Draw this up a level and you come to the crux of the matter. If Stalin is on a par with Hitler, is communism on a par with fascism? I am a million miles away from being a Stalin apologist and am far removed from that generation of the left who tended in that direction. Nonetheless I do not see a direct comparison between a man who attempted to wipe an entire race of humans from the face of the earth for twisted ideological reasons and a man who killed just as viciously to maintain political control. The basis of the killing is different in order (although, again, equally disgusting). But even if we were to accept comparability, this does not necessarily tell us anything about the core worth of the ideologies from which they emerged. For example, if for one reason or another Hitler had been unable to set up the programme of extermination of the Jews and his headcount was therefore zero, would this therefore make fascism a benign political movement? Or does the manner in which Indonesia destroyed East Timor 'prove' that capitalism is as evil as fascism? You can also select any religion (other than perhaps Buddhism but thanks to Israel now including Judaism) and find appalling levels of barbarity. Does this tell us something about the nature of religion? Possibly. Does it prove that religion is inherently evil? No.

The point of all of this is to cement an 'irrefutable' case on the evilness of communism to ensure that any attempt to alter capitalism in an egalitarian way can be discredited as evil. And also because there is a lingering hatred of a group of working men and women who had the audacity to challenge capitalism (it is not Stalin they really hate – in fact I suspect that many of them really quite admire him – it is Lenin). But this is a complete misuse of history. A philosophy cannot be judged on its misuse but on its intent. Communism failed because of what it became, not because of what it had wanted to be. Its aims were noble, and in this there is absolutely no comparison with fascism.

There is a more sophisticated distortion of the same type which actually illustrates the point better, precisely because of its sophistication. It has been argued that the operation of communism is inherently evil (in any form, not just a debased form) because of its necessary working methods. The evidence of this is given as Mao's Five Year Plan. The more sophisticated free-market argument is that this kind of central planning inevitably kills because it inevitably fails. The agricultural crises and famines of the late 1950s appear to demonstrate this. Communism kills.

But this is not looking at history, it is looking at a couple of years in one country. As Chomsky points out, there are other more instructive ways to look at it. China and India had very similar mortality and morbidity rates throughout history. However, communist China introduced a proper healthcare system while capitalist India continued with a free market *laisse faire* (*laisse mort*?) approach. Unsurprisingly, morbidity and mortality rates began to change in China while staying the same in India. If we assume that the Chinese system imported into India would have resulted in the same changes in mortality, communism would have been a very big net saver of lives in India. In fact, more Indians died from 'capitalism' in every seven years of the second half of the twentieth century than died from 'communism' during the Chinese famine. Capitalism is eight times more lethal than communism. Nonsense, of course. As always, it is much more complicated than that. But we can see from these examples how the distortion of history and its selective reading are an important part of the development of our collective political mindset.

So that is what the world looks like when we have only a few incidents rather than a history. What does it look like when we lose history altogether? Baghdad in June 2003 is the answer. Tony Blair is a past master at making history disappear. The 2003 Iraq war was sold to us on many grounds. The two that emerged as favourites were weapons of mass destruction and human rights abuses. Only a tiny proportion of the world's population was taken in by these blatant pretexts – the members of the House of Commons in London representing a disproportionate number of them. However, oppose the war, support the war or any shading in between there was general agreement that there would only be one way to effect change and that would be military. Saddam Hussein was a bad and unreasonable man and if it was decided that something had to be done there really would be no other way. Why? Because we had been persuaded that the world began in 1999.

In actual fact there were many things that could have been done. The West did not want a democratic revolution in Iraq because its leaders knew perfectly well that a democratic Iraq would elect a Islamist government which would be even more hostile to the West than Sadam (who was, bear in mind, a close ally of the West and not a natural hater). The UN sanctions regime ensured that Sadam controlled all food, medicine and other essentials. It seems reasonable to believe that this would strengthen his control. It would also seem reasonable to believe that someone in the West would be aware of this. Given that this was in their interests, it is difficult not to conclude that this was not, in part at least, the intention. Removing the food and medicine sanctions, funding a broad range of democratic parties, placing inspectors on the ground to slow down the human rights abuses with which Sadam ruled the country and sending out the clear message that the West would recognise, support and normalise relations with a democratic Iraq would probably have achieved significant improvement.

But we were required to forget that the West refused to support previous uprisings which they had encouraged. We were required to forget that Sadam ruled over Iraq because he had our support and that there was little reason for ordinary Iraqis to trust our words. We had to forget that far from being desperate to end human rights abuses in Iraq, Tony Blair refused to sign a motion in 1989 condemning Sadam for gassing Kurds at Halabja – presumably on the basis that he was an ally. We had to forget that UN weapons inspectors were not thrown out of Iraq in 1998 – America ordered them to leave. We had to forget that America overthrew the last democratic regime in Iraq. We had to forget everything which could tell us why Sadam was where he was, why he acted as he did, why our interests were not the interests of Iraqis, why there were alternatives. We needed to start shooting from the hip in a historyless world.

America is particularly bad for misplacing its history. The details of ethnic cleansing of the indigenous peoples, slavery, its radical trade union movement, the depression, segregation, McCarthyism, foreign policy, corporate scandal and many other scars on its conscience need to be lost. Why? Because they would tell Americans a lot about their country which it is not in the interests of the moral conservatives and the free-marketeers for them to hear. Remind me, what was Enron again? The United States of Amnesia indeed.

And this has been a central strand of New Labour since the beginning. A line was drawn right at the 'New' and the entire history of the movement was forgotten. Part of the New Labour messianic zeal came from the belief that the past was the past and that we had nothing to learn because 'Things Could Only Get Better'. The disappearing history of Blair is becoming

American in its proportions and we are now expected to forget what was promised/said/done a matter of weeks ago.

Milan Kundera wrote that freedom is the struggle of memory against forgetting. Like goldfish we are supposed to accept our world because we are supposed to forget its lessons. History is not bunk. If it was, the oligarchs would not be half so keen to rewrite it or blank it out.

Living in the spectrum

There was a time when being a millionaire was a pretty exceptional thing, but over the years inflation has eaten away at the prestige of millionaire-dom. The threshold for membership of the club has been lowered to such an extent that being a millionaire nowadays means being pretty well off rather than being stinking rich. Thus it is for radicalism. Once upon a time opposing private profit being creamed off the NHS by the corporate sector would have put you in the mainstream of politics. Now if you raise the same concern you are called a 'wrecker of reform', an 'unreconstructed social-ist', a 'usual suspect', a member of the 'awkward squad', 'loony left', 'Old Labour', a 'throwback' or – above all – irrelevant.

Political viewpoints exist in a spectrum. This spectrum has always been divided into three zones – moderate/mainstream, radical and ex-tremist. Those branded moderate or mainstream tend towards a political position which is usually characterised as the most commonly held or the consensual. This is the territory of Westminster (elected under a voting system designed to allow only parties who exist in this centrist sphere of politics to play). At any given time it is characterised by a number of core assumptions about what is the commonly held view of people. It is in some way a representation of the political culture of a country (and is often country specific) and is therefore taken to be a statement of what is 'right' – justification through apparent numbers. Thus in Britain we have a core set of assumptions about what we need and want which inform almost all political discussion – economic growth, law and order, core public services, sovereignty, infrastructure.

In other countries they are different – in America freedom of action is much more important than public services for example. Each of these general goals are signed up to in the centre of the spectrum and the shading comes between the approach taken to achieving each – Tories think economic growth and the application of market principles will in themselves result in better public services while the Labour Party (well, until 1997) believe that economic growth would only deliver better public services with some state intervention. And so on. The differences in approach are slight enough to square the circle of competing priorities. That is to say that the politics of the centre is based on the doctrine that all the core aims are signed up to and action to achieve one must not jeopardise the achievement of another. The result is a fairly close consensus with the biggest differences in policy occurring at the margins (the acceptance of social values such as tolerance of difference does not particularly affect key goals). The centre is a land in which most of the thinking has already been done. The assumptions inherent in defining this centre ground are flawed, but that will be explored in a minute.

The radical phase of the spectrum is that area on either side of the centre. This area is characterised by a general acceptance of some of the core values identified by centrists but usually without full acceptance of others. Thus the radical right certainly accepts the need for economic growth but often does not accept the need for strong public services. The radical left will undoubtedly support better public services but will often not sign up to the assumptions in the law and order debate. But what makes the radical fringes radical is that the means proposed to achieve the chosen 'consensual' aims is outside the spectrum of centrist politics usually because they would adversely affect other aims. The radical left might be happy to sacrifice economic growth for greater equality; the radical right will be happy to sacrifice equality for economic growth. The radicals tend to propose things which are of a different order to that which is proposed in the centre; where centrists debate whether something should be bigger or smaller, the radicals debate whether it should exist. The primary function of radicals is (or was) to shift the centre over a period of time. In principle radicals tend not to win but to force others to come closer to their position.

And then there is the extremist phase of the spectrum. Extremism tends to be characterised by rejection of what is accepted as consensual by others. The extremist position puts forward an entirely different set of principles which can only be achieved by a programme of action which is inimical to the aims and goals of centrism – the expulsion of racial minorities, repealing rights to private property. The extremist should not really have a role in mainstream politics and are usually dismissed and ignored. It is a position which is entirely one of conviction and is in effect entirely unstrategic.

All of this is largely nonsense. This is not to say that there are no such things as consensual views among societies, but the way they are shepherded into these categories is not governed by the consensus. The aims and goals of consensus are generally so broad that they can sit comfortably in many parts of the spectrum. Core values are in reality only excluded from the very ends of the spectrum. Law and order can mean tough on crime (jailing the parents of children who scrawl graffiti on walls) or tough on the causes of crime (tackling failing law and order by addressing the deprivation which causes much of it). The core value of being anti-crime could either mean 'bring back hanging' or 'tax the rich 'til the pips squeak' – currently both ideas are only to be found deep within the radical phase of the spectrum. The key is to recognise that the spectrum is characterised not by Newtonian absolutism but by relativity. The spectrum is not geometrically constant and the centre is seldom in the centre. Rather than reflecting political views the spectrum is about controlling political views.

To demonstrate this, let us consider the current shape of the spectrum. Where would we now find the centre of the spectrum? There is now a 'consensus' that the private sector should be allowed to deliver clinical services on a profit-making basis within the NHS. There is certainly debate about what this means – should it only be an emergency move when the core publicly-delivered NHS is temporarily overwhelmed or when there is internal failure or should it be a more fundamental part of public health service delivery? What we do not have much of is serious debate at Westminster about whether it should be allowed at all. So this is now the centre. But even five or ten years ago this would have been an idea very firmly in the radical right of the spectrum. Even Margaret Thatcher recognised that private sector clinical delivery in the NHS was too far out of the consensus for her to get away with. Thatcher was a radical rather than a centrist, but she knew perfectly well that if she was going to get things done she would have to function in the centre. Thatcher was desperate to privatise the Post Office but knew she couldn't weather the political storm which would ensue. Blair is about to do it without anyone really noticing. The 'centre' is not where it was. In this sense it is not a centre at all.

Equally, what was straightforward centre ground a few years ago is now considered radical left; crazy ideas such as the benefit of using income tax to create a civilised society or the basic wrongness of launching wars against sovereign states to achieve regime change for reasons of domestic self-interest. Meanwhile ideas which used to be in the realm of radical left thinking are now considered extremist – public ownership of industry has gone from being public policy to 'Stalinism'. Interestingly, it is now almost impossible to identify a radical right (in the old sense of the spectrum) – they are now running the show in the centre. It is the extremist right which is fulfilling the 'dragging' role of the radical fringe with the neo-Nazi parties across Europe dragging mainstream policies on issues such as asylum to the right and the Christian extremists of the America religious right overthrowing the constitutional separation of church and state to impose draconian social control over public America.

And yet it is all words. Despite what we are led to believe, none of this consensus is consensual in the old-fashioned sense of the word (i.e. a large majority of people agreeing). Rather it is 'acceptional' – people are willing (just) to accept what they are being fed. The spectrum does not reflect views, it makes them. Taking a certain position is branded in spectral terms and the media complies, leading the public to accept the implications. This is not an unconscious act; it is planned.

To demonstrate this, let's look at two examples. Perhaps the best known is the position of Noam Chomsky, the world's leading dissident. Chomsky is undoubtedly one of the world's great intellects. He is also one of the most informed and knowledgeable men in the world and chooses as his subject some of the most relevant and currently important issues in the world today. So Chomsky is a regular figure on the American domestic commentator circuits then? No, he's almost never seen on mainstream television. Why? Because Chomsky has been discredited. In what manner? His arguments refuted? His evidence questioned? His knowledge or intellect in doubt? His analysis flawed? No. Chomsky has been discredited purely and simply on the grounds that he is an 'extremist'. In fact, people seldom challenge Chomsky's arguments (largely because it is pretty difficult to do and very few would have the courage to do it head to head), and given that Chomsky largely deals in the recitation of accepted facts (economic indicators, death tolls, documented actions) it is difficult to see what the 'extremism' is. Chomsky himself has long resigned himself to his exclusion and works largely through other channels, but the impact of this type of exclusion on American political life is enormous.

Throughout America's recent global adventures Americans have been given virtually no context and are entirely insulated from many of the economic and geopolitical implications and motives behind them. If they had this information it would be much, much more difficult for military leaders to get away with the things they have. How many Americans were aware during the 2003 Iraq War that Saddam Hussein initially came to prominence when the CIA recruited him in 1959 to assassinate Abdul Karim Qasim, leader of the popular 1958 Iraqi revolution? Would this kind of information cast doubt on current motives? Yes. Is repeating what is established fact an act of extremism? Apparently so.

The Private Finance Initiative was a Tory means of privatising public sector capital (through lease-back agreements on hospitals and schools etc.). Labour renamed it Public Private Partnerships. They have both been a disgrace. In Britain there is an academic who has followed the progress of the PFI/PPP process in great detail. Allyson Pollock has monitored and analysed all the implications of these rent-back schemes which give private sector contractors guaranteed and risk-free profit from the taxpayers pocket. She has revealed over and over the extent to which the premises on which PFI was sold to Parliament such as value for money and risk transfer benefits have turned out to be false. The system of PFI costs more than the public building of facilities; that is no longer in doubt. The contracts handed out have been configured in such a way that the winning bidder faces little or no risk; harder to ascertain due to the secrecy surrounding the contracts but no longer in much doubt either. So when the BBC recently wanted to stage a debate on the issue it was natural that Pollock would be invited to contribute.

Well, not according to the Government who refused to put anyone up for debate if Dr Pollock was involved. The researcher putting the programme together was reportedly shocked. He asked why? The answer given was that she was 'discredited'. By whom? No answer was given. Dr Pollock is a highly respected academic and no-one in the academic community doubted her integrity, ability or veracity. Her work on the subject has been widely published and has not been seriously challenged. Discredited by whom? By the spectrum. She does not inhabit the new centrist zone so she must be a crazy woman and has nothing to tell us about the debate. Of course, the BBC did not invite her to appear on the programme and the 'consensus' was once again not only not challenged but was reinforced. The only voices were pro-market.

The spectrum is insanely narrow. In America it is more like a boa constrictor – breathe in just a little and the spectrum closes its grip around you even tighter. It squeezes the life out of politics and is handing total control over to a tiny, unrepresentative minority. In a sane world the current crop of neo-conservative 'thinkers' who now run the White House would be shunned in the same way the Klu Klux Klan are. Instead, we see the laughable spectacle of George Bush claiming in a televised presidential debate that "there is a mainstream in American politics, and John Kerry is right on the left bank". In fact, Kerry was perhaps the most right-wing Democratic candidate in the party's history. He is very pro-big business and the differences between him and the neo-cons on international affairs was a matter of nuance, not substance. The thought that he might be a radical left-winger is beyond laughable. Unfortunately, in American politics the dividing line between straightjacket and dinner jacket appears to have been misplaced. This is a society in which the word 'liberal' is now one of the ultimate insults. It really isn't so long since liberal was an insult because it meant lacking the courage of convictions and failing to follow through logic.

The extremists have stolen the keys and renamed themselves moderates. The first thing they did was to label the moderates extremist and jail them. They squeezed the spectrum so hard that it barely has room for a second opinion and then shifted the ground which is called the centre so far to the right that 'centre' now has no meaning. Anything which does not hand more and more power to the looters and pillagers of big business is considered outside the spectrum and is written of as extremism and then ignored. All the language of politics follows to the extent that the neo-Nazi British National Party now has more influence on policy in Britain than politicians who used to be considered on the right of the Labour Party (and who are now thought of as radical). And we are supposed to believe that this is consensus.

Signing up for the game

It has been argued that for change to happen there has to be three kinds of people taking action. The first – the stone throwers – exist outside the system and bring about change by criticising and revealing lies and wrong assumptions. These are the protesters, the critics, who force institutions to alter their behaviour. Then there are the alternative builders. They reject the institution and its means of organisation and try to create alternative structures elsewhere. These are radicals who generate new ideas and pursue them as models for better institutions; people who set up cooperatives, alternative communities, projects and initiatives. And finally there are the long marchers, people who enter the institutions and affect what change they can slowly. These are the radicals among elected politicians and so on. No single one of these types of action can by itself create fundamental change, but together they can make things change.

There are, of course, many organisations and individuals which want change. After all, the pro-big business agenda by definition is going to work against the interests of others in society (such as people). So how do these groups and individuals play? Well, they have learned that if their challenge is too direct they will quickly be 'discredited' and considered outside the realm of the spectrum. Once outside the spectrum it is very difficult to have any influence. It is therefore standard practice for the non-governmental, non-business sector (broadly the civic sector) to place themselves inside the spectrum where they can then have the greatest effect. So they take the 'long marcher' approach – play the game by the very rules they want to change and then try to subvert them. The problem is that the rules have become so rigid (and the spectrum so tight) that once you accept them it is hard to do anything other than conform. There was a time when there was enough space within the spectrum to enable people with different views to enter it and to achieve things. The scope for this has decreased enormously. In fact, it has reached the stage where by accepting the ludicrously constraining set of rules many organisations which would like to see change achieve quite the opposite – they shore up the status quo.

Let me give an example. When the Scottish Parliament was first set up, the portfolios of lifelong learning (higher and further education) were combined with the enterprise portfolio to create one department. This was generally seen as a good move and did indeed generate many benefits for the higher education sector. I was involved in developing lobby strategies for the higher education sector at the time and felt that the best thing to do was to go with the grain and work our way into the policy-making process by emphasising the economic potential of higher education. At first sight this strategy appeared to work. Higher education has a very strong economic role and particularly given that the Scottish Parliament has limited powers over economic issues (no macroeconomic policy powers, for example) it gave universities a fair amount of leverage. The outcome what that there was very great interest in the issue of the commercialisation of university research (taking academic research and turning it into commercially viable products) and new money was put into it. However, having achieved that first part of the strategy, our aim was to open the case up and demonstrate the other crucial contributions higher education makes (to the arts and culture, to civic engagement and understanding, to policy making, to international relations). Unfortunately, by that point we had reinforced the commercial imperative and the view of universities as glorified economic development agencies. They would nod in agreement when we highlighted the role higher education plays in the culture of Scotland or agree how important it was to gain an understanding of our society through the social research carried out in universities. But they simply didn't want to talk about it. The agenda was set. It didn't matter what other arguments were now made, the question which took precedent whenever any higher education issue arose in the Parliament was 'what is the implication for enterprise?'

When the assessment of the quality of research was considered politicians argued that the quality of the research didn't matter; it was the commercial applicability which was key. When course provision was discussed it was always in terms of whether universities were producing graduates with the skills industry needed. By accepting the rules of the game (profit motive comes above all else) we did nothing more than reinforce them. (It is necessary to point out that this is a slightly unfair reading of the political situation because there was significant discussion about the question of low participation in higher education among the poor. Nevertheless, if we look at the areas in which action was taken and in particular if we examine where extra resource was invested, the driver was consistently commercial or economic imperative.)

As the game has become more exclusive, more and more people are queuing to sign up to it. And the more who do, the harder it is to change the rules. This does not just apply to organisations, it applies to the full range of those who engage with politics. It includes the media commentators and what they choose to write about. It includes the dinner party set and the conversations they hold. It includes protesters who change the language of their protest to make it more palatable. It is another trick of control – co-opt the opposition. We have reached a point where there are far too many long marchers and not enough stone throwers or alternative builders. This is not conducive to change.

Editing out the maybes

In the summer of 2003 a journalist reported what were presented as the words of a leading intelligence source. These words were reputed to indicate that the Blair government repeatedly interfered with intelligence information to distort it and make it more persuasive as a justification for starting a war. The source was eventually confirmed after he committed suicide which in turn followed a process by the Ministry of Defence to release his name by stealth.

An inquiry was launched under a Law Lord called Hutton. Lord Hutton and his team caught a lot of people off guard by the rigour with which they pursued evidence. An awful lot of information was revealed which the key players could never have believed would be unearthed. Up to this point it made sense. It only turns Alice in Wonderland at the point at which Hutton publishes his report and his conclusions directly contradict the bulk of the evidence he has gathered and exonerates the government almost entirely. He does this by the strangest twists and distortions of logic. For example, the phrase which was used to describe the hardening of the material in the published intelligence dossier which was at the heart of the episode was "sexing up". Lord Hutton, probably quite rightly, concluded that he would have to provide a definition of this phrase if a judgement was to be made. In fact, he concludes that there were two possible definitions. One was that "sexing up" could mean adding large amounts of entirely false information to change the implications entirely. The other was that "sexing up" could mean making the presentation of the accurate information more interesting to the general public. His conclusion was that the government were innocent of the former and entirely entitled to attempt the latter.

The observant among you may notice that there are a range of other definitions of this phrase which fall between these extremes. It is like a trial which revolved around the question of whether someone was "hurt" when a building collapsed on them and concluding that there are two definitions of "hurt" – causing a persistent vegetative state or wounding their ego. The former didn't happen, the latter isn't illegal. Case closed. How about a definition of "hurt" which encompassed a sentient life but one confined to a wheelchair (say)? Or how about a definition of "sexed up" which meant pushing at the boundaries of the accuracy of information until it was verging on utterly dishonest or presenting things which were only assessed as being a possibility as certainty or expunging any equally valid information which is counter to the sought case, or simply removing any caveats which would leave room for doubt? What if "sexing up" means distorting real information to such an extent that it appears to show something that in a balanced reading it most certainly doesn't?

Let us dwell on a couple of specific examples from the Hutton inquiry. The dossier stated that Iraq had chemical and biological weapons which were a threat to the world and which could be used within 45 minutes. Everyone was deliberately led to believe that weapons of mass destruction could be launched on innocent countries and this was the headline which many newspapers led with. During the inquiry (that is, over ten months and 30,000 casualties later) it emerged that the 45 minute claim came from a single uncorroborated source, the reliability of which was not ascertainable. (It later came to light that the source was subsequently assessed as unreliable and there is more than a suspicion that experts knew all along that the information was at least suspect. Certainly no other intelligence supported the claim and a number of government intelligence experts who would routinely have seen this kind of information were denied access to it. They claim to have never believed it and think it was kept from them precisely because they would not have assessed it as accurate.) The government specifically asked for the initial wording from the Joint Intelligence Committee ("may be able") be changed (to "is able"). And in any case the claim related only to short-range battlefield weapons such as mortar shells; something which was known but omitted (Tony Blair claims never to have know this – either a lie or inexcusable incompetence).

Is the claim an outright lie? No – someone who might just possibly have known made the claim which makes it 'intelligence'. Was it distorted to the point at which it appeared to show something entirely at odds with what it should have? Absolutely. Is this "sexing up"? Unless you are Lord Hutton.

There are numerous examples of the same thing happening. The balanced intelligence assessment was that the greatest likelihood of Iraq using chemical weapons was if it was attacked. This far-from-inconsequential nugget failed to get anywhere near the final dossier. A subsequent 'intelligence' dossier turned out to have been mainly plagiarised from a decade-old student's thesis almost verbatim. Except the original essay refers to "support for opposition groups" and this was changed to "support for terrorist organisations". Misleading? No question. Sexed up? No question. (Hutton failed to even comment on this dossier.)

Finding examples of how the Hutton inquiry overlooked the 'editing out of maybes' is shooting fish in a barrel, and even the subsequent Butler inquiry into pre-war intelligence (run by another establishment figure and without the participation of any of the opposition parties who boycotted it on the basis of its fiddled remit) concluded that the 'maybes' shouldn't have been removed. But this sin of omission is endemic. There is no policy which is introduced by government anywhere which has any risk or any downside. It is unequivocally good on every occasion, for that reason the only option and if you have any doubt there is always plenty of evidence, none of which has the words 'perhaps' or 'alternatively' anywhere near it.

The point is a simple one; certainty is a precious thing and should be reserved for things about which you are certain. Doubt may be less persuasive, but when you are trying to persuade a country to support an illegal war, doubt is a valuable thing which everyone should have equal access to.

The dismissive discourse

As always, language is the first means of control. Whether we are constraining the sexuality of women by using words like 'slut' or 'frigid' or whether we are undermining the rights of refugees by calling them 'bogus', we shape opinions through our choice of words. This has always been so. The current vogue seems to be the dismissive discourse – encouraging us to write ideas off before even considering them. The dismissive discourse is everywhere in the new politics.

In the run up to the 1997 UK General Election when Tony Blair swept to power I worked for the Scottish Labour Leader in Westminster. During this time I lived among the thrusting young Blairites. One of the things that I remember puzzling me was the extent to which they could appear to be against *everyone*, though not at the same time. If I found myself arguing about the environment in the pub I would suddenly hear the aspiring researchers of aspiring politicians complain about 'the usual bleating tree-huggers'. Surprising, given that those with environmental sympathies are among the target voters for left parties. If the topic of conversation was civil rights it would suddenly be peppered with phrases such as 'Guardian readers' (an insult, apparently), 'muesli eaters', 'sandal wearers', 'chattering classes'. Arch-social conservative David Blunkett later used these same terms in an on-the-record briefing on a civil liberties matter.

Conversations about universal services became about 'subsidies for the middle classes' even though the party's entire taxation policy and election strategy was all a 'middle class perk'. They were contrasted with honest, hard-working, ordinary people. Until redistribution of wealth was raised in which case the 'honest hard-working person' became an 'unreconstructed cloth-cap socialist'. The French were either 'Third Way' fellow travellers or arrogant agricultural subsidy junkies. If single mothers were part of the wider category of 'socially excluded' they were to be helped, but when they were single mothers they were irresponsible and had to be shown the error of their ways. Daily Mail readers were either bedrock middle Britons or prejudiced Daily Mail-reading idiots. Human rights protesters were brave examples for us all when campaigning against abuses in the Islamic world but wrong-headed peacniks when campaigning against human rights abuses perpetrated by Britain or America (or one of our clients). Everyone was to be despised, although never all of the time.

Except, I came to realise, in two cases. Socialists (or the left generally) were always bad, while business leaders (or capitalists generally) were always good. You could probably add soldiers to the always good list, but even nurses are prone to occasional vilification (like on any occasion when they complain about their pay and conditions). That was when I realised what we were about to elect and resigned.

The language of New Labour has been surprisingly negative for a party which appealed to the positive aspirations of the electorate in 1997. People expected a new sort of politics with much less name calling. In fact, they got at least as much name calling as under the terminally declining Tory government. Since Blair has come to office he has attacked anyone who criticises him or his policies. Those opposing 'reform' or 'modernisation' (blanket terms which mean 'whatever Tony wants to do') became 'the forces of conservatism' or 'wreckers'. People who identify ulterior motives in any of Blair's actions are irrelevant 'conspiracy theorists'. Despite being quick to use mockery and satire against his opponents, Blair dismisses anyone who does the same back as irrelevant and lacking in credibility. Those using the veto against the Iraq war resolution at the UN were 'obstructionist' but he is clinging on to his EU vetoes for grim life. Blair's world is populated with usual suspects, awkward squads, obstructionists, the self-interested, the unreconstructed (his director of media tagged the word 'wankers' onto this when he referred to the Scottish media), the plain stupid and the plain wrong. Blair, in his ever deepening egomania, is like an excessively powerful Holden Cauldfield or Travis Binkle (*Catcher in the Rye* and *Taxi Driver* respectively) – seeing failure everywhere around him and assuming he is the only one to see through it.

However, Tony Blair's mental state is his own concern; what is important is the way this influences public debate. Blair and his Ministers use volleys of invective against anyone who attempts to open debate up or to challenge what they are doing. And this *does* influence people. Along with his spiritual allies in the Daily Mail (what more that paper wants from a government than Blair's economics and its Blunkett-style social policies escapes me) Blair briefly succeeded in making a lot of people believe that firefighters were lazy, greedy people. Firefighters wanted to be recognised as professionals and to have their pay regarded accordingly. They asked for a professional salary of £30,000 a year – hardly an extravagant target, particularly given that this was their opening gambit. Blair immediately decried their '40 per cent pay rise' as simply not acceptable. The fact that this wasn't a pay rise but a request for job regrading didn't slow his verbal assault one little bit. Public sympathy certainly started on the side of the firefighters but it dwindled rapidly. It would require some detailed social research to be sure whether this was down to people becoming informed about the details of the pay negotiations and finding the union position unreasonable or misguided or whether it was simple vilification.

Having observed the print media over this time and having heard the types of official comment that the broadcast media was required to broadcast, I have no doubt that the vilification played a large part. Blair's approach can be best summarised in a quote of his. He was commenting on the hundreds of thousands of protesters who had come to one of the big global economic summits to complain about policies he supported. The people protesting were incredibly diverse, from the pretty conservative British trades unions to the radical anarchists, with many in between. There were radical economists, mainstream environmentalists, human rights groups and gay and lesbian groups. There were many very intelligent people with a lot of important things to say. How did Blair respond? "These people have no arguments and as far as they do they are completely wrong and must be challenged at every level." Every single one of this enormous range of thinking people completely and utterly wrong. Not to be debated with, engaged, understood, listened to even. They were to be defeated, ignored, 'challenged'. Blair's message couldn't be clearer. These people were all idiots. Ignore them. And that is the Blair doctrine. "Anyone who disagrees with me has no argument and if they have an argument is it completely wrong and must be defeated."

Some of the most regularly used dismissive phrases are those to describe anyone on the left. Whenever you hear of 'Awkward Squads' or 'Serial Rebels', start paying attention. The fact that we are expected to accept that these people are what they are (arrogant, well meaning, psychotic, old fashioned, dangerous, whatever) and will always act in this way is a clear sign that someone doesn't want us to hear what they say. It is strange that New Labour – the party of On Message – should consider that someone who holds a consistent position should be dismissed immediately for that reason alone. We are supposed to believe that they are the political equivalent of an action movie – see it once and that is plenty. We are supposed to dismiss them immediately because they have done this before. In fact, we are expected to dismiss them before they have even done it. Well, they were bound to do it, right? Why would that be of any interest to you? You knew what was coming. It has become such an accepted fact that Blair even dismisses 'rebels' with an avuncular smile. They are, after all, the doted grandfathers you indulge but don't listen to.

Of course, it is not just Blair; everyone does it. It is actually much worse in America, a country which appears to think in glib soundbites where no-one is convinced by an argument until its merits (or shortcomings) can be summarised in a single catchy sentence. One more time; 'Axis of Evil'? How can you base a foreign policy on such blatant nonsense. We cannot subjugate democratic discussion to the philosophy of 'mud sticks'. We cannot allow ourselves to be manipulated to support a war by calling a country which opposes the war "cheese-eating surrender-monkeys". We cannot let the dismissive discourse shape our thinking. And yet we do.

Don't get involved

All over the world people are expressing great concern at the crisis in democracy. People just aren't turning out to vote like they used to. In Scotland 2003 saw an important election in which a fraction under 50 per cent of those registered to vote did so. All kinds of different people are panicking about why this is and what should be done. So far the suggestions include internet voting, postal voting, compulsory voting, voting in supermarkets, changing the voting system (this is nothing to do with turnout and everything to do with vested interests longing for non-proportional voting again), education campaigns and some sort of appropriation of the lessons of reality TV. Some people are even suggesting that the political parties have to produce a manifesto worth turning out to vote for.

All of it is missing the point. The truth that has to be faced up to is that low political turnouts are not a side-effect of the current international political project – they are one of its aims. For three and a half years of a four-year parliamentary session government politicians tell the public that politics is something which the public should not concern itself with. Throughout the world the free-market based political aristocracy has done everything it could to turn politics into a system of micro management. The leaders of free-market-government have not failed to engage people in politics, they have succeeded in disengaging people from politics.

Any sane person looking at any one-year period in international politics could not draw any comforting conclusions. 2003 was a particular case; the crude manner in which America seized control of the world's second biggest oil field (is anyone still pretending it was about human rights or international security?), the way in which Israel finally gave up on any pretence of a semblance of law in its mass execution programme (please sign here so we can kill you with impunity), Blair's blatant plans to prepare schools, hospitals and universities for eventual take-over by American corporations (section 15 of the foundation hospitals legislation allows for the sub-contraction of all aspects of running a hospital to the private sector), the Germany-in-the-1930s climate we have now adopted to asylum seekers (we're flying handcuffed people back to a country we bombed almost into extinction and where no more than a few percent of the land area is controlled by anyone other than vicious warlords). One of the key conditions for allowing rabid foaming-at-the-mouth free-marketeers to take control of the entire world is that the rest of us avert our eyes (or never hear about it in the first place).

Blair does not attempt to engage in discussions with the electorate. The reason he has given for falling in behind him on foundation hospitals/dismantling the NHS is that if we don't it will be "the biggest mistake for a generation". OK, that's fine then – the political, social and economic concerns some of us had are assuaged now. It is with wonder that we await to find out how he is going to persuade us to back him on his next looting mission into British public life. "If this Parliament blocks this move to hand the running of the home civil service over to Microsoft it will be an affront to God." We have been explicitly told that government is now about doing less in the notional belief that this will therefore mean it is being done better. We are not supposed to question politics; the media/corporate/government agenda does not encourage us to think about politics; we are not educated to understand politics; we are supposed to vote primarily on personality, scare story and vague vision. We are supposed to vote for them once every four years but we are not supposed to hold them to account for any specific thing they did. The new model of political engagement is not accountability but endorsement. We are supposed to endorse the personalities and what they did over the four previous years. If we *really* don't like what they did we *could* remove our endorsement. That would of course be a mistake, we are lead to believe.

This is the world of the partial democrat. Democracy, for the partial-democrat, is about giving legitimacy to what was going to happen anyway. If what was going to happen anyway becomes just too much for the public to stomach (or if they just tire of the incumbents or, on a rare occasion, are actually enthusiastic about an alternative choice) then they can invoke their right of veto and bring in the next lot. And then it is back to business as before. Blair is the partial-democrat *par excellence*. There are two ways in which this is easily recognisable. The first, and by far the most obvious, is the manner in which he views international democracy. In Blair's world view, the purpose of the United Nations is not to make a reasoned, debated, democratic decision but to give legitimacy to the actions of the powerful. A vote is a tribute, not a decision.

The second example of Blair's partial-democratic credentials is the slippery approach to 'the issues'. Blair often claims that what he is really talking about is what people really care about (down with a ban on fox hunting which no-one cares about, up with refugee-bashing 'cos the people ain't keen on foreigners). He would have us believe that this is the principled, issue-led politics which we elected him to deliver. But Blair does not actually fight on the issues. He has only two approaches; deference to values we can't disagree with and a simple "look, I'm a pretty straight sort of a guy so trust me". These have absolutely nothing to do with the issues, and if anyone attempts to pin him down on issues he instantly shuts up shop. "But surely foxhunting is simply wrong and a moral stance should be taken" will be met with either "what we want to do is improve schools and hospitals for the ordinary people of Britain" (nothing to do with the issue) or "no-one wants to see a fox hurt, so trust me and I'll make sure we get round to it" (again, nothing whatever to do with the issue). Whenever a matter needs to be debated, Blair makes out like an American General and fights the battle from such a height above the targets that you can't actually make them out one from another. And he expects us to act like American fighter pilots – just press the button and trust in those wiser than you.

The 1990s saw the boom in lifestyle marketing. This was of course in part an attempt to squeeze a bit more profit out of our lives, but it also had political aims. It was an attempt at fragmentation, an attempt to focus our minds on small, personal matters. It was about ending identity politics. Identity is a personal choice we make with our credit card. Politics is a marginal act we use ballot papers for. If we want to change the way we live we should redecorate. If we get angry, a good dose of top quality chocolate will get those endorphins going again. If we have social problems we can buy a different lifestyle and leave those problems behind (unless, of course, those social problems have anything to do with poverty). With the soothing voice used by all those who would trick us we are lured away from any activity which might change anything by someone who is selling us something. For 'Nike – Just Do It' read 'hey little girl would you like to come and see some rabbits'. In Aldous Huxley's Brave New World the underclass was kept occupied (and oppressed) by distracting them from the mundane unpleasantness of their life. This was done by providing them with inane, complex, pointless games to play in their time off (a sort of glorified crazy golf with machines) and by giving them mind-altering drugs to give them a chemically-induced sense of happiness. Quite what the difference is between this vision and contemporary Scotland escapes me. Except we have Playstations and Ecstasy.

It is the same big businessmen on whose behalf the government is now working who are quickest to discredit politics and politicians (and remember that the owners of virtually all the non-broadcast media are big businessmen with the same motives). In Britain, no political gift to the corporate world is enough. Lowest business taxes in Europe? Still too high. Weakest labour laws in the developed world (America aside)? Still too stringent. Dangerously low levels of health and safety checks? Still too much 'red tape'. But offer anything for people (minimum wage, employee rights, a moratorium on genetically modified crops until we find out if they are safe) is an outrage and loudly decried by the corporations. We are told that politicians are all second rate and that none of them understand business. Too few of them were businessmen. They're not that bright. They are petty and vindictive. It seems odd to me that the single group in society which gets by far the most out of government nowadays is the same group which hates government most. Of course, it isn't odd. They want politics discredited because they don't want people to realise what is going on.

Quite what it is that makes a businessman so suited to running a country anyway? Business has one simple aim – make as much money as possible. It is the fact that the goal is so simple which makes the corporate world view so simplistic. A government, on the other hand, has to manage a complex range of competing and sometimes contradictory goals. The job of running a company is a walk in the park compared to running a country. But don't expect humility from the businessman. In his mind shot put – throwing one ball as far as possible – will always be more significant than juggling

– keeping loads of balls in the air at one time. And he will make sure that this is the general view. So that self-seeking chancer Richard Branson keeps coming high up on polls of the most respected people in Britain. Most respected for what, exactly? What is this great good he has done our society?

Meanwhile politicians regularly come at the bottom of these polls, despite at least some genuine interest in doing some good (well, for many of them and initially at least). In Scotland over and over we are expected to look to 'entrepreneurs' in awe. The two examples which regularly crop up are mobile phone salesman Richard Emmanuel and bra manufacturer Michelle Mone. Why this awe? Emmanuel did no more than buy phones from companies and sell them in Scotland. The sum total of his achievement seems to be the creation of a few low-paid service sector jobs and the economic benefit gained by those restaurants he eats in. The case of Mone is even worse – almost her entire operation is overseas where she employs sweatshop labour. Why would we want our children to be like this? (More on this later.) Politicians, on the other hand... No, stop there. We know they're all second-rate chancers. Free-marketeers want us to hate politics and politicians because they want them all to themselves.

So what happens if people have a choice and actually vote? Well, the free market ideologues have reason to fear democracy. In the early years of the 21st century Venezuela was a virtual object lesson in the control of the social imagination. A leftwing President (but no further to the left than the post-war Labour government in Britain) had been elected democratically. Venezuela is one of the most grotesquely unequal countries in the world. It has under its soil the largest oil reserve outside the middle east, but that resource had been used only to further enrich a Venezuelan elite which was already powerful and rich. As an indication of the distribution of wealth in the country, 78 per cent of the farm land was owned by four per cent of the population. The new President, a dark-skinned man called Hugo Chavez, committed himself to diverting more of the income from the national oil company into healthcare, education and other social provision for the poor. Which meant it was a matter of months before there was an attempted coup – organised by business leaders and backed by the US government.

The coup installed a business leader as President, but only for 24 hours. When the landless peasants heard about the coup they literally descended from the mountains around the capital Caracas in their thousands and demanded Chavez back. The army, who were never entirely behind the coup (Chavez was a military man himself and retained loyalty among the armed forces), rebelled and even with the support of the Americans there was no way to keep the democratically elected President out of power. So, having failed to get rid of him through the preferred Latin American route the Venezuelan elite attempted the Western route and stitched up all the means of communication. The television stations were all owned by Chavez's opponents and broadcast relentless propaganda against the President. They started the strikes – but not strikes as we understand them. The managers of the national oil company (key Chavez opponents) closed down production and mobilised people to protest. This is directly akin to Lord Sainsbury closing all his supermarkets, instructing his employees to protest and then calling it a general strike. But there were mass protests (these seem to have been largely spontaneous) in support of Chavez. And with funding from the US government's 'Endowment for Democracy' an international campaign was run to discredit Chavez and his government. This was so successful that most of the world was completely fooled about what was happening in the country and many political commentators took events to be a popular uprising against a dictator. Finally, the opposition used a recall clause in the constitution (a democratic constitution which Chavez himself pushed through) to call a referendum on whether Chavez should be expelled from office. (The means for gaining the two million signatures required were dubious to say the least; everything from instructing employees to sign at pain of dismissal to simply making up names.)

The turnout for the election was larger than anything we have seen in the West for a long time. People who knew Venezuela knew that Chavez would win – even with the difficulties the dispossessed faced in voting there was such a majority of them that they were going to re-elect him. Even so, the Independent reported on the night before that Chavez was about to be beaten (there is a crisis in journalism when a respected paper can be sold a lie and fail to even check it out). Everything money could achieve was attempted to influence the outcome. Chavez won by a margin of two to one. The opposition disputed the result, despite international observers giving it their approval. Even after eight votes in six years in favour of Chavez and his party the rich refused to accept the result. That is why democracy can be dangerous to them, and that is why they don't really want you to vote.

So we have a sect of 'partial democrats' who pass themselves off as the democratic manifestation of the very souls of the people. But they hate the idea of accountability and instead favour occasional opportunities for endorsement. They do not want people to understand the nitty gritty of the way their lives are governed, and certainly have no intention of doing anything which would change this (such as including basic civics lessons at school). Government actively discourages scrutiny. Then there are the massively powerful forces of big business and the media (much the same thing actually) who want to discredit politics as much as possible partly to weaken a system which is still in the control of the people (if they chose to exercise that control) and who do this by the drip-drip of perpetual criticism and complaining. And at the same time we are being continually distracted from all of this by a cult of lifestyle marketing which has us gazing at glittering sparkly things which we are supposed to believe are 'real life'. The result is that we leave those who have our interests least at heart to shape our government. And then we complain about the state of our world.

Crisis in democracy? I should say so.

There is no 'there' there

After the Scottish parliamentary elections of 2003 a conference was organised to discuss the outcomes. Campaign managers from all the parties came and talked about how they had run their campaign; the strategy of how to target voters, the means by which messages were put across, the budgets and areas of expenditure, the canvass and so on. Then an academic looked at the results and analysed them from a number of angles; voting rate by constituency, age, region, patterns of party vote over a decade and trends and shifts between parties. Another academic considered what this would mean for how the Parliament would work in future; numbers on committees, majorities and how they would be formed, the importance of party discipline. And then a panel session of politicians discussed what this election had meant for Scotland. Much concern was expressed about the low voter turnout and what could be done to change that. Others raised questions about the governance arrangements within parties and how they could ensure both stable government and still allow some freedom for backbenchers. Many interesting points were raised and much was learned. However, in the course of this whole event, almost nobody thought to talk about politics. You know, competing political programmes and differences in views on how the country should be run. There was angst about how committees should be constituted but none on what the election might mean for what the committees talked about.

For those that don't know, the 2003 election saw the return of seven Green, six socialist MSPs, a party that campaigned on pensioners rights and a candidate who stood opposing the rationalisation of health service delivery (in an era when ideology is dead, remember). In every case their seat came at the expense of one of the two parties in Scotland which are considered centre left but which had drifted to the right over the previous four years (longer in the case of Labour). Surely this is a clear sign that the electorate was now on the left of the main parties and was forcing a conscious shift of

Scottish politics in that direction? Well apparently not. In the entire course of the day's discussion the theme of the protest vote and disillusionment with the big political parties cropped up a few times but that was it. The message was clear – a vote for a centrist or right wing party was a conscious choice while a vote for a left wing party was a protest. There is no politics here, only party brands and protest votes.

This strange omission can be found again and again. There is a whole generation of young(ish) commentators emerging in Scotland who are greatly concerned about governance and the way institutions of government are run. They are following on from a phalanx of 'centre left' think tanks in London which have fetishised governance. They never talk about political programmes – these are assumed to be consensual – but cannot find an end to their fascination with how the machine works. The effect of this is no surprise. It makes us all believe that the choice is about how rather than what. How is an important question – and nothing ever got done without a how. But it is only a meaningful question if it follows the what question. What do we do, then how do we do it; never the latter without the former.

Another manner in which politics has been ripped straight out of politics is the rise and rise of gossip as the correct form of political discussion. There are pages and pages of political commentary and coverage which is devoted to the idle gossip of the political classes. Did Gordon and Tony make a deal? Why did Alex Salmond/Alan Millburn/Estelle Morris *really* resign? Did the Prime Minister's wife *really* shower naked with another woman? This forms a large part of the bulk of our politics and it is insidious. When the political differences between the parties becomes negligible, something else has to be found to talk about and gossip has proved an easy column filler. Tony Blair is right to decry the focus on this tittle tattle at the expense of the real issues. As usual, though, he is being entirely disingenuous. Blair doesn't want us to ignore the gossip in favour of the meat of the politics. Quite the opposite. The thing Blair detests more than anything else is having to defend the detail of his policies (not the meaningless high principles – he can talk about that for weeks – the actual details of what policies mean on the ground). Blair would hate it if there was a genuine public debate about the impact of introducing a rampant free market into higher education or if people really understood the impact of allowing some hospitals to become profit generating. He would much rather stick to the woolly stuff and where that isn't enough he will find something else to preoccupy us. Usually gossip. Blair doesn't mean that he wants political commentators to stop printing gossip, just that he wants them to stop printing other people's gossip. The New Labour spin machine has lead the market in unattributable briefings, character assassination through hints and leaks and diversionary tactics. That is how the vacuity of his administration's ambitions and the insidious nature of the gradual sell-off of Britain are kept out of the press.

This is about the end of ideology, but it is the specific means. By talking about governance rather than policy differences we are led to believe that there is no choice in what we do, only choices in how we do it. By talking about the whole political process in terms of the interpersonal relationships of the key players we are gently led to believe that this is the important thing. The problem has got so bad that quite a lot of the professionals can't even see the politics anymore. To my knowledge there has been only one brief mention of the left-shift of the 2003 election in any of the mainstream print or broadcast media. Ironically, that was a passing and grudging sentence written by one of the most reactionary New Labour commentators. People can't see politics if it hits them in the face. Scotland fought for decades for a Parliament of its own, and then it comes along with no politics attached. Keep your ears open, listen to the so-called political debate and see if you can find anything to pad out the governance and gossip enough to call it politics. You'll struggle.

There are no side effects, only effects

Think of an imaginary community. Let's call it Blairton. Blairton is a medium-sized town with a reasonably affluent section but a significant amount of relative poverty as well. The middle classes of Blairton, like the middle classes everywhere, are fairly effective at getting what they want. They vote and write letters, you see. Well, the suburbs of Blairton are pissed off. They want their taxes lowered so they can afford that second foreign holiday. So that's what they get. But because the people of Blairton also want good schools for their children and decent free healthcare, more money has to be found. So a whole bunch of assets which were partly owned by the people of Blairton are sold off and the proceeds used to subsidise their tax cuts while keeping the schools and hospital running. But there still isn't enough money so spending on the schools and hospitals is cut. Only marginally, but it is cut nonetheless.

Meanwhile the assets which used to be owned by the people of Blairton are now owned by private individuals who got them cheap and are now making a profit from them; a profit which can actually be traced back to the wallets and purses of the people of Blairton. So they don't feel much better off and then gradually they start to notice that the school is starting to look a bit run down and the hospital isn't what it used to be. So they get pissed off again and decide it is time for a change. Now they want money put into the schools and hospitals again. So, because they always get what they want, these people get a commitment to more investment in the local hospital and the local schools. But because the schools and the hospitals are not in good condition, the amount of money that would need to be invested to get them back on their feet again is quite large. So targets are set which they cannot meet and they are deemed to be 'failing'.

The people of Blairton are told that this now means that something more radical is necessary. So to turn round these failing schools and hospitals they are told that they must modernise. For the school this means that it has to be knocked down, the land sold for houses and a new school built miles away. But it will be built by wealthy private individuals (by coincidence the same ones who made all the money from the sell-off of all those assets) who will have to take some profit – the price for 'saving' these 'failing' schools. For the hospital this means that all of the poorly paid jobs will be sold off to the same wealthy private individuals and those that survive will be even more poorly paid. And at first the locals are happy – they have a shiny new school (even if it is pretty inconvenient to get to) and there seems to be more money going into the hospital.

But eventually they begin to have doubts. First of all they discover that the new school is not quite what they expected – fewer classrooms, fewer teachers, built on the cheap. And there is more unruly behaviour. Then the hospital starts missing its targets by even more than the did before. The suburbs are confused and angry. This wasn't supposed to happen. Then they notice that the substantial group of poor people in the town has got both more substantial and poorer. And with no money and no hope they begin to behave worse, so now the suburbs don't feel safe. Of course, the suburbs aren't aware that these poor people used to work at the hospital before they were 'downsized', or had jobs that relied on the assets that got sold off, or used to work in the parts of the town which have largely disappeared as the shops all moved out to where the school used to be and the expensive housing now is. And their kids have to travel by bus for half an hour every morning to get to school (they don't have Range Rovers, these types) which makes organising childcare even more difficult. And the poverty causes deterioration in the health of the community and the educational standards drop which explains why the school and the hospital miss their targets by even more.

The suburbs don't know this. They just start demanding more policemen and stiffer sentences. So the wealthy individuals step in and build prisons. But, of course, this doesn't help. And so, in quiet moments, the suburbs try to think back (memories are of course hazy by now). They still can't afford that extra holiday – the tax breaks were all taken up by those Range Rovers without which their kids would be forced to sit on the bus with the troublemakers and on home security devices without which they wouldn't be safe. So they feel no better off. But now their hospital is in a mess and the school is in a mess and the town isn't safe like it used to be. The poor folk, meanwhile, are much worse off (though it doesn't do for the suburbs to dwell on this). In these quiet moments the suburbs might scratch their heads and wonder, who *is* better off here? A suspicion might sneak up on them at this point. The only people who seem to be really better off are those wealthy people who bought the assets cheap and got paid to build the school and cut the wages of the hospital janitors and then built the prisons. But it is only a passing suspicion, so when the wealthy people come back and say that the only option is for them to take over the running of the whole school and the whole hospital, the suburbs give a little nod of dumb acceptance. But it does play on their minds. Surely it is the middle classes that are supposed to get what they want, not those wealthy people who don't even live in Blairton?

If we are given a pill to cure our cough and it does but all our hair falls out, this is generally known as a side effect. It is nothing of the sort. It is just an effect. We have been conditioned to believe that if the primary aim of any given action is met, anything else which results from it is an anomalous and secondary issue. This is nonsense. Everything which results from an action is an effect of that action and the success or otherwise of that action can only be assessed by considering the overall impact of all of these effects. That, of course, is not how we are trained to think about public policy. Is modernisation acceptable if it means job losses? That, for those who currently govern us, is the wrong question. The correct question is 'is modernisation the right thing to do?' The answer to that is always yes – who doesn't want to be modern? So we modernise and the outcome brings misery to a lot of people. But this is a side effect and not the fault of modernisation.

Myopia is usually taken to be the problem with much of how the public relates to policy; a short-sighted approach which fails to consider the long game. Well tunnel vision is every bit as much of a problem – the ability to see only what is straight in front of you and blindness to what is happening just out of the line of sight. We are strongly encouraged to view the world as a series of disconnects. Things don't connect to each other but are supposed to function independently. So we have targets which are sprayed all over the place but which measure only one thing at a time. Thus we are supposed to believe that there is never any connection between Gross Domestic Produce targets and, say, greenhouse gas emission targets. Or health targets and inflation targets. Or poverty targets and stock market indicators. This belief is wrong. We knowingly sacrifice emissions targets on the basis that they would harm GDP (although unlike the Americans we don't say it). When we suppress pay to keep inflation in check this affects the health of the lowest paid. When we celebrate soaring share prices we ignore that they may be at the cost of the livelihood of many of the poorest people in our society. Everything is connected, nothing is incidental.

This problem becomes very much greater when the disconnect is across continents. It wasn't so very long ago that I really believed that the poverty in Africa was largely to do with the weather (it was sad to realise that Blue Peter was part of the conspiracy...). People in Africa starve because of our trade policies, designed to boost further our own wealth. Our second family car and a dying child in Somalia are not two random events happening in isolation. They are intimately, inseparably connected. Terrorism and oil exploration are bound together. The school run in that Range Rover and the death of the rain forest are bound together. Robert Mugabe and the Common Agricultural Policy are bound together. War and arms exports are bound together (and the fact that we don't make this connection very often shows how bad the problem has become). But because we allow others to maintain an endlessly narrow focus we simply can't see their binds.

Returning to Blairton, a quick scan shows that the very thing that people want is often the opposite of what they get, even though they get the thing they think they want. This is, in part, the root of the great disillusionment with politics. Sometimes it really does feel that change is impossible because even attempts to make modest change seem to fail so terribly. In fact, these changes haven't 'failed' at all, they have often fully succeeded. It's just that the baggage of what people have actually signed up to isn't what they thought they signed up to. It is the policy equivalent of the small print. It is the conjurers trick of misdirection. It is the beguiling tale of the confidence trickster. It is the doctor's cure which has to kill you before it can cure you.

We are not equipped to reconnect all these disconnects. Everyday people don't have the breadth of knowledge or understanding to put the whole picture together (who really follows all the changes in, say, penal policy and the full range of implications?). The rank and file politicians themselves are too busy trying to find the best piece of disconnected information to prove their case (either for or against). The leaders often have other motives (for example, you can be sure that Big Tobacco is very well aware of every connection in policy and they know where they are putting their money). The commentators, meanwhile, are often too bothered with commenting on what happened *today* and will rarely connect it with what happened two years ago last Wednesday.

If only the people of Blairton would talk to each other properly and think about what might happen to their neighbours and, ultimately, themselves if the step ahead of them is taken. If only they could think about what happens tomorrow if they eat all the fish in the river today. If only they could decide what they *really* want – not just one thing they have a hankering for today but the sum of all their hopes – then perhaps they might end up getting it.

Compared to what?

There was a time when it was perfectly reasonable to offer someone six loaves of bread for a chicken. It made perfect sense – I need chicken, you need bread, let's do it. Of course as the transactions became more complicated the comparisons became more difficult. 'I'll give you fourteen hours of use of my gym and swimming pool for one of your electronic hand blenders' is a much less intuitive proposition. Thus barter died and money was invented. But barter is back, certainly when it comes to public debate. One of the benchmark bartered goods, a currency if you like, is your average nurse. You see, whatever it is you do (if you are a public servant) you will always be compared to a nurse the second you ask for a fair pay rise. When the firefighters went on strike to ask for a decent salary, a host of New Labour ministers appeared on television asking why firefighters thought they deserved it more than nurses. No-one thought to ask the ministers why they thought neither of them deserved it. The crude act of comparison is a useful trick when you want to undermine the case being made by one group. Just pick any other group which garners more public sympathy and which is also poorly paid and there you go.

It is of course a sorry state of affairs when the poor nurses are being used to suppress the salaries of the rest of the public sector, but then there isn't much they can do about it. It isn't only nurses though – you can use which ever comparator suits your case best. If firefighters were pointing out that they risked their lives, then politicians would compare them to soldiers. If the argument was among the sympathetic left-leaning middle classes, it was suddenly social workers who were chosen as the representatives of the down-trodden masses. If it suited, international comparisons were used, so suddenly we all became familiar with how much French firefighters were paid. We learned nothing about how much French nurses and social workers were paid so I think we can assume that this is not such a convenient comparison. The chain of poverty comparison can go on for ever. Presumably if nurses go on strike sometime soon, we will be reminded of the sterling work carried out by those poorly paid hospital porters. If the porters strike, we will be reminded that hospital cleaners get paid a pittance. And if the cleaners strike, then we'll discover just how little those same cleaners would earn if they were working in the private sector. Of course, these comparisons never work back up the way again. So you never hear firefighters compared to civil servants or social workers to MPs.

It isn't only to justify the low wage culture that we see these remarkable comparators. Just before we blew it up we were very prone to comparing Iraq to prosperous Western democracies. This is of course a dishonest thing to do. The comparison isn't best made with Sweden or Switzerland. A better comparison would be Brazil or India; democracies, for sure, but ones with the kind of social problems that even Iraq didn't face. Equally, the comparison wasn't made with, say, Saudi Arabia, a much more obvious comparator. Neither of these types of comparison are of any use because they prove, respectively, that democracies do not necessarily deliver justice and that the West doesn't actually have any problem with dictatorships anyway. Saddam is compared with Hitler or Stalin, but successive American presidents have been responsible for not dissimilar levels of casualties in countries such as Nicaragua, El Salvador or Chile, Vietnam or Cambodia. He is never compared to Suharto whose crimes were similar.

Then there is the more mundane comparison, but still designed to discredit and skew any debate. For four years the Scottish Parliament received nothing but media attacks because it had the temerity to criminalise the practice of chasing foxes to petrified exhaustion and ripping them to bits with dogs. For fun. Few of these media attacks actually justified the practice (although the land-owning, right-wing proprietors were itching to raise their blood-smeared faces above the parapet) because editors knew that there really was very little public sympathy for the barbaric practice. So instead the line of attack was a simple comparison of what the Parliament spent its time on. Why are you banning fox hunting when the economy is in such a mess? Or when crime is rising? Or whichever item of right-wing orthodoxy was convenient. How quickly many on all sides adopted this as a legitimate argument – as if there was some great act of Parliament which would have transformed Scotland if it hadn't been pushed off the Parliamentary timetable by the couple of hours in four years which had actually been spent debating the Hunting with Dogs Bill. Any commentator with a shred of intelligence ought to have dismissed this puerile piece of nonsense out of hand. Instead they collectively agreed to trade four bottles of French wine for a three piece suite.

There is also a more subtle form of comparison in which Lords of the Manor suddenly appear (because this comparison has nothing to do with pay). This is a particular favourite of the bandit capitalists who are posing as a Labour government. Of course it is fair to charge fees to go to university because it is the middle classes that go to university and why should the poor pay for their education? Or more specifically, why should a cleaner pay for a Lord's education? This time the purpose of the comparison is to create a distraction. The question is, of course, nonsensical. There is certainly a problem with the social class profile of university students – far too high a percentage are from wealthy backgrounds. But the problem is one of early years education and not one of reverse redistribution of wealth. The problem will be solved by reducing poverty and increasing early years and school educational standards for all. It will not be solved by charging for entry. It makes no sense whatsoever. The question can, and has, been applied to other public services. Why should a cleaner pay for a Lord's heart bypass operation? Well, for one very simple reason – from each according to ability to pay to each according to need. If these faux-socialists are worried about the perks available to a Lord, tax them at a proper rate and put the money into the health service. But if the Lord falls ill, let's cure him to the best of our collective abilities for the simple reason that he too is a human.

You will find these kinds of comparisons everywhere. Why put money into the arts when it could go into hospitals? Why put money into hospitals when it could go into preventative measures? Why put it into preventative measures when we could give it in tax cuts and let people choose their own level of health? Why put it into tax cuts when we could put it into the arts? We are faced with an endless role-call of competing choices, none of which are real choices but are actually false comparisons. The bartering of public policy is, like so much else, a race to the bottom.

Too far, too far

The spectrum, as discussed above, has a more flexible, issue by issue use. It might be typified as the exception which disproves the rule (as opposed to the exception which doesn't disprove the rule discussed below). This is to cowboy politics what a faulty washer is to cowboy plumbers; a marginal and insignificant factor used to persuade us that a perfectly sound whole needs scrapped. But in the case of the cowboy politician it is often grasped at in desperation rather than confidently asserted from the outset.

Let's look at two examples. In both cases you have to start from the assumption generally accepted at the time that many things are negotiable in the Labour movement (such as its values and principles) but Tony Blair's divine right to rule is beyond debate. So it is that we see the Labour movement turn against the firefighters who went on strike at the end of 2002. Initially the firefighters looked to be in a strong position. They are really quite poorly paid for such a dangerous and important job and for one which requires a high level of performance. They had asked in effect to be regarded as professionals (moving from about £22,000 to £30,000). The Blair Government's response can only be described as Thatcherite. Their immediate first step was to ridicule the call for a 40 per cent 'wage rise' (a wage rise and a regrading are different things, of course). Then they were compared to nurses and virtually called greedy. Then they were told that they might get an above inflation rise but only if restructuring (i.e. job losses) was part of the deal. Like every negotiation the firefighters started high in their demands. Unlike successful negotiations the Government started not from a position of trying to reach a reasonable settlement but from a position of being seen to be tough on the unions. The aim was not to reach a settlement but to be seen to beat the firefighters.

This caused big difficulties in the wider Labour movement as well as in many parts of the party. The Labour Government is still heavily funded by the unions because they are supposed to represent the interests of workers. The firefighters had a very good claim for better pay. Many people were sympathetic to the firefighters – among the public they began with high levels of support – and in the Labour Party this sympathy was widespread. No-one expected the Government to give the firefighters everything they wanted, but many did expect an outcome which gave the firefighters something meaningful while leaving all the parties involved with credibility. So when the Government took their desire to be seen to be tough to the point of overruling an agreement between the firefighters and their employers because it wasn't tough enough (specifically because it didn't involve job losses), many Labour Party members were either pretty disgusted or certainly very uncomfortable. Even a lot of the loyalist activists were unhappy with their Government's approach.

So the dispute dragged on and the Government rhetoric got stronger and stronger, the attempts to vilify the firefighters more and more pointed. This did nothing to calm the nerves of activists. But then Fire Brigades Union leader Andy Gilchrist made a speech to a political conference. In that speech he voiced the opinion that Blair no longer represented the interests of the unions or of the workers more generally. He went on to say that the dispute should mark the watershed when the unions should wrest back the Labour Party from the right-wing New Labour clique which had hijacked it. And that was all it took. Suddenly Gilchrist was being talked about by every cabinet minister as the man who was trying to destabilise and destroy a Labour government. Most activists knew that this meant very little, and many people had expressed the desire to see Labour becoming a left of centre party again. But just as that broken washer allows a dishonest plumber to persuade you that the whole kitchen needs replaced, so this 'gaffe' enabled Labour activists to pretend that irrespective of the strong and perfectly fair claims of the firefighters and despite the jack-boot behaviour of the Government, the whole case had been undone. The firefighters were unmasked, either as communist revolutionaries or as gullible fools who had been allowed to be used by communist revolutionaries.

This was a fig leaf of a reason to fall fully behind the Thatcherite attack on a trade union. But a second example is in some ways more worrying. This one related to the build up to the war on Iraq. Neither defence nor foreign affairs are devolved to the Scottish Parliament so throughout the build up the Scottish Executive held the line that this was not a matter on which they were able to comment or take a position. However, while the Scottish Parliament cannot legislate in areas of defence or foreign affairs it can express an opinion on any matter it wants. The issue had become so controversial that after the enormous peace march in Glasgow in February it was clear that the 'head in the sand' position could not hold for ever. By the time that the SNP had come out and opposed the war and the Liberal Democrat coalition partners were clearly getting restless, the Scottish Labour Party realised that some sort of vote was coming and started to support the war quite vocally.

In the end a number of motions were put before the Parliament. Labour backbenchers were of course as uncomfortable with Blair's blood-thirsty rush to war, but it was easy for them to reject the SNP motion – in the schoolyard yah boo of modern politics it is apparently acceptable to reject something solely on the basis that it is from another party. (Indeed, this is another example of exceptions disproving rules. Even if an opposing party puts forward a motion which is correct in every way, you can simply call it a publicity stunt or a cynical ploy and throw it straight out. Thus it was that the Liberal Democrats voted *against* an SNP motion calling for proportional representation for local government – their number one aspiration.) So the amendment which became the focus for all the anti-war MSPs came from Labour backbench dissident John McAllion. The Liberal Democrats chose to support this one, and when the SNP motion fell they were happy to back it too.

There were always going to be a number of Labour rebels on this one and this meant that even with the support of the Tories the McConnell administration were perilously close to defeat. This put an enormous amount of pressure on those who knew they ought to be rebelling but had become serial loyalists in a 'no matter what' sort of way. They were at real risk of infuriating and losing the support of their constituency parties, they were going entirely against the grain of public opinion and, frankly, they knew they would have been plain wrong to support an illegal war. This was a dilemma indeed. So they were all looking for straws to cling to. On the morning of the vote John McAllion gave an interview to BBC television and, as usual, he was passionate and persuasive. There was almost nothing in what he said that could be disagreed with. But he made the 'mistake' of saying that this was an important step in reclaiming the Labour Party from the unrepresentative clique which had taken it over. A collective sigh of relief went up among the loyalists without a cause which make up much of the Labour back benches in the Scottish Parliament. "He's gone too far, too far" they chanted. Finally they had an excuse (!) not to vote for the McAllion amendment. Was this because the war would not now go ahead? No. Was it because it was now legal? No Was it because it now had international support, or because it would no longer mean the deaths of tens of thousands of Iraqi civilians and many more poor conscripted soldiers, or because Iraq was suddenly shown to pose a genuine threat to the world or because it had stopped being about American control of oil? No, no, no and no. It was because one man had dared to suggest that Blair was in the wrong and should be called to account. Thus it was that McConnell won his vote (or rather how he won Blair's vote for him) by a tiny majority. In the end, only five Labour MSPs rebelled. Anyone with basic cognitive powers and any traces of a morality would find this hard to comprehend. Let's be clear – the Scottish Parliament came to support this travesty of international justice and this wholesale slaughter and pillaging because one well-meaning politician dared to suggest that something should change. I wonder what these MSPs tell their constituents when they ask about those civilian deaths. Do they reply "yes, but they deserved it because John McAllion criticised Tony Blair"?

Pulling down an entire edifice on the pretext of one minor flaw is, of course, an American speciality where you only have to hear a single moderate comment for the whole argument to be dismissed as the 'usual liberal crap'. Israel makes a speciality of it. You can spend as long as you like making a serious and carefully argued point about the country's abominable behaviour and without fail the pro-Israel lobby will find one phrase that it can pull out of context to prove that you are an anti-Semite and so to be ignored. It is nothing more than yet another way to silence people and to protect the established lies.

Be afraid. Be very afraid.

The right thrives on fear, the left on hope. It has always been thus. Part of the reason that the right has been so dominant is that it is easier to make people afraid of the problems that exist than it is to offer hope that things will change. That is why fear of all sorts – logical, illogical, founded or unfounded – is crucial to the right wing project. Fear, and its close partner hate, is the fuel which runs the Daily Mail and its equivalents. If you doubt this take a glance at the paper for a week or two. Draw two columns on a piece of paper. At the top of one column write 'makes me feel better about my world', at the top of the other write 'makes me feel worse about my world'. Then spend some time allocating the Mail's stories and editorial comments into one of these two columns. Education is doomed, crime is everywhere, asylum seekers are swamping us with deadly diseases, our taxes are rocketing, paedophiles are after our children, gays are destroying marriage, the poor are scrounging off us. There is very little to put in the 'feel better' column. If the Daily Mail published this during a war its editors would be shot as traitors. It has one function and that is to make us hate and fear almost everything around us.

And the remarkable thing is that very little of this fear is grounded in anything like reality. We are told that education is dumbing down, but the only evidence for this is that more people are doing better (you are expected to draw your own conclusions from this). Crime is actually pretty static and lower than in previous periods. Doctors deny that there is any 'epidemic' stemming from diseases brought in by asylum seekers. Tax take is still among the lowest in a developed country. Paedophilia is probably significantly less common now than in previous eras where we can assume a much higher degree of unreported incidents. Marriage was on the road out well before 'gays' were even given basic rights. And if the 'us' is meant to mean 'hard-working upper middle class types' (the Daily Mail's perpetual 'us') then 'we' are doing very much better in relation to the poor than 'we' ever were. Meanwhile the things we really ought to be worried about such as global warming, the highly dangerous power of big corporations or the vicious foreign policy of the US are presented as benign.

The bizarre impact of fear is well explored in Michael Moore's excellent documentary *Bowling for Columbine*. Here we see interviews with Canadians who have been burgled and who still have no fear of crime (to the extent that they actually leave their doors unlocked). Meanwhile Americans who have never been the victim of crime seem permanently petrified. Moore points out that this is almost entirely down to the media, some of it intentionally generated, some just a by-product of the sensationalism endemic in American television. Moore recounts the tale often told (in my school at least) of the evil man who hid razor blades in the sweets he gave out to children on Halloween. Except Moore points out that there have only been two poisonings ever recorded on Halloween, neither involving razor blades and in both cases a specific child was targeted for family reasons. I then recall the horror we felt as kids when we heard the story of 'casuals' (football gangs) wedging razor blades in the flumes at Edinburgh's Commonwealth Pool and the stories of children being sliced horribly.

But while this generalised fear has the effect of bringing out our red teeth and claws and making us much more susceptible to illiberal right-wing policies, it is also targeted at specific cases. Asylum seekers have become a particular target, for instance. The idea that we are all going to catch a horrible and deadly disease from these people (actually, they are beginning to be presented as almost sub-human) is now a key part of allowing ourselves to hate them. The fear of crime is also designed with a specific end point. The evidence shows that, give or take fluctuations in types of crime committed (more gun crimes as we become more Americanised, for example) we are much less likely to be the victim of crime than we were in 1979. And yet we are way, way more scared of crime than they were. How can this be? If it isn't the experience of crime – and it isn't – then it has to be the presentation of crime. Check those tabloid editorials again. Fear of crime is used to justify all sorts of illiberal posturing. Crime is the result of the permissive society – women going out to work, marriage being undermined by homosexuals, basic welfare provision encouraging the poor to think that they can take what they like. Poverty is never fingered as a cause, but almost anything else the right wants to target is. There is no evidence for the fear and no logic in the way it is used, but it is everywhere.

Advertising fear has a slightly different kind of effect. As usual, advertising is much more subtle than other forms of campaigning. Adverts don't tell you that you're ugly, but they certainly leave you feeling as if you are. The whole basis of modern advertising seems to be to make you feel basically shit about yourself one way or another, or at the very least to make you feel as if someone else has it much better than you do. Consider some of the current adverts on the television. Again, take a piece of paper and write down what you think each advert was intended to make you believe about yourself and how you think it was meant to make you feel. Read it back. It will probably look something like:

> My car is shit
> My house is shit
> I'm boring
> My clothes are old
> My family life is inadequate
> Everyone is cooler than me
> Everyone is funnier than me

I smell
I'm lonely
I don't have enough money
I can't cook and best not to try
My job sucks
I'm ugly
My girlfriend is ugly

This happens over and over and over. In the pages of magazines the women always seem to look better than the women I know. Of course, if the women I knew were made up, lit, photographed, digitally touched up and put on the glossy page like these women I'd be wondering why I didn't know women like them. When I park my car I only have to walk fifty metres to find a picture of a car which not only looks much better but is zooming round the scenic coasts of Europe rather than crawling around the streets of Edinburgh during rush hour, not gleaming but in need of a good wash. Every shop I pass to get to the bus has something in it that I feel is better than the equivalent that I have. The bus has a big picture of a movie star on the side of it. His hair looks better than mine and despite the fact that I have clothes similar to the ones he's wearing, they just don't look that good on me. In the bus there are newspapers and magazines with people behind them. I can't see the people but I can see the perfume adverts on the back. Do I smell OK? There are adverts on the inside of the bus. By the time I get into the office in the morning (a maximum one hour commute) I must have seen hundreds of things which are better than my things. I am scared that this will somehow count against me. When I switch on my computer some guy called Eric has emailed me to tell me that I can easily afford a penis enlargement. Someone else tries to sell me Viagra.

Hypercapitalism is every bit as much about controlling the desire for consumption as controlling the means of production. We have to keep buying so we have to be at least a bit passive, suggestible, open minded. But passive people don't do all that much, so we need to be motivated. So we are made to be afraid of not buying. We have to be scared to be seen in last year's jeans. And yes, it sells products and at a rate never seen before in human existence. But what is the cost? My generation seems to have problems. We seem restless, unfulfilled, disorientated, unhappy. No wonder – we have been undermined constantly for as long as anyone can remember. Nothing we can ever have will match the platonic ideal which is used to drive us onwards and onwards. I try to imagine the alternative. I think about advert breaks on the TV in which one in every three adverts consists of someone reassuring speaking in a friendly calm voice telling me "Don't worry. Your car works fine, it's reliable and it's comfortable. Your clothes look good on you. You smell perfectly fine and I really like what you've done with your house. Your friends are really nice and your girlfriend is lovely. Don't buy anything today, just enjoy the wonderful things you've got."

In the '90s the manipulation of politics through fear and the sale of goods through fear met up in the misdirection and sleight of hand of lifestyle marketing. As already mentioned, we were told to worry about achieving the 'life' we wanted and not waste our time with big matters which would be taken care of for us ('you worry about your snowboard, we'll manage that war on your behalf'). In the '50s all we had to worry about was communists. That was fine – you didn't meet them every day and people were paid to catch them. We have drifted into a world in which we are expected to be afraid of everything. So we are. The psychosocial and psychological effect will probably not be felt until my generation is retiring. By then the country will be run by boys who had reached their 20s too afraid to leave the house in anything that wasn't a designer label and girls who were scared at the age of nine that their underwear wasn't sexy enough.

But the king of all fear is American fear. Nobody is scared like Americans are scared. It is of course ironic that no other nation is quite as petrified as the most powerful one on the planet. It is partly the cultural history of America – frontierism, the threat of savages (actually, the people who lived there, but fear makes us see squint), the 'fear of a black planet' as Public Enemy memorably put it, the fear of lawlessness, of witches, of Hellfire preachers. Whatever it is, it has never been stronger. Because the king of all American fear has become the fear of foreigners. The attacks on Manhattan on September 11 2001 generated a fear which must surely be unique. An entire country is petrified of a terrorist attack which will almost certainly not harm them. To stand a chance of harming anything approaching a meaningful proportion of Americans terrorists would *actually* need to set off a so-called 'dirty bomb' or *actually* release large amounts of chemical or biological weapons. How easy is it to get large amounts of this stuff into America and distribute it? No-one should be dismissive or complacent about protecting their citizens from genuine threat, but surely threat and fear should be in proportion?

Well, they would if the fear was about protection and not precisely the kind of manipulation that was discussed above. If you aren't yet aware of the Project for the New American Century, type it into Google and check out their website. But be warned, it may be some time before you sleep soundly again. PNAC is an alliance of rightwing extremists in America. Their open doctrine is that of 'full spectrum dominance' – the control of every aspect of everyone's life to ensure the perpetual supremacy of America. By controlling the world's military power they can control the world's economic power. By controlling the economic power they can control the military power. Once you can control these you can control everything. PNAC realised that this was possible as soon as there was only one superpower left. By the second half of the '90s, much less than a decade after the fall of the Berlin wall, PNAC was putting forward a pretty brutal strategy for ensuring that no-one and nothing could ever again stop America from doing exactly what it wanted. PNAC would under usual circumstances be a cult. Unfortunately they found themselves a frontman and now they run America. The names of the signatories to PNAC's 1997 masterplan (of which Blofeld or any other Bond villain would have been proud) are pretty much the same names appointed to virtually everything in the Bush White House. Rumsfeld, Cheney, Wolfowitz, Pearle and so on.

The PNAC plan has many elements to it – the breaking of various international treaties to allow America to militarise space (almost done), the overthrow of Iraq and Afghanistan (done), the rolling back of environmental protection (being done), the destruction of the UN (underway). They wanted tax cuts and got them. They wanted more powers for the security services and got them. They wanted big changes in civil liberties and got them. And this was published in 1997, more than four years before 'terrorism' was something the US public had to worry about. But what is most worrying is that PNAC knew that they couldn't get what they wanted without fear. In a passage which would be enough to get an Arab detained indefinitely without charge or trial, PNAC recognised that progress towards these goals would be slow without a shock to the system, something of the magnitude of Pearl Harbour. This was their precise reasoning. Funnily enough they got that too.

Generations to come will look back at the cabal running America in the early years of the 21st century with nothing but distaste. They took the greatest human tragedy to hit America for 50 years and used it brutally and cynically to further their extremist views. Given the convenience of events, future generations may also discover some level of complicity. Of course, there is nothing new in any of this. Hitler was very well aware that fear and hate motivate men and women in ways that hope and reasoning can't. The Holocaust was about genocide, but it was also about control. We cannot live our lives in fear, or at the very least we cannot call it living. The truth is that we are safer now than we have ever been (in the rich north at least). We have a much better chance of living a long and healthy life, we are much less likely to suffer and we have levels of luxury that our grandparents couldn't have dreamed of. It is actually perfectly possible just to wake up one morning and decide not to be scared anymore, and as soon as we do it will be much harder to drag us around by the nose.

Henry Adam's 2003 play *The People Next Door* explores the issue of illogical fear. A quiet and slightly simple Asian man has a tenuous connection to someone who may or may not be a terrorist. The police try to use him and as a result his neighbours, who had previously been friends, start to become afraid and suspicious. The elderly lady upstairs is thinking to herself about the nature of fear. She thinks about the fears of her other elderly friends who refuse to go out because they're too scared to be on the streets. No wonder, she says; if they don't see it but instead imagine it they're bound to become scared of it. So, she says, "they all rush home from the sewing bee and lock their doors, waiting for the psychopath who never comes".

The Cult of 'We'

They're everywhere. They populate our country. They fill all the jobs. Their children fill the schools. They own the cars. They hate political correctness. They hate tax. They may not know what art is but they know what they like. They respect a strong leader. They look up to captains of industry. They look down on politicians. And yet statistically you are unlikely to meet them very often. Who are they? They are 'we'.

'We' is one of the more curious political groupings. 'We' are a mythical people who neatly fit into any contortion of a certain political view which means that anyone else who isn't of that view is a 'them'. 'We' are the supreme invention of the current ruling classes, the perfect inversion of the order that preceded them. A majority not only silent but invisible. They melt into air as soon as you try to touch them. Let's have a look at some of the characteristics of 'we'.

Firstly, 'we' are always hard-working and earn a fair day's wage for a fair day's work. Because of this, 'we' are fairly well off, or at least 'we' would be if it wasn't for the iniquities of taxation in a Britain which has become a tax-hungry worker-penaliser. 'We' live in our own house with 'our' spouse and 'our' children and this is what we consider to be 'our' family. 'We' never divorce, 'we' marry, 'we' are obviously heterosexual and 'we' never commit crime. Well, when 'we' do it is because the law is an ass and anyway tax fraud isn't proper crime and if the burglar chose to come into 'our' house he deserved to be beat into a coma with a handy bottle of chardonnay. 'We' want the best for 'our' children and that is why 'we' work hard to pay for their fees so they can go to a good private school. 'We' aren't interested in politics, at least so long as there is a strong leader there to look after 'our' interests. 'We' love 'our' car because it is a symbol of 'our' freedom. But above all, 'we' are inherently right, irrespective. It is precisely because 'we' are good, hard-working people that it is OK for us to sometimes say 'Paki' or 'poof' and even though 'we' sometimes make jokes about 'our' wives' innate inferiority, 'we' love them really so that's OK. 'We' can look at naked pictures of seventeen-year-old girls pretending they want to have sex with 'us' because 'we' are good people who would thump anyone who looked at 'our' sixteen-year-old daughter that way. 'We' are incapable of harm because 'our' vices are by nature harmless, and you can prove that simply by observing how anyone who objects to 'our' vices so obviously has No Sense of Humour. Welcome to Britain.

This is, of course, a mythical fantasy dreamt up by a rightwing media to justify every prejudice and is transparently wrong. Let's take a look at the above 'we' and see how much of it stands up to scrutiny. There is an assumption that most of us are doing pretty well financially and that it is only the last, the undeserving and the terminally unlucky who are poor. But then most of us simply don't have a clue what our real position in the economic pecking order is. One simply question exposes the lie of our mistaken belief in our wealth. If you ask people if they think they are in the top 20 per cent of earners, you can find more than 50 per cent of people who do. It does not take a mathematician to conclude that we are deluding ourselves. Oh yes, we work hard – harder than any other country in Europe – but that doesn't mean we are doing well. The real 'we' – the majority of us – are being left behind as the real rich pull away from us, and a big majority of people are closer to the incomes of the 'poor' than they are to the incomes of the 'rich'.

Survey after survey has shown that people are not inherently antagonistic to taxation, and indeed are almost always happy to pay more tax if it is well used. And in any case, the UK is virtually a tax haven with some of the continent's lowest rates of tax (especially at the top end of the tax bracket). Yes we have become a nation of home owners, but 40 per cent of the country does not own a house. And with the majority of children now being born outside of marriage, divorce rates as high as one in three, birth rates dropping rapidly, average age of first marriages tipping into the 30s and most new net households being single occupier, the four-bedroom-three-kids nuclear family is the exception, not the rule. When it comes to crime, the assumptions about who commits it are often wrong. Domestic abuse, child abuse, car crime, financial crimes and many others are often at least as likely to be committed by the middle classes as by the 'underclass'. In fact, a 2004 study by a criminologist revealed that 64 per cent of professionals admitted to breaking the law compared to 43 of those from low income groups.

By far the biggest myth about 'us' is that we send our children to private schools. Whenever the issue of the charitable status of private schools is raised, or proposals to weight university applications from state school pupils or any other move which the establishment sees are a threat to one of its biggest perks, the outrage is immediate. The line is always the same – normal, everyday hard-working parents who just want to do their best for their children scrimp and save to be able to afford the best education for them. They forego summer holidays, they drive modest cars, they live on cardboard and water (pick your cliché) just so their children can get the best start in life. These are people like you and me, the middle classes, and it is a blatant assault on all of us. It may therefore surprise you to discover that in Scotland only four per cent of schoolchildren are at fee-paying schools, the UK average about three percentage points higher. Given that most of the landed class and almost all of the superwealthy are almost certain to have their offspring educated privately, that doesn't leave much space for the kids of the rank-and-file middle classes. The reality is that a private education remains a highly expensive perk for the elite, and the interests of the fee-paying schools represent the interests of less than one in 20 people.

The car is definitely a badge of the middle classes and it would be wrong to pretend that there isn't a strong attachment to the car by those with reasonable incomes. However, it is not the love affair we read about in newspaper 'think pieces'. Cars cause more sensations of frustration than of freedom for most and many express a desire for an efficient and reliable public transport system. In many families at least one person of working age is reliant on transport other than the car for commuting. So when there is another outpouring of tabloid outrage at the increasing cost of motoring, it is interesting to compare it with the rather muted outrage that meets underfunding of public transport. And it is also interesting that 'we' are supposed to be apathetic about politics while at the same time being greatly concerned about taxation, transport policy, law and order, immigration, education policy, Europe, 'restrictive' labour laws and much more. So 'we' are apathetic about politics except for 'our' politics of 'personal liberties' and 'common sense'. In fact people are greatly concerned about government and have strong views on many matters of politics. They feel alienated from the political process, but as discussed above that is part of a fairly deliberate campaign of disassociation.

And does the distaste for 'political correctness' evident in the right-wing media's 'we' correlate to the real general public? Perhaps more than I'd like to admit, the answer is at least partly 'yes'. But then, given the propaganda about what we're supposed to think if we are part of the mainstream perhaps that isn't so surprising. This 'we' is positively encouraged to be misogynistic (the Sun ran a viciously personal 'Save Topless Female Models' campaign after left-wing MP Claire Short suggested they might be an embarrassing anachronism), racists (any coverage of immigration), violent (the glorification of war, the 'defend you and yours with force if necessary' approach) and ignorant (modern art-hating, anti-intellectual, disinterested).

The use of manufactured collective identity is an element of all so-cial control. "If you're against the king you're a traitor to your country"; no, because a king is not my country. The attempt to create a focal point around which we are supposed to gather and with which we are expected to identify is in fact an inherent part of human society. It defines kingship, it defines empire, it defines nationalism, it defines religion, it defines com-munity, and it defines all political movements (even anarchism in which the cause is no less collective than is, say, Roman Catholicism). It has (at least) three purposes. The first is to marginalise those who do not subscribe to the collective identity. At the near end of the scale they can be indulged as eccentrics or oddballs; at the extreme end they are burned as heretics. It ensures that those who sign up to the collective identity are unlikely to be influenced by those who don't and it weakens radical or alternative views. The second purpose of the collective identity is to encourage conformity. A model is defined into which it is easy to fit, a cloak of acceptance which can be slipped on with ease and which aids passage through day to day life in the wider community. The icy coldness of being ostracised is contrasted with the warm glow of being a part of a wider whole. The third purpose is to alter the way people think and respond. Once someone has signed up to a collective identity they gradually come to identify with every aspect of that identity. If that collective identity has a belief then the individual is much more likely to sign up to that belief. Agreeing to join the club has the effect of changing what you think and believe.

In most models this three stage process is fairly obvious – the indi-vidual cannot face the life of a heretic so he or she becomes a believer and through living the life of a believer they eventually become a true believer. But what is interesting about the Cult of 'We' is that there are no members, you cannot choose to join and someone else decides whether you are a heretic on the basis of rules you don't know. Most collective identities have some sort of rite of entry – you are baptised into the church, you pay a mem-bership to join a political party, you are granted citizenship to a nation and so on. With the Cult of 'We' your involvement is not actually necessary. The closest there is to a rite of entry is the purchase of the Sun or the Daily Mail. The three purposes of collective identity are just as evident here. Firstly, you are made to feel part of the group by setting up a number of values which are contrasted with others (as always the language is essential). So modern art means nothing to ordinary people (ordinary, real, sane, god-fearing, whatever). They like pictures of things that look like real things. Look at this stupid dead sheep in a tank. That is only liked by snobs and the chattering classes (snobs, chattering classes, pretentious gits, smart arses, whatever). And eventually, through bombardment, the reader is encouraged to see any-thing other than figurative painting of the most insipid kind as crap (boring, stupid, pointless, ugly, a waste of space, whatever).

What is essential about the Cult of 'We' is that it is enormously political. It is a conscious attempt to recreate a McCarthyite climate of reactionary political militancy which is almost invisible to the carrier. They are encouraged to see all sorts of violent behaviour towards women as normal (whether they are men or women). That is because this is a backlash against feminism (in itself a loathed *bête noir* of 'we'). They are encouraged to hate racial minorities in a way that they can view as acceptable. That is because it is a backlash against progress in racial equality. They are encouraged to hate collective public provision. That is because it is part of a 'survival of the fittest' free-market ideology. And so on.

And of course it works, because most people are content to be led towards what they are supposed to believe. Icelandic folklore strongly believes in a tradition of what they call 'hidden people', trolls and goblins who live in the lava fields on which much of Iceland is built. We are supposed to believe that we too are living among a population of 'hidden people' who engage in mythical life quite unlike the one we live ourselves. However unlike Icelandic folklore, we're supposed to believe that we are the hidden people.

The new deities

Where gods don't exist, humans quickly create them. It is a Platonic ideal; we long for a 'perfect model' which we can look up to, which we can follow, which can tell us how to live. And which can keep us in line. So who are our gods? Why, entrepreneurs, soldiers and the little man, of course; these are the groups of people which it seems we are currently supposed to regard as above reproach. So let's have a look at our new deities and see what we can learn from their elevation to that position.

First by far come entrepreneurs. The current Scottish government is so in thrall to the cult of entrepreneurs that it is now making entrepreneurial education compulsory in every school in the country. This is because entrepreneurs are the single most important people in a modern society. They are the ones who create the wealth which keeps the rest of us alive and without them society as we know it would collapse. This is held to be true (without irony) by the political classes and is celebrated with a messianic zeal by the right-wing media. The theory is that in every society it is the charismatic leader who takes an idea and turns it into a reality. It is only in the actions of these leaders that anything is invented, made or distributed. The more of them we have, the more chance we have of creating a society which is successful. In Scotland in particular we have ranks of serious-faced 'commentators' (one recently described himself, again without irony, as an 'ideas entrepreneur') who are queuing up to tell us that Scotland is a failed, dismal little country because we are either genetically or socially ill-disposed to creating entrepreneurs. This is particularly galling to some because we used to produce the world's greatest entrepreneurs.

So if this is the theory, what do our entrepreneurs look like in the flesh? Scotland has a first-team of entrepreneurs who are repeatedly called on to show the rest of us where we are going wrong. They are invited *ad nauseum* to speak at conferences, to lecture children, to educate politicians. They are gurus to show the rest of us the error of our ways. We can't afford a music teacher or a decent playing field for our children but we will pay whatever it takes to ram the lesson of our entrepreneurial saviours down the throats of our children. Let me pick five entrepreneurs who are currently viewed as being in the premier league of Scottish gurus – Michelle Mone, Tom Farmer, Brian Souter, Tom Hunter and Richard Emmanuel – and let's take a closer look at these deities' feet of clay.

Let's start with Michelle Mone, by far my favourite of the five and the one which demonstrates the problem best. Michelle Mone is a former underwear model who now runs a company which makes bras stuffed with some sort of jelly which makes women's breast look bigger. Hardly the cure for cancer, but let's try and pretend that the existence of a generation of women who are so encouraged to make their breasts look artificially large that they will pay extra for a bra is some sort of 'good thing' (and no sniggering at the back). What is interesting about Michelle Mone is that, at the time of writing, her company has been going for three or four years and she doesn't seem to have actually made any money (yes, she's a millionaire but that's because she *married* a millionaire). Certainly she terminated the contract of her figurehead model – a C-list celebrity known only as the young girlfriend of wrinkly and aged Scottish rock star Rod Stewart – reputedly because the £200,000 a year contract was too expensive. And then asked her to allow her image to be used for nothing after the contract was terminated. This is *not* Microsoft.

But let us pretend that Michelle is doing something useful *and* profitable. Why should we be delighted? Because she creates the jobs that keep the rest of us in a decent standard of living. Well, if the rest of us work in a sweatshop somewhere in the developing world we may have reason to be grateful. Alternatively if we are one of the handful of administrative staff who work in Scotland we might be inclined to believe some of the rhetoric. Or perhaps the creatives working in an advertising agency – but now you're going to have to pretend that advertising jobs are by nature a good thing for the world too. Now imagine that this mediocre self-publicist were cloned and set loose across Scotland. To pretend that this would be a good thing is one pretence too far. Many of us out here are good at what we do, we contribute something useful and we don't need to be told otherwise. Give me a teacher or a nurse over a bra saleswoman every time.

This is of course an unfair comparison, so let's chose someone successful. Tom Farmer has been a remarkably successful businessman and has certainly employed a lot of people. He set up the tyre and exhaust company KwikFit which through a combination of convenience, low prices and an insidiously catchy advertising jingle became the major UK player in this sector (he later sold it for a very large sum). KwikFit provided something useful and valuable, created jobs and did it at a price which saved motorists money. Surely this is the prefect example of what we need more of in Scotland. Well, try and think this through a bit. For all his success it has to be remembered that he didn't invent tyres and exhausts and that before he came along people seemed able to secure tyres and exhausts for their cars just fine. It is also fair to assume that given that keeping tyres to an acceptable level is the law there is little reason to believe that proportionately more tyres were sold. From that I would conclude that someone else must have been fitting those tyres so can I therefore hazard a guess that those jobs existed previously? And if I can also assume that part of the reason that he was able to sell us those tyres so cheaply was that he increased worker productivity it seems reasonable to further conclude that there were probably proportionately more jobs in tyre fitting before his arrival than after. Proportionately because I assume we are not going to credit the increase in car ownership to Tom Farmer himself but rather to the large car manufacturers who reduced and reduced the real cost of a car. Not entrepreneurs but good old fashioned engineers and businessmen.

So where were these jobs that KwikFit put paid to? Well, probably in all those struggling little garages you see all over rural Scotland, and those you don't because they've been knocked down. But we can at least be grateful for the cost savings. Unless we were one of those people who lost their jobs. Or were dependent on their income. Or came from their communities in which the loss of those jobs was part of the decline which affected us all. Or if we were taxpayers who footed the social security bill during the '80s. There is no taking away from Tom Farmer's achievements – he played the game fairly and well and won great rewards for himself and his shareholders. Whether Scotland as a whole should be grateful is another matter.

Next comes Brian Souter, who can be dismissed fairly quickly. After all, his bus company was only successful because he was virtually handed suitcases full of money when the public provision of bus routes was deregulated. A business practice which included suppressing wages and crushing trade unions only helped him so far. Then he had to trade in a larger market place which hadn't been rigged in his favour and his share price has been plummeting pretty well ever since. If we had more Brian Souters in Scotland it is fair to assume that no-one would be better off. In any case, he is no longer entrepreneur *de jour* since he ran a campaign to stop the government in Scotland repealing anti-gay legislation.

The next two – Tom Hunter and Richard Emmanuel – are both successful, achieved what they achieved without blatantly harming anyone and provided something which wasn't there before. These are closer to our deified entrepreneur, and yet the case for the defence still seems weak. Both made their money retailing products at a point at which they were just about to boom in sales. Tom Hunter established a successful sportswear chain at just the point at which sportswear became the ubiquitous uniform for the young. Richard Emmanuel opened a chain of shops selling mobile phones at just the point when they started to become affordable and when you had a fighting chance of getting a signal anywhere outside London. Both expanded rapidly – creating jobs along the way – and then sold out at a large profit. So far so meretricious. And yet why are we supposed to be excited? Yes, they provided a service, but it is daft to argue that this wouldn't have happened anyway without them. And yes they created a fairly large number of routine and relatively poorly paid retail jobs. Neither made so much as a single phone or a single training shoe. They bought from abroad and sold here, took the profit and split. Good luck to them I guess, but what has this got to do with the greater good of Scotland? There is no meaningful wealth creation there – not in the sense of adding value to something. It was just an import-export exercise which got a couple of people rich. If there were hundreds more of them nothing would be better or worse – they would just continually knock each other down in the rush for the same amount of expendable cash which was generated in the economy by activities such as manufacturing.

Entrepreneurs today – with a few exceptions – don't really make anything. And in the case of the exceptions it is questionable whether we wouldn't all be better off if they hadn't. If you invent something really valuable for the world, wouldn't you be better off licensing it to someone who is an expert at making it and invent something else valuable? Why is it a good thing that you use your creative energy messing around with accounts and dealing with rent and staffing? Surely someone else could do that, someone without the capability of inventing valuable things? If you are a talented jewellery designer wouldn't it be better if you spent your time creating beautiful things rather than slaving over a hot business plan? In fact, surely it is the person who created the technology in the phone that we should be swooning over, not Richard Emmanuel? Sure, someone's got to sell them, but that's hardly a complicated process.

As usual, the deification of entrepreneurs is another simple matter of ideological manipulation. We are encouraged to view the unequal appropriation of wealth as more important than its actual creation. The clear message which is being sent out is that the goal is money not value. If we were to spend time teaching children the value of science or art or of the many social contributions they could make which really and genuinely improve the world we would get a much better return than spending our time indoctrinating them into the belief that making profit on the back of other people's innovation is the goal. It is part of an ideology which underpins the free market and shifts our value system. If we want to believe in feudal social systems, we better make people think that lords are important, even though it is the peasant farmers who created all the wealth. These neo-lords perform exactly the same function, and it is time their worth was interrogated a little more rigorously.

Another modern deity is the soldier. It is now de rigeur for anyone who pulls on camouflage to be described as a 'hero'. Every one of them who goes out to fight on our behalf is above reproach. So what is so heroic about soldiers? Britain only sends troops to fight under circumstances in which the opponent is unable to defend themselves with anything like success. We pick fights primarily against third-world countries and the tiny losses we have suffered despite fighting four wars in five years rather attests to that. What is notionally heroic about soldiers is their sacrifice; their willingness to sacrifice their own lives for the greater good. The possibility that the army attracts the psychologically flawed with a desire to dress up, be told what to do and to kill people is not to be mentioned. Some drift into it because they really don't have any idea what else they want to do, have no good alternative (often underperformers academically) and a recruiter came round and made it sound fun. Often good people, but hardly heroes. Some are coerced or encouraged into it by family, often those with a military tradition. Again, nothing inherently heroic about it.

But many (to my eyes the most frequent) are borderline psychopaths who have a genuine desire to shoot guns, stab knifes into inanimate objects and ultimately kill people. This category is one recruiting sergeant away from a life in prison for assault or murder. There are virtually no soldiers whom I have ever heard in person giving a humanitarian reason for their trade (apart from officers performing a public relations role for the benefit of the media). They are paid killers who almost never make any moral judgement about their actions. A few soldier during the 2003 Iraq war raised some concern about their involvement in the wholesale slaughter of a poorly armed army of conscripted adolescents. If they had become conscientious objectors then that would have constituted heroism.

This hero-worship was dealt a blow when the pictures emerged from Abu Ghraib, the American-run military prison in Iraq. Naked men being piled on top of each other, cowering from attack-dogs, led around in dog leashes, hooded and threatened with electrocution and much worse which isn't discussed because we haven't seen the pictures. Suddenly soldiers were seen for what they often are – violent people who find it easy to dehumanise anyone they deem to be 'the enemy'. We saw in the leering faces precisely the carefully cultivated combination of amorality, sadism and perceived superiority which is necessary to make people effective killers of other people. There was genuine shock (although quite why people were surprised that this kind of thing happens during war is a total mystery), but after a short interval it was possible to prosecute a few 'grunts' (even though they were almost certainly following policy) and write the whole thing off as a 'few bad eggs'. Yet from Chechnya to Abu Ghraib, the endemic bullying (and probably murder) in the Deep Cut army training centre in the UK to the vicious assaults and rapes perpetrated around American military bases in Europe (not to mention millennia of exhaustive evidence of the barbarity of those who engage in war) we all have at the least a suspicion of just exactly what these 'heroes' are like as soon as controls are lifted.

If this sounds callous, it is not intended to be. Many good people have been killed in battle over the last ten years and we should of course mourn their loss. There are also essential peacekeeping duties which need to be carried out and which do put people at great personal risk. And no, I have little intention of signing up for these duties myself. But the blanket depiction of the soldier-hero has nothing to do with the people involved. It is a way of making us believe in the cause by believing in the protagonist. We can't criticise the conflict because our protagonists are heroes. By elevating them to heroes we elevate the conflict to heroic. By pretending that the slaughter of civilians is being carried out by 'heroes' we are conditioned to accept it.

A man who is in a multimillion pound jet fighter launches a missile from a height that means he can't see what he is launching it at purely on the basis that someone else told him to do it. The missile falls and one hundred meters above the point of impact it disperses into hundreds of tiny bomblets the size of a soft drink can. These fall over an area of many tens of square meters. When these hit the ground they are designed to explode shrapnel in a manner best suited to ripping human bodies to shreds. On this particular occasion the man has dropped them on a frightened crowd of fleeing women and children who are torn to pieces. About a fifth of the bomblets don't explode. Well, at least not until months later when a child comes across one of them and is attracted by its bright yellow colour and is also torn to shreds. The fighter pilot meanwhile returns to base and, quite happy with his day's work, hunts out his favourite porn mag and celebrates. What a guy.

Another of our local heroes is the amorphous 'little man'. These are ordinary people who by any usual standard have just done something rather horrible. By a twist of logic, however, they become 'heroes'. Our most celebrated recent example is reclusive retired farmer Tony Martin. He was a clearly mentally unstable man who lived in a desolate and barely habitable farmhouse. Certainly he had suffered a fair degree of harassment by a group of travelling people who lived in the area, but to most that would hardly justify his actions. One night he caught a couple of young, unarmed men – one only a teenager – escaping from his house having stolen what can only have been goods of a modest value. As they ran away, Tony Martin shot the teenager in the back from close range with a shotgun, killing him instantly. Dangerous sociopath in need of help? No! Vicious thug in need of punishment? No! Our tabloids decided that he was a 'have-a-go' hero who was only protecting his own property from the really bad people – a couple of small-time thieves. One tabloid actually ran a campaign to have him freed when he was jailed for a derisory five years.

What we are supposed to internalise from this is that violence is fine, property is more important than life, and that travelling people are evil. We have a hero to justify another set of right-wing political prejudices. Another deity elevated to a position from which we can see clearly what is right and wrong, fair and unfair, important and unimportant. Our gods are greed, oppression and hate. So how come they look like heroes?

The War of All against All

Universities are good things, right? They educate people, help them to learn. They create knowledge and pass it on. They are bastions of civilisation and civilise and enlighten all around them. They shaped what is good about the modern world (and yes, some of what is bad about it) and drove us forward. So who might be the enemy of the universities? Perhaps some anti-intellectual cult plotting their downfall. Perhaps it might be unintelligent people who feel excluded by them. There really aren't many potential enemies of institutions which, on the whole, are so benign. It certainly isn't nursery schools.

OK, actually it *is* nursery schools. Take a second because this requires some effort to get your head round. In the early months of 2004 MPs were asked to vote for a piece of transparently right-wing free-market ideology which will introduce not only charging for universities but variable charging for universities according to their marketability. It will soon concentrate the vast majority of the resource available to the higher education sector into the top few universities; the rest will be left to decline. Soon English higher education will look like a small, deformed version of the American system with a small proportion of students going to fabulously wealthy universities and the majority forced into underfunded community colleges (Scotland chose not to follow suit). Who is doing this to the universities? Not the right-wing think tanks which now pass for all wisdom in America (or so we are told to believe) but the aforementioned nursery schools. Why is this? Well, Tony Blair has made it clear that if he has a spare penny (which he doesn't) he will give it to nursery education (which he won't) because that is his priority (which it isn't). For this reason the universities will have to find another way to find investment, so variable fees is the only way. You may want to run through that again.

Let's get over the main points of disagreement here. Firstly, anyone with the slightest awareness ought to have noticed that Tony Blair hasn't promised any real money for nursery education as the MPs troop into the voting lobbies. It's just that the nursery schools are getting the first cut of nothing. Secondly, anyone with any memory ought to be aware that Tony Blair's first preference for any money he has available is to start a war. He has been involved in far more warfare than any British political leader since Churchill (five in five years and in rather different circumstances than those Churchill faced). So if he doesn't actually have that much of a regard for nursery education and if he isn't giving them anything anyway, why are we hearing about them? Well, mostly because they aren't universities. Nursery schools are briefly Mr Blair's priority because they just seem more deserving than universities. Universities are not universal – everyone is a toddler at some point but not everyone will go to a university. Nursery schools do not grant their participants an obvious immediate material advantage, while universities clearly do. There is no class bias in those eligible to go to nursery school but due to the uneven distribution of social wellbeing the rich are simply more likely to do well at high school and are therefore more likely to be eligible for university. And nursery schools are endlessly photogenic while universities are full of post-adolescents who by trying to establish some independence and individuality are easily portrayed in a pretty negative light. Nursery schools are for everyone, rich or poor, while universities are the home of the self-indulgent rich who are about to make a fortune because of their studies.

This state of affairs is actually made more deplorable by the fact that proper provision of nursery education is actually one of the most important things a government could do. For reasons ranging from increasing the birth rate by giving young couples the chance of children and a career at the same time to the positive educational benefit of structured early years education, it is a national disgrace that pre-school education has been almost entirely neglected. That Blair, after six years of doing nothing, now claims to be committed to nursery schools would be good if a commitment from him meant committing something other than rhetoric. He has pledged not all that much to pre-school education. Rather he is using our toddlers as a battering ram to force through another attack on the British tradition of the welfare state and to squeeze a free market into education for the first time. To Blair, nursery schools are a convenient weapon to use against universities in his endless war of all against all.

The war works like this: we have a limited amount of money and time, many worthy causes are in need of that money and time and it is therefore our responsibility to make the 'tough choices'. In this vision of the world, government is not about choosing the kind of world we want to live in and then delivering it but is a simple mediator adjudicating between the competing cases put before it and spending its budget accordingly. This managerial approach to government is often commented on as if it is somehow flawed by a lack of 'vision'. Quite the contrary; this is the means for delivering the vision of a minimalist government which is ever more selective and ever more reliant on the free market. It embeds the idea of finite opportunity and allows any case whatsoever to be neutralised by another case, indefinitely and forever. Just as soon as someone puts Blair under pressure to deliver on his 'heartfelt' commitment to nursery education we will find another counterweight. This will probably be that we cannot just give nursery education to everyone but that will be nothing more than a subsidy to wealthy parents who were already sending their children to nursery schools and would therefore be a bad use of money. So universal pre-school provision will suddenly find that *its* mortal enemy is existing pre-school provision. And before you know it the universities will have been to all intents and purposes turned into nothing more than Kentucky Fried Degree so that Blair could part subsidise the nursery education for a tiny proportion of parents who are so desperately poor that they may find it hard to take up the option anyway.

In the meantime Britain's Most Gullible (backbench Labour loyalists) will troop into the voting lobbies to destroy universal entitlement to education in England because they think this is a vote for toddlers. And the war of all against all claims another casualty.

The war has many odd pairings. For example, why are we asked to pick sides in a war between cars and the environment when it comes to fuel duty but a war between the environment and economic development when it comes to motorway building? Or why do we need to choose between firefighters and nurses when it comes to public sector pay settlements but between nurse's salaries and patient care when it comes to allocation of the NHS budget? If we are so petrified about losing jobs in the economy when it comes to setting a level for the national minimum wage, why are we so little concerned about these jobs when it comes to acquisition and mergers policy? Minimum Wage vs. jobs, jobs vs. prosperity. International law vs. war in Zimbabwe, war vs. human rights in Iraq. Middle class rights to the good things when it comes to tax, middle class's excessive perks when it comes to public expenditure.

What is produced is a public sphere in which nothing has intrinsic value in itself but only consists of a relative value when compared to something else. And the comparator changes depending on the desired result. It legitimises a lie – that there is nothing we can do but choose how to cut the cake. Wrong. As has been shown again and again, people will vote for tax increases if they can be convinced they will be used well. If Blair wants to establish proper pre-school provision for every family he simply has to draw up the plans and tell the country that they will make an enormous difference to their lives, persuade them of the benefits and tell them that part of a one pence rise in tax is the cost. People can be persuaded. Meanwhile if we want to fund universities we can follow the proposal to create a new tax band for those earning over £100,000 a year which would hardly leave them destitute but would easily pay for higher education and a number of other very good causes. It really isn't a matter of either nursery schools or universities.

There is an old card trick you probably saw at school – probably only at school because it really doesn't take much figuring out. Write "six of hearts" on a piece of paper and put it face down under something you can't move without being seen. Then put the six of hearts at the bottom of a pile of cards. Cut the cards in two and ask someone to pick one pile. If they pick the pile which was at the bottom (i.e. the one with the six of hearts in it) tell them "OK, you want to keep that one" and dispose of the other. If they pick the pile which was at the top (i.e. the one without the six of hearts) you tell them "OK, you want to throw that one away". Then cut the cards and keep doing this until there is only one left. Imagine your subject's surprise when they turn over the piece of paper to discover that it says "six of hearts", exactly the card you have chosen at 'random'. No, not many people fall for it. So why is exactly the same trick so effective in privatising universities?

Binary decision-making – an endless series of yes/no or on/off – is a stupid way to run a country and has only one real purpose. This war of all against all is designed to postpone the real question – what kind of world, what kind of country do we want to live in – until it is too late. Until we have been duped into answering so many irrelevant yes/no questions that we wake up in a dystopia that we never wanted.

What language is this?

It is an axiom of all modern linguistic and critical theory that words do not simply describe things but also create them. There is no such thing as a 'slut'; the word is a pejorative which is used to demonise someone for their actions. If there was no word 'slut' then sexual promiscuity in a woman would not necessarily be identified as a bad thing. Which is in turn the corollary of saying that if female sexual promiscuity was not viewed as a bad thing, the word 'slut' simply wouldn't exist. Language is the human species' most remarkable creation. Its subtlety, complexity and power is quite remarkable. It is able to describe something, create something, change something and control something all at the same time. To say "he's a fat bastard" is to describe his size. But it is equally to designate him as a category of people who are flawed because of their weight, in some way a failure. It creates a victim. Who, precisely through that pressure, is urged to change, to escape that classification. Who goes to slimming class, and who therein voluntarily signs up to the linguistic designation, strengthening it and ensuring its power to control people and their behaviour on the basis of their weight. There is no such thing as neutral language, so it all has a purpose and an effect. This is something we must perpetually keep an eye on.

This is an argument which is very well known and it is therefore unnecessary to labour the point. Indeed this book has already explored numerous examples of this kind of linguistic use; 'bogus asylum seeker', 'freedom of choice', 'natural order', 'one of us', 'entrepreneur', 'there is no alternative'. Every one is an attempt to use words to control the way we think. So all I would want to do here is to draw attention to the political euphemism.

The best known type of political euphemism from recent times is the war euphemism. This is the bizarre language which turns a butchered mother and child into 'collateral damage'. It seeks to dissociate as far as possible the words 'dead' and 'civilian'. Indeed, it seeks to dissociate any two words which might bare any relationship to what it actually describes. If you came across the phrase and didn't know what it referred to you would find it very hard to work out or even guess. And to show just how ludicrous a phrase it is, even a dictionary wouldn't help much. "Collateral: *adj* side by side, parallel, descended from a common ancestor but in a different line; subordinate, secondary; additional". "Damage: *noun* injury, harm." So the best you could do to work this out would be to conclude that it referred to 'secondary or subordinate harm'. Given that damage as a noun is not associated with harm to a person but to an object, you could perhaps get as far as thinking that it was the damage to property during a firefight. Each of the two words is carefully chosen for their lack of association with what they are describing. And so we find a way to talk about something which should turn our stomachs, but in a way that sounds technical and unimportant.

There are others which haven't really been rumbled yet. The one which is a particular bugbear is 'red tape'. The phrase originates from the use of red ribbon to collate papers and files in the early days of detailed record keeping but is now used to denote any form of unnecessary and onerous bureaucracy. 'Red tape' is associated with the filling-in of mountains of forms in triplicate and is generally assumed to be A Bad Thing. So what are these forms about that are such a waste of everyone's time? Well, they are taken to be the petty rules and regulations of business life imposed by an interfering government or local authority. We are supposed to associate red tape in part with a dystopian vision of modernity as penned by Kafka and in part with the bumbling and ridiculous fastidiousness of Captain Mainwaring in *Dad's Army.*

When the CBI and others call for less red tape, the average tabloid reader is encouraged to think that this means that they should no longer be required to fill in piles of forms which are destined to be filed in giant filing cabinets and never looked at again. It is exactly not what the CBI wants an end to. If you were to glance over the shoulder of a 'small businessmen' (it is always this virtuous type who are afflicted) to see what these pesky forms are about you would find that they related to such insubstantial matters such as 'health and safety', 'basic employee rights', 'prevention of tax avoidance', 'environmental protection' and 'the law'. No wonder this poor set-upon creature is in need of saving. How can he be expected to get on with making a giant profit for himself if he has to waste valuable time on matters such as not killing his workers, not pouring gallons of highly toxic waste into his local river or paying his fare share of the taxes that the rest of us are expected to pay. 'Red tape' is a euphemism for 'controls on illegal and unacceptable behaviour' and when businessmen want less of it they really want to be able to do whatever they want unchecked. It makes no more sense to listen to the CBI when it calls for less red tape than it does to listen to a petty criminal claim that his court appearance is 'just another example of red tape getting in the way of my business'.

A currently popular example which very few people have come to terms with yet is 'flexible labour market', which more accurately means 'flexible employment laws'. One should be immediately concerned about laws which are designated as 'flexible' on the basis that they tend only to flex in the direction of the powerful. Blair and Brown are forever telling us that we should be grateful for our flexible labour market. What they are really saying is 'workers, be thankful that we have made it easy for your boss to bend the rules that are supposed to protect you'. 'Flexible labour market' is designed to sound like the kind of desirable economic model we are always being bamboozled with. The word flexible is chosen because it is positive (and implies 'the opposite of inflexible'). What it really means is that people can be paid less, fired more easily, treated worse and receive fewer perks. It is 'good' for 'us' because it brings more employment by making Britain more attractive to employers. Of course, even if that was true, it is only true because they know that as soon as there is a downturn in the global economy they can pay British workers off more easily than they can the workers in other countries. Hooray for us!

A final example and the linguistic manipulation *par excellence* of the Blair era; 'modernisation'. The dictionary does not help to pin this word down to a specific meaning; the trick, of course, is that it means "Modernise: *v/t* to make modern, to adapt to modern tastes" and so relies on its entire meaning for the associated meaning of 'modern'. This is defined in turn as "Modern: *adj* of or in present or recent times; not old-fashioned". So when Tony Blair says that something needs modernised, he is actually saying that it has to be converted into a thing of our times. But then, our times are currently the times of Blair and it is his philosophy which is the one that determines the bulk of how our modern world is to be run. It is therefore actually quite helpful to know that 'modernisation' actually has the almost literal meaning of 'turning them into whatever Tony Blair wants them to be'. And that is exactly what it has come to mean. It matter not in the slightest what the starting point is and much less what the end point is. All you have to know is that the process which moves between these two points is modernisation.

A very quick illustration. Blair has told us that the NHS has to be modernised. The NHS as we currently have it (well, depending on when you are reading this) is one underpinned by the principle of collective provision of healthcare delivered at no direct cost to users purely on the basis of medical need and organised by the state on a non-profit making basis. The NHS as we are about to have it following Blair's reforms is one which is moving towards a system of contract managing between private profit-making providers with the scope for user charging. So we start from a system which (in terms of core principles) is unrivalled for efficiency and effectiveness and has never been equalled or bettered by any alternative system anywhere in the world. We move towards a system which in most regards is the private-practice-and-charitable-support model of the Victorian age, the main difference being that the government will be the primary source of charitable support. So we move from the 20th century to the 19th, but because Blair chooses that the present times will be dominated by the philosophies of a less enlightened time it actually represents 'modernisation'.

What language is it that means something completely different to the sum total of the words that make it up?

The rule and the exception

It is worth remembering that an exception always disproves the rule. If heavy objects started floating then there would be something seriously wrong with the theory of gravity. If small groups of wildebeest started organising and picked off any predatory lions they came across we would need to rethink the natural balance of animal life. A car which never ran out of petrol would pose real problems for petrochemical engineers. It is the very fact that these things don't happen which enables us to create the rule in the first place. Gravity was 'discovered' by Newton precisely on the basis that things *always* fall down. Our understanding of the food chain relies on the fact that wildebeest *never* eat lions. A lot of money is spent on oil exploration because we know *beyond doubt* that in propelling a car forward, the fuel in it is used up. Observably, empirically invariable.

This applies equally to the world seen by politicians. The only basis on which society can function is that productive energies are released purely by the interaction of need and greed. That is what makes markets such a successful means of producing and distributing goods. They are propelled forward and kept in balance by the twin forces of the needs of people (including their desires) which controls demand and the greed of those with the power to produce them, which controls supply. When the greed outstrips the need, the greedy fail because there is no market for them. When the need exceeds the greed, eventually someone else will be greedy enough to meet the need. A perfect balance. And how do we know that there is no alternative? Well, because the only exception proved it by not working. Soviet Russia attempted to buck the natural order of markets by seeking to propel productivity by other means. Rather than the twin forces of need and greed, a strategy of central planning attempted to propel the economy forward. The physical law of action and reaction which is at the heart of the free market was lost and an intellectual attempt to know what could not be known (the balance of supply and demand) was put in its place.

We know that gravity is the only possible way to understand the universe because when we let go of a stone it falls. Every time. Without exception. And if we attempt to break that rule – perhaps by building a tower block with unsupported foundations floating ten metres above solid earth – it fails. The Soviet Union attempted to let go of markets in the hope that things would hold up anyway, but they didn't; they fell. We know that capitalism is the only way – look at Russia. Collective ownership results in queues, famine, instability and stagnation. QED.

Sure, Russia was one of two superpowers. Sure it was the main reason for allied victory in World War Two (if you doubt this read some objective history). Sure at seventy years it outlived many free market economies and proved more stable during much of that time. Sure it managed to be the first nation ever to put a satellite into space. And then a man. But rules is rules.

Some of you may also remember the dark days of nationalisation. Remember when trains were always a bit late and sometimes they were cancelled. Fares kept going up. The service was basic at best. Yes, we were left in no doubt that nationalisation didn't work. Gas and electricity were expensive. The steel and coal industries were flabby and uncompetitive. In the '70s there was a clear distinction to be made. Industries which were nationalised were crap, while private companies working for private profit were lean and efficient. By the '80s this was so obvious that there was only one option – the whole lot had to be nationalised. Thatcher saw that the rule was being broken and the fact that those things which broke the rule were failing simply proved the rule. Running a company without making private profit is like getting a wildebeest to headbut a lion. Remember and tell Sid.

Or take the case of a man who was jailed for a violent crime. Five years later he has served his time, has earned his right to parole, has been assessed as reformed and is released. Two months later he gets drunk and gets in a fight with a man in a pub, hits him on the head with a pool cue and kills him. It is simply one more lesson which proves the rule we should all have remembered from the beginning – early release from jail never works. All we are doing is putting the same scum back onto the streets that our hard working police officers have spent their time trying to protect us from. How long before we learn? The rule is that you put bad people behind bars and you don't let them out. Just like you put petrol in your car if you want to drive it somewhere.

There is something else it is worth remembering, and that is that an exception doesn't always disprove the rule. If lots of sheep were born with two heads we would need to rethink our biology. If you toss a thousand different coins a thousand times each and they all comes up heads we might need to take another look at the laws of probability. And if we uncover a man who can always guess what card any other person is thinking of then perhaps we might need to alter our views on telepathy. But just because in every lambing season there will be one or two poor short-lived lambs which are born with a deformity, that doesn't alter the fact that as a fairly consistent rule sheep have one head. One coin which seems to always land heads up may be defective and doesn't alter the 50-50 nature of the coin toss. And a conjuring trick does not mean that we can all read each other's minds. From time to time atoms collide in a slightly unusual way; it doesn't change the fundamental building blocks of our reality. Rules are resilient to exceptions.

So the unbending rule of the market – that a broad range of self-regulating sub-markets is the best way to organise society – need not be reconsidered simply because there is the occasional failure. So Argentina may have been the model pupil, following the free-market instructions of the IMF throughout the '90s. It may have followed the rules to the letter. But the fact that it collapsed into very real bankruptcy by the end of the decade does nothing to disprove those rules. And we know that because most people who follow those rules – America or Europe, say – are a roaring success. Well, apart from Japan and the East Asian subcontinent. Or capitalist India. Or the African continent which has to abide by international market rules. The corrupt energy giant Enron may have collapsed in great scandal but that proves nothing other than that it was the exception. Well, it and Worldcom. And earlier the Bank of Credit and Commerce International. And Parmalat the Italian dairy conglomerate. Or all those dot com companies. Nor does internal failure prove anything, so starving Chinese show the flaws in central planning but starving black Americans on the periphery of their society are no flaw in the theory, any more than starving Indian 'capitalists' are. Queuing for the 'must have' Christmas present for your children is an entirely different thing from queuing in the old Soviet Union. These cases are nothing more than two-headed sheep and they do nothing to dent out confidence in that vibrant one-headed ram that is global capitalism.

Meanwhile the giant privatisation purge once again shows the primacy of private enterprise. Services have got better and prices have fallen precisely because of the inherently more effective and efficient functioning of companies in a free market. Well OK, trains haven't got better. In fact the massive failure of our national rail service is one of the starkest examples of decline in the quality of life in Britain. So many people spent so much of their precious time waiting on trains that came late or not at all or trapped in the stationary train itself that they just stopped using them. The infrastructure is decaying and there is no longer any coherence to making a journey because it has all be divided among a bewildering array of profiteering companies and regulators who regulate other regulators. And that is before we even get to the fact that passengers have died or been badly injured because companies cut back on expenditure on maintenance to increase profits.

Meanwhile the price of fares just keeps rising as subsidies prove insufficient to bail out a phalanx of failing companies whose shareholders continue to exploit the taxpayer and the passengers. But that has nothing to do with the principle of privatisation which is proved by the lower price that you can now get your gas for. If you buy it from your electricity supplier – the same gas from the same source down the same pipes but at different prices and sold to you by an endlessly stream of salesmen who are at best irritating and at worst out-and-out conmen who were caught swindling elderly customers. Oh and at least one family was killed when their house was blown to shards by under-maintained pipelines. Deregulated busses run on profitable lines and have to be bribed to run a minimal service to anywhere else. It is true that the coal and steel industries are no longer inefficient, but that is only because they no longer exist. And most recently we were forced to adjust to a dozen different numbers run by different companies for directory inquiries. And many of those had accuracy rates of below 50 per cent before they went bust. But not to worry – the industry leader had a success rate of almost 80 per cent so only one in five of the numbers they gave you were wrong. But they have nice adverts and that shows that privatisation works. Dead passengers and wrong numbers are a fluke just like a coin that always lands heads up. The rule remains.

The penal system is no better a place to expect to find rules broken by inconsequential exceptions. Remember that jail works and it protects you and me from the bad people. People who are sent to jail deserve to be there. Well, apart from a wide variety of miscarriages of justice from Nelson Mandela to the Birmingham Six to the mothers convicted for infanticide over recent years who it is now accepted were condemned on the basis of an unsafe theory. But that changes nothing, any more than the thousands of ex-offenders who are released early on parole who go on to live valuable and honest lives. Naturally, they don't make the papers. Jail works, and where jail fails or where alternatives are more effective we are seeing a simple conjuring trick – passingly interesting but not significant.

There are no rules, only guidelines. All of you who still believe that gravity is a constant should give yourselves a shake and drag your understanding of the world into the 20th century, never mind the 21st. Einstein showed that gravity and time can bend almost a hundred years ago so you need to catch up. Newton died a long time ago and we need to get used to living in a world of contradictions. We need to stop thinking about the world and the way it is run as a matter of discovering the right rules and start thinking about it as a process of reconciling contradictions. In early 2003 we saw the run up to the war in Iraq. During this time we were presented with a case for war which was based on the simple premise that there was a contradiction in what we knew about Iraq and its weapons and what we were being told. The rule is that innocent people have nothing to hide and willingly confess everything. We know that Saddam Hussein *used* to have chemical weapons, partly because he used them and partly because we helped to supply them. Therefore when Sadam told the United Nations in an enormous declaration that he had no weapons of mass destruction but there was insufficient information on exactly how he had destroyed them, that contradiction was irreconcilable. He wouldn't be hiding things if he was innocent so the contradictions show that he is guilty. And so we started a war which led to the death of probably about 100,000 people.

Move forward a year and a half and we found ourselves faced with another bemusing contradiction. It turns out that there *were* no weapons of mass destruction in Iraq – absolutely none whatsoever. The legal case that Blair made was that pre-emptive strikes were legal where a threat exists (which incidentally has no basis in international law where the threat is anything other than immediate). So there is a very real contradiction when we discover that this legal basis was actually entirely flawed to the extent of being totally and utterly untrue. However, this is not a contradiction which changes anything because a guilty man is a guilty man irrespective of whether he broke the law you claimed he was breaking. And thus it is that Blair still believes he was right to go to war. Of course, there are many more contradictions yet to be found in the matter of the 2003 war on Iraq and we can fully expect to see them dealt with in exactly the same way; put forward as conclusive proof where convenient and dismissed as irrelevant side issues where inconvenient.

Consistency is not an important matter; ideological zeal trumps consistency every time.

Fun

How can a chapter describing the distorting and manipulating power of the industrial-military-intolerance empire be entitled 'fun'? Fun is undoubtedly a good thing. There is very serious medical evidence that those who experience fun, happiness and laughter are likely to be protected from a range of maladies to a much greater extent than those who are miserable, depressed and bored. People who have fun and who are happy are very significantly less likely to engage in all manner of antisocial and violent behaviour. But above all, how can I be about to decry fun because it is, well, fun? Totally enjoyable and with no need for guilt.

And that is precisely why it is such a useful tool for those who would manipulate us. That isn't because they intend to offer us something that we enjoy, but because they will use the fun justification to excuse all manner of things and to distract us from all manner of other things. We have already explored the use of 'fun' in encouraging us to decline to be involved – the cults of lifestyle marketing and the endless denigration of the political process as 'not fun' in an attempt to keep us away from it. This point can be expanded a little. It is a slightly unpleasant phrase but 'dumbing down' is now the accepted terminology for the drive towards anti-intellectualism. We are now surrounded by acres of worthless things which are sold to us entirely on the basis that they are 'fun'. We have extremely bad music (all novelty records fall into this category), excruciating television programmes (most reality television – at least the stuff that doesn't pretend to be a social experiment), horrendous clothes ('humorous' ties and socks), pointlessly expensive leisure activities (how did we survive before we could drive a racing car round a track?), puerile films (comedies which don't have jokes and action films with no plots) and so on.

Now, part of the point is that none of these things are necessarily objectionable (although people with 'funny' Christmas ties singing 'funny' Christmas pop hits while quoting catchphrases from some lame sitcom are really pushing their luck) but they are certainly two other things. Firstly they are very profitable because by selecting a lowest common denominator and by challenging no-one they are ultra-marketable. And secondly, they are habit forming because they lower expectations to such a level that they are easily fulfilled through endless facsimile. Dumbing down helps to stop people getting involved in the political process in any manner which would change society but it also creates an ever-expanding opportunity to squeeze profit from people. It is the intellectual equivalent of cutting someone's legs off and then selling them crutches. It is essential to note whenever someone tells you that something is 'just a bit of fun' or 'harmless and passes the time' that they are virtually never cost free. When did you last hear anyone with something to sell describe lying in a sunny public park reading an engrossing library book as 'fun'? When you try to think of something fun to do with friends have you ever seen anything which encourages you to buy a 50 pence Frisbee and go for a walk in the countryside? Fun means profit, and they want you just dumb enough not to realise the lie in this. They want your imagination crushed under a half-tonne of promotional material for your local multiplex. Fun is no longer your friend.

In fact this kind of 'fun' is even more like a drug than a simple dependency. Psychological assessments of happiness raise big questions about whether all the 'fun' we are now having has made us the slightest happier. We can trace the analysis of the problem back to 19th century French sociologist Emile Durkheim. He developed the concept of anomie and described how it left people feeling disorientated when there is an expansion of options and a declining social context to help make the choice. We can do what we want but we have no way of knowing why. Stopping in a service station, we are faced with a barrage of chocolate bars and the only rational response seems to me to be total paralysis. With endless shading from chewy to crunchy with or without nuts, toffee, mint, biscuit – the options are simply too vast to consider – how do we make a choice? But take a look at the brightly coloured wrappers. Focus on the fun. Purchasing endless 'fun' designed for someone a bit like us but with a dimension missing does not seem to make us happier. It just repeatedly leaves a gap which we feel we need to fill with more fun. A mesmeric narcotic, but one which doesn't really work.

So 'fun' distracts us from the important things, reduces our horizons and develops in us a dependency which we can only address by generating ever more profit for someone else. But this is not it; fun ain't done. Fun continues to justify all forms of discrimination and suppression and to oppose all sorts of vilification and victimisation is an act of the 'humourless'. It should be of great concern to women across the Western world that well over a century after women began the fight for equal rights under the law and forty years since modern feminism emerged that we are now surrounded by more exploitation of femininity than ever. It is virtually impossible to pass a day without being bombarded with pornography. Advertising, pop music, films, magazines and newspapers are dominated by endless pictures of naked women in submissive and suggestive poses. Much more now than in the '60s we are expected to look at women as sexual objects. The ludicrous Spice Girls celebrated 'girl power' (can you imagine men celebrating 'boy power'?) by dressing like teenage prostitutes.

By selecting soft-porn poses which don't show pubic hair men's magazines have worked their way down from the top shelf. The annual lists of most attractive women have reinforced a deep socio-psychological slant to the way men (and by extension women) are supposed to value women. The lists place you according to looks alone and there is no other measure which appears to affect your ranking.

The women are usually described as 'glamour models' and what we know about them is virtually zero (they appear to exist primarily to fill up these lists.). At best we might discover a hobby or two or something about their preference in men but, given that these always seem to be just a little too conveniently tailored to the readership of the sole domain in which they exist ("I like nothing better than spending a Saturday afternoon watching football with my man"; "what I really go for in a man is a down to earth bloke who doesn't mind getting his hands dirty and loves sex") it seems reasonable that these have been scripted for them. These women are 'Stepford singles' – not real people at all but idealised objects.

The language used to describe them and to contextualise them comes in basic shades of demeaning, dismissive, suggestive and aggressive ("taking a look at those" is an aggressive act). But we are supposed to disassociate this from rising sexual assaults, widespread domestic violence, continued employment segregation, teenage eating disorders, rising divorce rates and very possibly a greater dissatisfaction within relationships generally (men are not immune to the effects of all of this). And why no association? Because "sluts getting them out" is just a bit of fun.

If much of the state we're in can be in part traced back to a reaction against the perception in the late '60s that a change might indeed be coming, nowhere is this more obvious than in gender politics. For more than 30 years we have been actively encouraged to take a wholly negative approach to 'feminism' and 'feminists', a noun that is now almost wholly pejorative for most people.

But 'fun' is all around us when it comes to the suppression of minorities. It doesn't matter whom the joke is against or for what reason – religion, race, sexuality, gender – it is possible to justify it on the basis of 'fun'. In fact, there is almost nothing short of that which is defined as illegal which appears to be outside the realms of the 'fun justification'. I have seen people physically hurt and humiliated to a state of tears only for the protagonists to say, "come on, it's just a bit of fun". No it isn't, and it really is about time we stopped pretending it is.

The end of complexity

As every human on the planet is officially required to know, on September 11 2001 two commercial aircraft were hijacked and flown into the two towers of the World Trade Center in New York. Approaching 3,000 people died in the attack, almost none of them having chosen to be part of a war. It was a vile and disgusting act which can only be abhorred by anyone with any regard for humanity. And yet it really does seem that the only people who could speak with conviction or integrity about the horror committed were those willing to speak out against any such horror wherever it occurred and irrespective of which innocents perished. There is a large segment of the world who felt sick when they saw the starving people of Ethiopia in the '80s, but a much smaller segment who took the time to notice Rwanda, Srbrenica, Chile, Nicaragua, the Turkish Kurds, the Australian Aborigines (the list is too long to contemplate). We all decried Saddam when he invaded Kuwait, but few of us condemned the 'liberators' who mowed down tens of thousands of fleeing Iraqi conscripts in the 'turkey shoot' and then ploughed them (many still alive) into mass graves in the Kuwaiti desert. And it is nothing short of hypocrisy in us to be glad to see the back of the Taliban while being content to allow Uzbekistan to continue on its barbaric path. There can be no half way here. You can't pick and choose. Either you will join a protest march against the occupation of Palestinian land or you were glad to see 3,000 people killed in the attack on Manhattan. We are humanity, and you're either with us or against us.

That is a difficult paragraph; full of truths which lead to lies. It simply isn't possible to take an active stand against all injustices. Nor are they all directly equivalent in a strange blood algebra. There is no standard response; I abhor the Palestinian suicide bomber just as I abhor the murder of civilians by the Israeli army, but my reaction to each is not identical. Why not? Well, because it is complicated.

Let's look at the official narrative of the same event. Three thousand people minding their own business and full of good intentions were going to work as usual when a handful of evil terrorists killed them all out of a mixture of envy of the life they had and insane religious ideology. But terror can never be allowed to win, so America has to fight back, to send a crystal clear message that it remains unbowed. Every supporter of the terror which did this terrible thing must be hunted down and destroyed. They are the embodiment of pure evil and must be shown no mercy. But they are hiding everywhere, and that puts the onus on everywhere to play its part in destroying them. It is a simple battle between good and evil, and when it comes to the eternal battle of right and wrong there can be no equivocation. To fail to do everything in your power to destroy or to help to destroy the terrorists is tantamount to helping them. So the answer is simple; you're either with us or against us.

An equally difficult paragraph which also contains some truths that lead to lies. The truths are more difficult in this one, but there is no doubt that what was done to New York was wrong (the meaning and genesis of the word evil is so complicated that no-one outside Hollywood should use it if they are seeking to mean something real). It is equally true that it is incumbent on all human kind to act to right an injustice where they can – in Voltaire's words "every man is guilty of all the good he didn't do". Equally, a form of religious fundamentalism undoubtedly played a significant part in the attack. But then, so did many other things; poverty, anger at American foreign policy, intelligence agency incompetence. So it is much less straightforward to put these things together. Do I think it is right to stand by and do nothing when 3,000 innocent people have been killed? No I do not. Do I want those responsible held to account? Yes I do. Do I therefore want George W Bush to overthrow another country's government? Well, not unless they were responsible. Am I content to see hundreds of people charged with no crime locked in tiny cages in a Cuban wasteland? No I certainly am not. So George W, am I with you or against you? Well, it's complicated.

And that is the nature of life. It is packed with contradictions, complications, subtleties, uncertainties, doubts and disagreements. Just as contradictions are not something to be afraid of (see above), equally complications are something to be celebrated. Doubt is not necessarily a bad thing where certainty often is. Good politics, good decisions making, should seek out the complications and uncertainties precisely because these are the points at which the limits of a decision can be found. Doubt should act as a brake to recklessness and uncertainty is the best anecdote to unreason. These are things which can help to prevent us making stupid mistakes, or equally they are things which can help us to stop others from forcing mistakes upon us. And this is precisely the problem for those who wish to take action not because it has been thought through and is the best thing to do but because the decision was made before the reason arrived. The flaws in the actions of the galloping American monster after 11 September 2001 were numerous and thinking them through should have checked the rampage of the beast. But the beast was not for being checked and so it trampled straight over the top of any flaws. It was essential for the completion of the project that all complexities were exiled from the debate. So a single overriding doctrine was needed to get rid of those complexities and that was the clumsy old white-hat-black-hat trick; are you a goodie or a baddie? We have been attacked and this is what we are going to do about it. And you can either be with us or against us – there is no third option. Hegelian dialectic proposed that a thesis should meet an antithesis and that from the interplay of these will emerge a synthesis, an answer greater than the sum of its parts. The Bushian dialectic works differently; not thesis, antithesis, synthesis but thesis, intimidation, reprisal.

The end of complexity can be found in all sorts of places. The debate about the funding of higher education in England discussed above should have been full of complexity. There were three key stakeholders – society generally (and the government as its representative), employers and students/graduates. Each of these saw very great benefit from higher education – society got doctors, teachers, engineers, medicines, new technologies and enlightenment, employers got high-skill employees at no cost to them and graduates got an education and greater earning power. So there are a number of sources of income it was worth discussing. Each of them might have made a contribution in a number of ways; government could have raised income through all sorts of progressive or regressive methods which could have been generalised or targeted; employers could have made a contribution on all sorts of bases again generalised or targeted; students or graduates could have paid in an endless combination of ways. So how come the entire debate was summed up in the simple duality either students pay a regressive free-market fee or universities will continue to crumble before our eyes? In fact it is much worse than that; unless you back variable top-up fees we will be unable to expand places at university for poor students so it is fees or eternal elitism.

The complexities in this debate should have been the proving ground where we discovered if it was the best possible policy. At that point it was the most controversial piece of domestic legislation of the Blair government and following an incredibly bruising campaign for and against, a government with a majority of more than 160 won by only five votes. It is therefore reasonable to suggest that the arguments for this policy were tested to the limit – that is to say that the complexities were laid bare and thoroughly explored. Well, not really. There were three alternative proposals which were put forward during the (almost year long) debate. The first was the idea of a graduate tax – an extra amount paid by those with degrees on top of their income tax. It was certainly progressive and much fairer than a rigid fee system. The second was simply to increase the existing flat rate fee and raise more money without introducing a market into higher education. The third was that an extra tax band should be introduced on those earning over £100,000 a year which would have raised enough money to fund universities properly as well as meet a number of other spending requirements. So a detailed debate then.

Well, no. All three were answered in the following way; a graduate tax would be too expensive to administer, flat rate fees would be unfair and rich people can pay accountants to avoid paying tax so there's no point in trying. Quite a lot of people blinked when they heard all of this too. It's all a bit technical but given that the variable fee will be collected through the Inland Revenue, why can't the tax code used simply be implemented in a way that does not terminate when the set debt is paid off? Or if it is really that technically difficult, why not set each student's debt at a notional £5 million and right off any of that debt not paid back 40 years later (there will be a write-off clause written into the legislation as a concession to opponents)? How is charging people variable fees according to what the market will bear fairer than charging everyone the same? (And no, markets will not link fees to potential future earnings whatever Ministers think.) And how is charging people more or less but with no reference to ability to pay fair? And is Blair really saying that the fact that some people will try to break a law targeted at them is a good reason not to impose the law? Saying that tax should not be levied on the rich because they will avoid it is like saying murder should no longer be an offence for terrorists because they will just do it anyway and lots of them won't be caught.

So people really tore into these complexities? No, because when they tried they were quickly told to stop carping and pick a side; for fees, healthy universities and loads of students from poor backgrounds or against fees, for crap universities and for elitism. No, complexity and ideology do not sit well together.

But the greatest example of the ending of complexity is the case made for the 2003 Iraq war. We have all become armchair intelligence experts ever since Blair decided that he was going to back America in its invasion of Iraq and then realised he would have to justify it somehow. It would be naïve to think that wars are usually started because of something the enemy nation did (as if there would have been no conflict if they hadn't done that thing) but it is true that they are generally started *when* someone does some-thing. Suez, Korea, Vietnam, Iraq 1991 – all these were going to happen for geopolitical reasons but each appeared to be triggered by some sort of act of aggression. Iraq 2003 was equally going to happen – the puppet-masters who sneaked into the White House behind their stooge Bush were openly lobbying for it as early as 1997 – but this time Saddam didn't actually do anything to start it. In fact, given that a decade-long war encouraged by the West followed by a rout at their hands in another war, followed by a decade of vicious sanctions, seven years of stringent weapons inspections and five years of continual aerial bombing had reduced Iraq to a third world state virtually incapable of defending itself, there wasn't really anyone they could have been aggressive towards. So to persuade us to attack a defenceless country which was not an active or potential threat was going to be difficult. Not for America where international law had been filed under 'quaint odd-ity' for years but for Britain which remains stubbornly unenthusiastic about unnecessary wars.

So Blair needed a reason and the only one he had was that Iraq posed a threat to the world which couldn't be seen but which we knew about be-cause of intelligence. He released his two dossiers and inadvertently dragged the question of the complexity of real decision-making out into the open. In-telligence is by its very nature complex. Satirists John Bird and John Fortune performed a sketch lamenting the loss of the "golden era of intelligence, the days when you had solid information such as Hitler having enslaved most of Europe and bombs falling on London". But that is information (or news, or fact), not intelligence. Intelligence is a multitude of partial scraps of informa-tion, overheard snippets of conversation and endless rumours. If they were indisputable they would move from being intelligence to being facts. The point of intelligence is that this host of random bits and pieces needs to be put together and assessed for probability.

Not according to Tony Blair, though. At the time he told the country, in no uncertain terms, that Iraq posed a current and imminent threat through a programme of weapons of mass destruction which was "current, detailed and growing". Except that we now know it was none of these things. If you were to read the first of the dossiers closely you would find that there were actually only two pieces of evidence for the existence of chemical and bio-logical weapons in Iraq (and none for the existence of nuclear weapons). The first was a negative sort of evidence – we knew he used to have them and we have no conclusive proof he has destroyed them. The same sort of evidence which would convict me of having a slice of strawberry cheesecake in my fridge because I did once and would be totally unable to prove that I had eaten it. The only other solid evidence was the claim that Saddam could order the deployment of chemical weapons in 45 minutes. Except that this came from a single uncorroborated source which was not known to be reliable, passed through a third party which while assessed to be reliable was known to have a personal agenda. Meanwhile, there was other evidence that Saddam didn't have any such weapons, such as Saddam declaring that he didn't (unreliable, perhaps), his senior director of his weapons programme who defected and admitted that they had developed weapons but had destroyed them all in 1993 when they knew the weapons inspectors were coming and the report of those weapons inspectors who after seven years concluded that Iraq had "fundamentally disarmed".

Now I am willing to accept the complexity of this. "Fundamentally disarmed" allows for the possibility that sufficient materials were retained to restart the programme. Destroyed in 1993 and still unable to resume production by 1995 still does not mean that by 2003 there was nothing. But it does cast doubt and raise some complex questions about what we believe to be the truth. There can be virtually no-one in the intelligence service who would now support a pre-war assessment that – without any doubt or uncertainty – Iraq posed an imminent threat because of the possession of weapons of mass destruction which it had the capacity and intention to deploy and use against other nations. In fact, the CIA has since clarified that they never said there was an imminent threat from Iraq and declassified intelligence now makes it clear that the intelligence showed no certainty in the first place.

These are complexities which simply didn't suit Tony Blair. And that is why they were, well, 'simplified' for us.

The box of arguments

Science likes consistent arguments. Why do things fall? Gravity. Hydrogen and oxygen combined through combustion? That'll be water. It is generally a sign of good science that one argument provides a solution to a question in a manner which consistently proves to be true, even in the face of counterarguments (even though it can take quite a while to deduce which of the arguments is correct and some may never be resolved). Other areas of knowledge are much more forgiving of inconclusivity. Take something like literary analysis. Here it is possible to put forward an argument which may face alternative arguments and neither one wins outright but neither is therefore without value. For example, is the personal experience of an author a necessary piece of information if we are to understand his or her text? Or rather does the nature of writing down words on a page create within them a delimited whole which requires only those words to establish the meaning of the text? Feel free to discuss this for the next 60 years but don't feel any need to reach a final conclusion. Nature/nurture? Social theories are exactly the same; no final answer is available. The same for economics (which notably exists to make astrology look good).

However, in none of the above or any other similar cases – from astrophysics to a debate about football in the pub – will five bad arguments make up for one good one. This should also be true of political, social and economic debate. But it isn't. If you have something which is indefensible, just keep throwing half-baked arguments at its opponents until they finally give up. Sure they will swat away each of these arguments one at a time. But, just like Gulliver under a hail of Lilliputian arrows, sheer volume will eventually result in defeat.

There are a variety of models of how this works, but they generally conform to something like the following. 'X is right because of A.' 'But A is wrong.' 'Don't be so stupid, what about B?' 'But B is wrong too.' 'And next you're going to tell me C is wrong.' 'Yes I am.' 'Look, you can stick your head in the sand all you want but there is no denying A.'

Unfortunately the run up to the Iraq war is again the best example of this, so we'll look at it quickly:

> Iraq has weapons of mass destruction.
> If we know that for a fact we could destroy them.
> But he is hiding them.
> So we have to let the UN weapons inspectors find them and disarm them.
> But we've waited long enough.
> Surely another few months won't make any difference.
> Yes they will, he is an imminent threat.
> Do you have any evidence of that?
> We can't wait until we have conclusive evidence because then it would be too late.
> But there is no-one he could threaten without facing an immediate and massive retaliation.
> But he's insane.
> Even if he is, he appears to be complying with our requests.
> He's just buying time.
> To attack us?
> Yes.
> But how can he attack us if his country is crawling with weapons inspectors?

He could supply chemical weapons to terrorists.
But Saddam Hussein has no links with Islamic terrorists who
hate him for running a secular state.
That isn't a chance we can take.
But surely the biggest risk of him passing on weapons is if
he is attacked?
We can't afford to wait for a mushroom cloud before we
act.
Surely there can't be a mushroom cloud because we know
he doesn't have nuclear weapons.
He might within a matter of a few years.
So there is time to let weapons inspectors in.
We know he has other weapons of mass destruction now.
But we don't know where they are?
No.
So how do we know?
Because of all the information supplied by previous weapons
inspectors.
So inspections work?
The risk is too great to wait any longer – Sadam had his
chance.

You can therefore summarise this pro-war argument as follows. We
don't know for absolute sure that Iraq has illegal weapons. We certainly
don't know where they are but we don't have time to look for them. That
is because we can't wait for evidence of a threat. And although he is doing
what we are telling him and has no alternative, he might attack us anyway.
If not he could give weapons to terrorists he has never met and who hate
him. He might give weapons to terrorists if we attack him which makes it
all the more important that we do. And despite knowing that he hasn't got
nuclear weapons we still have to attack him because weapons inspections
worked. But can't be allowed to work again. This is almost exactly the basic
argument which persuaded a majority of the Westminster Parliament to
vote for war.

But you can find examples almost anywhere:

We shouldn't provide free nursing care for every elderly
person.
Why not?
Because it is a ridiculous perk to the middle classes.
Why so?
Because they can afford to pay for it themselves.
So why not tax them more to ensure that we can afford it for

everyone?

Because the middle classes already pay enough tax.

So they have to use all their savings to pay for essential care?

Which is perfectly fair.

But then they'll become very poor pensioners.

Yes, but we will look after poor pensioners.

How?

By targeting free care on the poorest.

Scotland's economy is underperforming so we should stimulate it with big tax breaks for small businesses.

But this gift of public money will either bail out failing companies or be taken as extra profit.

No, it will be put into research and development which will stimulate the economy.

But almost no small businesses invest in R&D irrespective of their profit margins.

Well, in any case it will attract big businesses to settle in Scotland.

Unless someone else offers them a bigger incentive.

So we have to stay competitive.

But the average wages in China are a fraction of ours and they have a well educated population.

Which is why we have to get the financial climate right for small indigenous businesses in Scotland.

Trade unions must continue to support the Labour Party.

But the Labour Government presides over the worst legal working conditions in Europe.

They are still better than they were, and more will be done when it is right to do it.

So why does the Prime Minister brag about our poor working conditions to international corporations?

A sound economy is the basis for job creation.

So to create jobs we must make them insecure and poorly paid?

Labour has introduced a minimum wage and some trade union rights.

But they are the lowest and weakest respectively in Europe.

But the alternative is worse.

Not the Liberal Democrats or the Scottish Socialist Party which are both proposing better policies.

They will never get into government.
But they will put pressure on Labour to change its policies.
The trade unions need a strong Labour Party and must keep funding it. That is the bottom line.

And so on and so on indefinitely. It's that disappearing Hegelian dialectic again. Debate used to be a sort of intellectual game of tug of war where strong arguments pulled against each other and the more forceful brought the debate onto their ground. It has now become a bit more like a boxing match where one boxer just keeps running away until the time is up and he wins by default. Instead of good arguments we are now presented with a box full of non-arguments.

Inaction is not an option

Despite all this wealth of manipulation there remains a problem. Even where you have the power to alter what people think through deception and control there is always the risk of inertia. What happens if people are made to vaguely agree with what you are saying but still don't feel inclined to support the actual action you are proposing? It is much easier to persuade people that exercise is good for them than it is to make them jog.

And that is why we need to be kept on our toes by a world of crises, a world where we are surrounded by potential disaster and inaction is not an option. This can be the dissemination of fear as discussed above, but it is usually a little more mundane than that. Let us look again at the genesis of the university tuition fees debate.

This all started almost a year after the beginning. At the end of 2001 a Spending Review was underway. This is a tri-annual process when notional budgets are set for the following three years. Every UK spending department has to put its case for more resources to the Treasury and it in turn has to hold the jackets and adjudicate while the others fight it out. Organisations funded from UK spending departments know this is their main chance to secure adequate funding for the succeeding three years and therefore put in their own cases to their sponsoring department. Following this plan Universities UK, the representative body of all the universities in the UK, submitted a bid to the Department for Education and Skills. In this they calculated what was needed to restore the physical infrastructure of universities, partially restore staff pay to where it ought to have been, expand their valuable research work and invest in the future. Unfortunately, the bill which they arrived at was £9 billion, a frankly implausibly large amount of money. Shortly afterwards the then Higher Education Minister responded in precisely the manner anyone would have expected her to; by dismissing the bid as "cloud cuckoo land". The universities got barely a fraction of this money and they whined a little bit. And there it ended. By the middle of 2002 no-one remembered the universities and their problems.

Then a curious thing happened. The universities knew that there wasn't much scope for securing more money and continued to make the case but with little effort or focus. So far so expected. But then out of the blue members of the Government from the Prime Minister down started raising concerns about the funding of higher education. Cloud cuckoo land suddenly didn't seem quite so remote and a cry of penury which had declined back to a mere whimper was suddenly foregrounded. But not by the universities; it was Ministers who started to talk about 'crisis'.

This was the point at which people should have started to become suspicious. If you look in the *Little Book of Basic Governing* you will find an important section which is headlined NEVER ADMIT A CRISIS. You may discover that you have soldiers fighting in a foreign land equipped only with teaspoons and homemade catapults, but this is a 'supply chain difficulty'. A hospital may be overflowing with flu-ridden pensioners who are left to suffer while strewn across floors throughout the building, but this is an 'unpredictable and temporary medical epidemic which will be under control in the near future'. Ministerial corruption is tittle tattle, massive budget deficits are minor accountancy issues, collapsing peace negotiations are steady progress. Whatever these things are they are never crises.

Now, there is no doubt that UK higher education is underfunded, but the buildings aren't falling down, the output quality remains high by international standards and lecturers are not yet in open revolt over their meagre pay. It is not exactly what you would call a textbook crisis – more of a brewing problem. So given the usual governmental crisis-aversion and the scale of the problem, why did we discover politicians so willing to use the 'c' word on our airwaves? Well, because they had a solution. They realised that they were going to have to do something major (because of this crisis) and they had gone away and thought about it and, hey presto, within a month or two they came up with the idea of introducing a free market into UK higher education. Variable top-up fees (yes, the very thing they promised not to introduce in their election manifesto) would be a fair and equitable way to solve the higher education funding crisis in one go. Problem solved.

This is of course all a piece of Alice in Wonderland claptrap. You have to read that paragraph in reverse to understand what was actually happening. It was well known that a tiny cluster of free-market ideologues in the Downing Street Policy Unit had been keen on forcing the idea of a free market somewhere into Britain's education system for a while. After all, transport and all the public utilities had already been completely privatised, postal delivery privatisation was a done deal, so-called 'co-payment' (charging for services that used to be free at the point of delivery) was creeping in all over the place and the Foundation Hospitals legislation had sneaked private clinical services into the Health Service by the back door. There was only education left, but that is a notoriously difficult nut to crack for the profiteer; the commitment to free education is strong in Britain. There was no chance of getting it into schools (yet) and there was no profit to be had in college education. This only left universities, and the earlier introduction of flat-rate tuition fees had left the door open. The problems were the sticking point of a manifesto commitment and the thorny issue of a Parliamentary Labour Party which simply wouldn't swallow top-up fees as a piece of ideology. So manifesto commitments were going to have to be superseded and the Party was going to have to be made to swallow something unpleasant on the grounds of pragmatism, not ideology. Momentum was going to have to be engineered.

There were a large number of rebels on the Government benches and they were going to have to corralled and forced into some form of action. Had the natural course of things been allowed to run, the likelihood is that the universities would have been given modest increases in funding from within the general budget, perhaps in combination with a real-terms rise in the flat rate fee. If Blair had tried to introduce the variability into this political climate it would not have been accepted, so a new climate had to be engineered. This had to create a situation in which the imperative for change seemed unavoidable and in which it would be impossible for rebels to promote the status quo or a variation on it. And that's why the crisis was needed. It was a localised form of permanent revolution, and it worked. Much else was required – bullying, coercing, manipulation of facts, setting up of false contests with other spending departments and so on – but it couldn't have begun without that very spur to action.

Foreign policy is the natural home of this sort of arbitrary urgency. This is the case for a number of reasons. For one it is particularly difficult to gain public approval for expensive or risky activities which take place in faraway parts. It seems too remote from people and it is hard for them to understand why it is that we can't just keep out of it. Another reason is that people are both notoriously ignorant and suspicious of anything beyond their doorstep. If an official source tells us that a certain country is a threat most people do not have the base knowledge to assess that claim and they have also been led to be suspicious of many of these countries over a long period of time.

Any country outside Europe and North America is generally viewed by the public as being unfathomable and probably hostile (this in part because we get so little news about these countries and because when we do it is seldom reassuring). The simple mouthing of the name of an African nation can be enough to cause The People In The Street to screw up their faces. Tell them that there are dirty deeds going on in Chad and they will nod sagely as if to say 'I thought as much' despite possibly having never heard of Chad before and certainly knowing next to nothing about it.

So when we want to make some sort of incursion somewhere in the world, more often than not for economic or political reasons, the public needs to be persuaded that something has to be done and that the government has just the answer. And it proves easy because people know so little about foreign affairs. So Iraq's human rights abuses were something we couldn't overlook while Uzbekistan's human rights abuses are 'improving steadily' (i.e they only boiled seven political opponents this week). North Korea is a threat to the world because it has Nuclear Weapons which it actually has little desire to use while Israel poses no threat to world peace despite having a nuclear arsenal which many hardliners in the country are just itching for an excuse to use against one of its Arab neighbours. Bombing Kosovo was the only way to stop ethnic cleansing while in the Democratic Republic of Congo the best way to deal with the problem is to leave them alone. The fact that Iraq had oil we wanted but was no longer playing ball while Uzbekistan had oil we wanted and was playing ball is a coincidence. We have to be dragged into these things because we have no inherent desire to bomb people so threats and crises must be established and it must be very clear in our minds that inaction is not an option. And we are rather too ready to believe this.

In fact, inaction is almost always an option and certainly seems to be the one favoured by governments when it comes to the agendas of poverty, taxation, social equality, corporate crime and environmental degradation. If a government had the will to seriously go after corporate tax evasion it would be easy to manufacture a suitable crisis. The billions of pounds of money which are in effect stolen could easily be categorised as destabilising public services and could equally be presented as the scourge of small businesses who are carrying a disproportionate amount of the tax burden because they are less able to avoid paying it. Poverty is a genuine crisis and lies at the heart of most of our major social problems from ill health to crime. We are in a genuine tax crisis in Britain. We are trying to run a European-style welfare system on American-style taxation. We have sold almost all of the family silver to subsidise artificially low tax (the privatisation of the '80s and '90s) and are currently trying to disguise it by running public services on the never never (the Private Finance Initiative and its offshoots). The environment is being daily eroded, racism is on the rise, approaches to gender and sexuality remain fraught. But none of these are to concern us because the possibility of a weak leader of a distant country using shoulder-mounted rocket launchers to fire mortars of out of date chemical weapons (which turn out not to exist) for literally hundreds of yards is more worthy of our billions than poverty or the extinction of species.

So don't just sit there – panic!

Oh, and then there are the plain lies

It would of course be remiss to list the ways in which we are brainwashed into an alien way of thinking without pointing out that sometimes they simply tell us lies. There are two categories which work best – those which are complicated and which most people can't pick out as lies and those which it is hard to disprove.

A very good example of the former occurred in an edition of the television political debate programme *Question Time*. It was the aftermath of the Iraq war and Government minister Patricia Hewitt was defending the situation in post-war Iraq. She told us that the problems with starvation and lack of medicine was Saddam Hussein's fault. The story goes that we acted like good and civilised people and put an embargo on Iraq which stopped him getting anything which might help him build weapons of mass destruction but would allow food and medicine in. This would be paid for by Iraq by supplying us with oil – the so-called Food for Oil programme. The problem was that Sadam hoarded the food and medicines that he received from the West and kept it for him and his henchmen, leaving his population to starve. We acted in good faith and have no blood on our hands. Both the other guests on the panel and the audience fell silent at the evil mendacity of Sadam Hussein.

Meanwhile I was jumping around the bed in the hotel room I was watching this in. Almost every word of it was a total lie. The United Nations carried out a major report into the Food for Oil programme and concluded that they could find no evidence of the stockpiling of food or medicine. On the contrary, Iraq was actually praised for a distribution system which was remarkably efficient under the circumstances. The real problem was two fold. Firstly the West simply didn't supply enough food or medicine and where it did it often knowingly supplied materials which were worthless (Iraqi hospitals are apparently well stocked with medical manuals on plastic surgery which America supplied because it has a surplus with no domestic use – and they took the oil money for these). Secondly, more than half of what was nominally provided never got to Iraq. America had a veto in the form of blocking orders which allowed them to prevent the delivery of anything which they deemed to be of 'dual use' or of any other threat. This applied to a lot of medicines which they designated as 'chemicals' and things such as incubators for premature babies which were impounded on the basis that they contained microchips which might have been used in missiles. Again, they took the money for these. They just didn't deliver.

The career civil servant who was responsible for administering the Oil for Food programme was a man called Dennis Halliday. He was hardly what you would call a radical – he had worked as a bureaucrat with the United Nations for more than 25 years and was personally selected to be put in charge of this highly controversial project. Dennis Halliday resigned from the post publicly saying that his conscience would no longer allow him to be involved. He said that in the end he could only find one way to describe the policy being inforced primarily by America and Britain, and that was genocide. He did not use this word lightly. His deputy, a man called Hans Von Sponek, succeeded him. Again, this was a steady career diplomat. Six months later he too resigned, and he too described the policy as an act of genocide. The state of Iraq was not a product of Saddam's mendacity but of deliberate British and American policy. And yet not one person on the panel or in the audience appeared to know any of this (a virtual news blackout made sure of that). So a Government minister appeared on national television and lied about what those who knew it best described as an act of genocide and she strolled away with no-one appearing to be aware they had been lied to.

The second way to get away with lying is to make sure that no-one can prove you wrong. During the Miner's Strike of 1983-84 a front page story appeared in the Daily Mirror claiming that miner's leader Arthur Scargill had stolen from the strike fund to pay off his mortgage. The source for this story was an insider who leaked documents. It was incredibly damaging. It was also entirely untrue. Seven years later and well after the miners were defeated it emerged that the internal source was in fact a covert agent working for the secret service. Almost two decades later the editor who published the story, a man called Roy Greenslade who was by that time a media commentator for the Guardian, finally admitted that the story was almost certainly a lie. Which must have been a great consolation to the communities who had their faith in their leader seriously questioned at what was for many of them the most difficult time in their lives. Lies are constant and perpetual, and people in power generally get away with them. That's because we generally believe them.

And there you have it…

This hasn't been an exhaustive list of the ways in which debate or lack of it has shaped the public consciousness and the social imagination. Some of these overlap each other and there are plenty of other ways in which we are manipulated. Nevertheless, it is helpful to take apart what we are actually being told to enable a better understanding of why we are being told it. In quick summary they are as follows.

Tools for controlling the social imagination

Hiding ideology	Presenting ideological arguments, policies, analyses and approaches as if they have no ideological basis but are purely pragmatic or inevitable
Denying alternatives	Portraying any given course of action as the only possible course of action by burying or discrediting alternatives
Assuming inevitability	Describing events and circumstances as if they are the only possible outcomes and are therefore part of a 'natural order' which it is pointless to try and alter
Controlling space	Ensuring that the places in which information can be transmitted are controlled by those with a vested interest in the interpretation and use of information
Defining importance	Filtering information, particularly news, to create and reinforce views on what is important and not important and what is positive and negative

Manipulating evidence	Presenting as 'facts' information which is only partially true, which is open to interpretation or which might be contradicted by other information
Predetermining outcomes	Setting the remits of inquiries or posing questions in such a way as to ensure that a predetermined answer is likely to be arrived at
Repetition	Reinforcing and embedding a message through continual use
Graduating change	Introducing major change in small steps each of which on its own seems insignificant
Removing values	Conducting debate on subjects that require value judgments without any reference to values or principles
Eliminating history	Treating history selectively and ignoring any aspect of history which might lead to undesired conclusions
Delineating mainstream	Defining a narrow and selective range of views as conventional and marginalising anything outside that range
Co-opting support	Forcing external actors to conform to the terms of a debate if they wish to participate and thereby reinforcing those terms
Simplifying complexity	Presenting complicated or contradictory information in a simplistic manner to avoid debate
Deploying pejoratives	Dismissing or undermining people, organisations, ideas or analyses by describing them in dismissive or hostile language
Discouraging engagement	Seeking to prevent ideas and views being challenged by discouraging people from becoming involved in issues

Depoliticising politics	Discussing and practicing policy and politics as if it were only a process of micro management
Ignoring outcomes	Denying the outcomes of actions altogether or identifying only those outcomes which reinforce the original reasons for action and ignoring any others
Distorting comparison	Selecting comparisons or measures not according to appropriateness but according to the transforming effect it can have on perceptions of that being compared or measured
Selective invalidation	Claiming that an entire point of view is invalidated by any action by one person which itself appears to be invalid
Generating fear	Controlling action and views through fear
Manufacturing identity	Creating a false collective identity and using it to manipulate views and attitudes
Deifying archetypes	Promoting role models with the aim of making people believe that the characteristics and goals of these role models are desirable
Creating artificial conflict	Undermining the case made by one group by setting that case against the case made by another group even though they are not in reality in competition
Distorting language	Using euphemisms and jargon to disguise meaning
Inconsistent contradictions	Exaggerating contradictions to undermine certain cases while ignoring contradictions which appear to undermine other cases
Justifying oppression	Using oppression to control views but justifying it in terms of 'fun'

Eradicating doubt	Claiming certainty where none exists
Parallel justification	Distracting opponents from flaws in an argument by supplying multiple explanations for action
Inventing volatility	Portraying situations as unstable and the status quo as not an option to coral people into unpopular action
And lies	

Section Four

Recapturing the Social Imagination

Reason for hope

A quick summary: almost every change in the history of mankind has come from an idea or vision which was shared by a small group of people which grew bigger. This is the social imagination. Almost every one of those ideas was opposed and resisted and almost every one of those people was persecuted or marginalised. This is the control of the social imagination. While we no longer burn our heretics, they are now caught up in a complex and powerful web of control which discredits and silences them. A sense of resignation – or even hopelessness – is encouraged in order to suppress new ideas at source. The result is that we live in a grossly unequal society in a grossly unequal world and yet we have no widely-shared persuasive ideas about how things should be changed for the better.

This in itself might induce hopelessness. But it shouldn't; it is very clearly an aberration. To believe that we have reached the end of ideas (the end of history) is to believe that humankind has given up on hoping for a better world. This is palpable nonsense. The examples in this book are not a statement of defeat but a call to action. Yes, there are barriers to new ideas and to change, but they are surmountable. Certainly, some need to be worked around (media ownership and the control of space is a real problem) but many can be easily overcome and some disappear just as soon as you choose no longer to believe in them.

There is an alternative set of maxims which can guide how we see the world around us. If we can adopt these we can begin to recapture the social imagination. This will bring ideas, and those will bring change.

There is always reason for hope.

Change can happen

It is odd that we haven't learned the lesson that change always happens, or rather it is odd that we have failed to believe that lesson. This truth is perhaps the most constant rule which can be applied to the observable universe. It was believed that only the speed of light was constant, but even that is no longer believed. In fact, the concept of time is the expression of inevitable change.

So we know that things will change, the only questions being when and how.

It is of course important to realise that change may take a long time. If you want to find the place where time starts to bend, you need to travel an inconceivable long way out of our galaxy. In the same way it seems unlikely that a mode of law-making and government which is not tied to territorial boundaries is unlikely to emerge in the foreseeable future (and probably not in our lifetimes). There are reasons for inertia of this sort. At the moment humankind remains in a primarily consuming mode – our existence remains reliant on natural resources without which our way of living becomes impossible. Many of these natural resources are territorial – certain parts of the surface of the earth contain certain minerals. These resources are necessary to our way of life and are therefore valuable, a fact which means that they will inevitably be controlled in some manner. The territorial concentration of resource means that there is almost certain to be a territorial control of that resource. If there is to be territorial control then there must be a division and delimitation of the powers of control. This fact combined with other determinants – the widespread acceptance of the principles of democratic sovereignty, limitations in transport technology – means that it is likely that government based on territory will remain; the nation state is safe for just now.

But if change is inevitable, inertia is not. To illustrate this fact, let us consider the two limiting variables above. Firstly democracy. It is far too early to say how enduring a form of social organisation democracy will prove to be. From the beginning democracy has been a qualified form of social organisation. Initially democracy was specifically limited, for example to those who possessed land or who were male. But even with universal suffrage there are quite a few limits on democracy. These are voluntary opt-outs such as the independence of judiciary and the acceptance of inalienable property rights. The structures of democratic processes also limit the meaning of democracy – electoral systems (how people vote, what they can vote for, how likely their vote is to change things, how often they vote) can and do mean that even in a democracy there is a good chance that 'the will of the people' will not be met. The implications for the future of the nation state are numerous. Disillusionment with government could lead in many directions, including new forms of fascism. It is not impossible to imagine a circumstance in which one powerful nation facing domestic economic crisis might tip over into being aggressive and expansionary (and post-2004 it is worryingly easy to imagine in relation to the US). So it may not be safe to assume the inevitability of nation states (rather than, say, new forms of empire).

A less dramatic possibility is the ceding of power from nation state to corporation, something which is well under way already. Privatisation programmes for the developed world and their all-consuming sibling 'structural adjustment' for the rest mean that most of the world's most valuable resources are not in the hands of nation states anyway. In Scotland we have had the debate over whether North Sea oil is 'ours' or 'England's'. The answer is of course that functionally it is neither. The UK treasury does not make a 'profit' from North Sea oil, it charges royalties to and taxes the profits of private companies and it is those who make the money from the oil. Nation states do not so much control natural resources as hold the jackets while private entities fight over those resources, taking a cut as a fee. The state's job is no longer to take the wealth out of its land but to build roads so someone else can.

The abortive Multilateral Agreement on Investment would have moved this process very much further. This was a WTO-driven scheme which would have forced governments around the world to sign up to a legally-binding agreement which stated that the rights of trans-national corporations would always take precedence over the rights of a nation state. If a company invested in your country, it would then be illegal for you ever to change the terms on which that investment had been made. Those terms would include all taxation and regulation. Governments would no longer have the right to regulate companies operating on their land. Corporations would explicitly be placed above national law. It would have been a small step from this position to one in which nation states as we now understand them had disappeared in favour of solely domestic law-making bodies; community councils with limited local powers, always subservient to an unelected global law-making body (the WTO) which had an explicit remit to look after the interests of big global business. This almost happened – until people woke up (fairly late in the process) to what this would mean.

So these are possible political drivers of change, but there are others. The other limiting variable suggested above was the limitation on transport. So long as technology means that we have to live and work in a comparatively limited space (as a guess, a life lived beyond a radius of about 100 miles would necessarily be a nomadic one) then we are tied to a land and thus tied to a form of territory-based governance. But what if this changed? What if a new form of transport was discovered which could overcome this? What if something such as 'teleporting' became a reality? The fact that we could chose to live under any system of governance and work under any other would mean that the nation state as we understand it would quickly become meaningless.

So don't vote – just wait for teleporting? Of course not. This is just an attempt to illustrate the surprisingly fine balance which is history. On one side of the scales, there is always a very good and persuasive reason why nothing will change. On the other is a good and persuasive reason why things will change. Once you are able to recognise these different factors you are in a position to begin to influence them. This is exactly how the

Multilateral Agreement on Investment was defeated – people saw what was happening and acted to prevent it. But it applies equally to causing change as to preventing it, especially when one feels empowered to look for persuasive reasons for why change will/should/can happen.

Let's apply this optimism to our current economic system. Yes, there are very good reasons why change will not happen, and they all relate to the fact that capitalism is 'resilient' because it grants almost all power to those whose interests are best served by maintaining the system as it is. But it is equally true that there are many good reasons why the system is precarious. There are internal reasons; for example, capitalism's effectiveness in resource allocation through market mechanisms (and 'effective' here means on its own terms rather than any implication of fairness) is both the cause of and threatened by the concentration of wealth and control. Capitalism is a system which contains inherent instability (its strength and its weakness) which means that minor crisis and correction will be an ever-present. In 200 years it is possible to argue that the longest period during which capitalism 'worked' as it is supposed to was less than two decades, and then primarily because it followed the most devastating war that Europe (then the heart of capitalism) had even known. We seem far too quick to forget the great crisis in capitalism in the 1970s (which we now call the 'oil crisis' rather than the 'capitalism crisis' as if it was all down to black liquid) in favour of a brief boom (for some) in the late 1980s. And then we forget the crisis in the early nineties (a 'housing slump') in favour of the boom of the late nineties. Which is just in time for us to disregard the crash of 2000 (just an aberrant 'dot com bubble bursting') so we can get to a place where we are currently pretending that the failure to get back to a boom is down to a 'pensions crisis'. Capitalism (compared to, say, feudalism) is a fairly unstable economic system and it is therefore reasonable to believe that something will change.

Then there is the small matter of people. Tony Blair is known to be 'terribly worried about Africa' which is suffering because of 'corrupt governments' and 'bad weather'. The fact that Europe and America (in particular) deliberately sabotage Africa's economies through subsidy, domestic protectionism and a hostile 'aid' policy which undermines local production, imposes damaging market reforms and makes sure that, while they may be starving, they are never short of expensive Western weaponry. One axis along which we can see a very real pressure for change is the peoples of the developing world. In Latin America there has been a revival of radicalism which the US thought had been tortured out of them in the 1970s and 1980s. The campesino activists of Brazil, Argentina or Venezuela are only part of the picture. If the World Social Forum and all its offshoots turns out to be significant in the long term, we would do well to remember that it couldn't have happened without the activism of the developing world. Starving people across the world no longer seem willing to be lectured by

Bush and Blair on why things are going so well for them because of 'labour flexibility'.

Not that the human drivers for change are only to be found on arid plains. Inequality in the West is on the rise. Every American knows that the nineties were boom years in which American wealth simply couldn't stop growing. They know that an awful lot of people got awfully rich. What they ought to know but generally don't is that over the period of the economic boom in nineties America, average wages did not rise at all in real terms. The average American got not one little bit of benefit out of the good spell of capitalism. You can be sure, however, that they will be the recipients of the bulk of the suffering which the current downturn is bringing (as social benefits and healthcare drift further out of the grasp of millions). If only they knew (and understood), what would happen?

We are in no better position in Britain. For 18 years it was government policy to increase the gap between the richest and the poorest (Thatcher's 'enterprise culture'). So when a 'Labour' government gets in and just keeps making the poor poorer in relation to the rich, the conditions for serious disgruntlement are surely there. It is generally accepted that we are now 'better off' than we were in 1945, but it is much more complicated than that. Absolute (what we might define as life-threatening) poverty might seem to have decreased, but to believe that entirely would require us to disregard the reality of mortality rates. Those living in the poorest parts of Britain can expect to die almost a decade younger than those who live in the most affluent. This is to say that poor people die at a significantly faster rate than rich people. Which in turn is to say that poverty kills, every bit as much now as it did in 1945.

Relative poverty (which we might consider to be the ability to achieve quality of life) might also seem to have been on an inexorable rise. But quality of life is itself a relative measure – if it becomes harder to achieve an average quality of life because the average is rising faster than the means of many to achieve it, then relative poverty is also increasing. This analysis is contended; average wages have risen, everyone has a television and a fridge, many people now go foreign holidays and so on. But it is to suggest that if a man with a loaf of bread gives a starving man a slice the man should be happy, but if a man with a thousand loaves of bread gives a starving man a slice he should be twice as happy. When we slip further down the statistical wealth pole we are being deprived of our fair share of riches which are being given in evermore disproportionate amounts to those who need it least. That is the bottom line. And government policy has been explicitly pursuing this goal. We work longer, are less secure, feel less happy and are supposed to be grateful. To be unhappy about this is not selfishness but is anger at the selfishness of others. This is without doubt a power to be mobilised.

There are of course many, many more human reasons to believe that capitalism will have to change, but let us now consider another final and external reason. This one is the one which above all shows that capitalism will change dramatically, and that is the question of environment. Capitalism can be complicated but works on one simple premise; that in a system of perpetual growth, perpetually greater value can be extracted. As soon as growth stops, capitalism as we know it is no longer able to function (hence the pathological fear of recession). But growth cannot continue indefinitely. We (in the West at least) already live a lifestyle which is entirely unsustainable. This is one of those truths which people find both so banal and so unattractive that it is left to one side. But let us be clear about what this means: even if the Western lifestyle remained the preserve of the few, it cannot be sustained indefinitely.

In fact, the rate of resource use we have now may become unsustainable in a worryingly short timescale. We are already seeing some of the signs of the end of the period of uninhibited growth. Growth is particularly predicated on energy use and production of our core source of energy (oil) cannot grow at the rate of our current economic growth. Analyses vary, but the peak of oil supply – the year in which the largest amount of oil is pumped – will probably occur in little more than a decade or two and possibly less. And in any case, demand is already rising faster than supply, not least because China is becoming as oil-insatiable as we are. We are already seeing the first responses to this reality in the 'oil wars', but these are no solution. We will see renewed investment into research into alternative energy sources, but we are a long way from developing these to a position where they can replace oil. Renewable energy may in the end save humankind, but it seems much less likely that it will save hypercapitalism. From what we currently know about physics, chemistry and economics, the inescapable conclusion is that, one way or another, human existence in 100 years' time will not look like it does now. Our current model of capitalism will either have to change radically or it will die.

So even in light of the structures and methods of controlling the social imagination outlined in this book it is not difficult to see how change is not only possible but likely. The purpose and responsibility of those who seek social change is to recognise the different factors which lie in the balance and to restructure them in a manner which speeds up change and moves it down a route which is more positive. It is sometimes tempting to hope for a monumental crash in the system that we have, but that is as likely (perhaps more likely) to create a dystopia as it is to create a utopia. Change can happen, but change is an active process.

A final note on change; by its nature change looks unlikely right up until the point at which it happens. Slavery never looked more secure than the point just before it fell apart. Civil rights in America never looked less possible than at the point at which progress became rapid. Change can be slow (although more often than not it is fast), but it is always in a binary state. It is either happening or it isn't. And like all binary states, it is 'off' right up until it is 'on'.

There are always alternatives

That change can, indeed will, happen is only one part of the equation; it is, of course, just as important to consider what direction change takes. One response to the environmental limitations of hypercapitalism could be greater segregation. Enclaves in the developed world could accrue greater military power which required fewer and fewer foot soldiers. Along with greater restrictions on movement and perhaps even physical barriers, small elites could thereby insulate themselves from the threat of conflict with the dispossessed. The developed world could use that military power to accrue resources from the no-longer-developing world to ensure that, as far as possible, a small elite would be able to maintain its way of life. This process is of course already well under way (under the banners of anti-terrorism and asylum laws, spreading democracy and national and regional security). But this is an alteration and not an alternative. It is precisely the sort of redrawing of the bars of the cage which this book has been discussing. The system might operate differently, but it achieves almost identical aims – protecting a disproportionate appropriation of resources by a small elite.

Change in itself is not enough because change can be for the worse, or indeed change can come while leaving most things substantively the same. Recognising that change is not only possible but inevitable is the first step to recognising that things can be better. The second is that we face down the greatest and most damaging lie of the last thirty years – that there is no alternative. We have come to recognise that there are alternatives in many areas of our social and moral lives; it is only necessary to look at the changing attitude to racism in the UK to see it. When England played Spain at football in late 2004 there was a disgraceful racial taunting of the black English players by large sections of the Spanish support. The two commentators – hardly stalwarts of British liberalism – were admirably disgusted and spoke of their surprise that this kind of intolerance was still around in the 21st century. Barely 20 years earlier it would not have been difficult to find people who held the view that this kind of racist conflict was inevitable and unavoidable, that there was no alternative to racial intolerance in football. Because people expect changes in their social surroundings and because such changes are comparatively easy to imagine, they don't generally find it difficult to imagine a more tolerant world (whether or not they want it or whether they believe it is likely to happen soon).

Economic change, on the other hand, is something we find much more difficult to believe in. We have seen throughout this book how a narrow economic orthodoxy has been drilled into us all and the extent to which any dissent from that narrow view is marginalised. But it is important to try and escape this conditioning. There are alternative ways of organising our economy and we know this because we have seen them. The capitalism of 30 years ago is very different from the capitalism of today. Thirty years of deregulation and privatisation has removed many of the checks and balances which were in place to control the excesses of free-market capitalism. It would of course be a simple matter (in practical terms) to reinstate these and revert to a different kind of capitalism. Of course there would be consequences, but it could easily be done. Were you to propose it, though, you would be quickly told that while in theory it could be done, the practical implications of the consequences make it impossible. For example, you would be told that deregulation had unleashed the forces of growth on which our pension funds now rely. You would be told that the legal ramifications of greater regulation would be so overwhelming that it would be impossible to get it through without being bogged down in an interminable fight that would block any progress. You would be told about destabilisation and capital flight and hostile money markets. And the sum of all of these arguments would very possibly be persuasive.

On the other hand, it would be no more difficult to 'prove' that the existing economic system and the means by which we arrived at it were also 'impossible'. For example, is it plausible that the global economy could be based on a global system of currency flow which was almost entirely speculative? In 1971, 90 per cent of global financial transactions were 'real' (trade or long-term investment) with about 10 per cent being speculative (gambling on exchange rates between currencies, for example). Within 25 years 95 per cent of global currency flow was entirely speculative – all but five per cent of the world's currency was being used to gamble with. How would investment and trade be supported in such a crazy system? In fact, the amount of money being gambled every day on international money markets is larger than the total cash reserves of the seven biggest economic powers. Put simply, every day the developed world is betting more money that it has. And if the craziness of this system needed any further illustration, 80 per cent of that gambling money returns in exactly the same direction it came from in a week or less.

The idea is preposterous. To get there we would need to privatise as many state monopolies as possible, but they would have to be sold off at well under their value if the right economic stimulus was to be achieved. But these monopolies were owned by the public; how could anyone expect them to be content to have their own property sold off for well under its value? It is inconceivable. How would anyone be expected to believe that there could be a decade of sharp economic growth which created no jobs and did not raise average wages without an outcry? How could an economy function with big chunks of it based on share capital being invested in companies which had not only never made a profit but were so young that they hadn't even made *anything* yet? A financial system in which companies have to reduce the quality of their products to keep theoretical value assessments high or be taken over, despite the fact that their valuations are mainly capricious? How could anyone defend an economic system which discourages proper research and development? Which encourages people to take successful companies and close them down because there is more money to be made from stripping them of assets than for waiting a year or two over which time they would have produced the same amount of profit? Any other system in which the rules and regulations are mainly in the hands of those being regulated would be dismissed as inherently unworkable, but still we have the WTO and the IMF. No, there is simply no way in which our economy can work.

And yet, in its own twisted way, it does. There are two reasons for the disparity between the theory and the reality of our economy. The first of these is that it is possible to make anything which doesn't currently exist sound impossible. For every inventor obsessed with the possibility of making a man fly, there was someone who would prove that it was impossible. The laws of physics (if applied in a certain set of ways) prove it and the laws of God (which of course are infinitely adaptable to any circumstance) prove it. So until we have an aeroplane, there is and can be no alternative to travelling by land and by sea. The second reason for the disparity is that economies are enormously complicated things and cannot actually be modelled very accurately. To model and understand them they need to be greatly simplified. Large-scale economies are treated and understood as if they are mechanical (sets of fixed relationships like the moving parts of a machine) when in fact they are organic (complex arrays of eternally interacting and evolving relationships). If any enormously complex and evolving system is reduced to a simplified analogy it will be easy to pick holes in it. The human body cannot be easily explained in any way which makes it sound likely that it will work. There are so many weak points in the description of the process of human recreation that it simply sounds impossible ("right, so this DNA contains not only all the information required to make a person, it actually makes it out of basically nothing?").

To say that humans walk and don't fly is not the same as to say that humans walk and therefore *can't* fly. To say that the detailed process through which humans recreate is difficult to fit comprehensively into logic is not to say that human recreation is impossible. This results in two rules which ought to govern our belief in alternatives; something's non-existence is not the same as its impossibility and not every aspect of something's functioning needs to be understood in advance.

Let us imagine these two rules in relation to a climbing rose. A climbing rose, in the context of a garden, can't climb on its own. Take any given wall with a piece of earth below it but which doesn't have a rose growing; it is impossible to know if a rose will grow or not because there isn't one there. And indeed it may be impossible for a rose to grow (wrong type of soil, not enough soil, not enough sunlight, lack of drainage and so on), but that certainly doesn't prove that it can't. So plant a rose and see. But if one is to think ahead, it is impossible to know how or where the rose will grow – it could take years to really take off or could flourish almost immediately. It is impossible to know what direction it will take up the wall. If someone were to demand in advance the details of how such a rose was to be supported, the answer would need to be 'wait and see'. In the context of a garden we are content to believe that something which doesn't now exist might very well do one day, and we are also content to accept that we'll need to deal with certain aspects of growth as they emerge. If we didn't there would be no gardens.

The same thing applies to any change. Capitalism doesn't work very well in theory – Marx correctly identified significant problems inherent in the system before it had even properly developed. (In fact, by a lot of measures capitalism doesn't work very well in practice, but we'll leave that aside for a moment.) But it survives because it adapts, changes and corrects itself. Ironically, despite the fact that those who defend capitalism most are those most likely to be sceptical about things which don't exist and who are most likely to criticise things by squeezing them into a greatly simplified framework, capitalism survives precisely because of the creation of the new and the complexity of the unpredictable. Let us imagine that economic order and social change was put on the futures market. Investment in it would not wait until every aspect of it was proved beyond doubt. Nor would that market function on the assumption that nothing new would ever happen. The whole of capitalism is predicated on the concept of alternatives; alternative and better ways to make things, alternative and better things to make. In these alternatives lie profit, and it is profit which drives the system. So let's apply this idea backwards. We need to find an alternative and better way to organise our world and we need that because we are greatly in need of an alternative and better world. It is in these alternatives that we will find collective happiness, and it is in the pursuit of that collective happiness that change will be driven.

Alternatives are always possible – of course they are. Of course, some of those alternatives might not work very well, but that doesn't disprove alternatives because some will work. And of those which do work, not every one of them will work in a way which is better than what we have. But some will. Moving from capitalism based on laws to protect property to a system of complete lawlessness would probably not work in any productive sense. Returning to feudalism could work, but would in many – though not all – ways be worse than what we have. But if these alternatives are possible then so are others, and it is entirely counterintuitive to imagine than none of them could ever be better than what we have. The Enlightenment is becoming more important than it has been for centuries; it is time to remember that through the power of our own labours and ideas, things can be changed and be made better. We know this perfectly well, but we need to believe it and fight for it just a little bit more.

Ideas are important

Of course, all this consideration of 'alternatives' is a bit vague. Had the Wright Brothers got no further than deciding that manned flight was *possible* then we'd still be earthbound today. Yes, we have to believe that alternatives are possible, but that is a starting point that would have been taken as a given were it not for the factors outlined in this book. What we need now is a sense of what the alternative might be. We have to paint a picture of what change might look like. In other words, we are greatly in need of ideas.

Let us think of the impact of ideas by considering the analogy of the fabled cure for cancer. It starts from the presumption that there *can* be a cure for cancer and moves quickly to the 'how'. A scientist knows that cancer is the result of a rogue cell which multiplies voraciously and kills other cells around it. He or she knows that these rogue cells can be caused by a fault in the code which creates all the cells in the body (genetic cancers such as leukaemia) or by external pathogens which cause healthy cells to mutate (environmental cancers such as lung cancer or melanomas). Given the variety and complexity of the potential causes of these rogue cells (not to mention the fact that there are lots of these cells which are rogue but benign) this particular scientist decides to focus on the multiplication of the cells. Many ideas are generated by our scientist in trying to identify ways to stop the multiplication. New cells are imagined that might destroy any rapidly-multiplying rogue cell. These cells might be a variation on the cells we already have to fight bacteria or other pollutants in our body. Changing them to make them attack cancerous cells will require their genetic make-up to be altered. There is already a wide body of work on genetic manipulation in existence, so this is explored. Examples in this literature suggest a number of ways in which a cell might be altered to make it effective in curing cancer. Various forms of adaptation are considered and eventually a few are singled out as being most promising. Now these have to be tried and tested. If just one of them works, then cancer can be cured.

What we can see here is that the cure for cancer will be mainly driven by ideas. One of the biggest revolutions of the Enlightenment (created here in Scotland) was the shift from empirical medicine to theoretical medicine. Before the 18th century medicine was purely a process of 'throw it and see what sticks'. If making a tea from a certain herb helped a certain condition then it was adopted and used. There would probably be no understanding of *why* it worked; it just did. Now that might seem fine, but there are two giant problems with this approach. The first is that unless we understand why something works it is very much harder to improve on it. If we know that the herb tea is thinning the blood and thus reducing clotting, we can try to identify the element which is causing the thinning effect and concentrate on strengthening its effect. If we don't, it is very difficult to make progress. The other is that great confusion is likely in empirical medicine. For example, if people believe that leeches are good for them and show psychosomatic improvements in their condition then leeches become, empirically, a cure – even though they have no beneficial effect. Theoretical medicine, on the other hand, starts from the assumption that the body is a system, something like a machine, and that if we can understand how the machine works then we can understand how to fix the machine. Now, the Edinburgh medics who expounded this theory didn't actually get very far down the road of understanding how the human body works – in fact, some of their cures were every bit as ridiculous as those who preceded them – but the framework they left behind revolutionised not only medicine but all of the sciences. This framework suggests that ideas can be the largest part of a cure.

This is something we need to relearn when it comes to curing other problems. Obvious as it may sound, the cure for cancer will come from someone identifying what is wrong and trying to find ways to fix it. Social and economic problems are no different. Let's take the problem of pay inequality again. We should not be content with the massive disparity between the rich and the poor, and the disparity is now caused as much by low pay as by unemployment. There are large swathes of the workforce that work hard and yet don't earn sufficient wages to maintain a reasonable quality of life (and in many cases the wages on their own would not even enable subsistence). The Labour government, to its credit, did something about this. That it did the wrong thing can almost be forgiven in the context of the many other things it hasn't done. The response was to introduce a minimum wage at a level below subsistence (to root out the criminally low pay) and to make up for the rest by providing means-tested tax credits for working families whose collective income fell below certain levels. What this did was subsidise low pay. The issue of subsistence should have been dealt with by a minimum wage set at a level which did not require further state support to enable a worker to survive. However, this would not address the issue of income inequality.

To do this we need to consider not only income at the bottom but also income at the top. There are a number of things which might be done. The traditional way to address this issue is to redistribute income through taxation. But redistribution will always be unpopular so long as the wealthy are allowed to believe that this was 'their money by right' which was taken from them. Another option would be to match a minimum wage with a maximum wage. This would of course also be unpopular, and it doesn't take long to work out what the complaints against it would be. Or what if there was to be a link between these – particularly a link which left people free to pay what they want but with incentives to close pay gaps. What if there was to be a pay ratio introduced which meant that the best paid person involved in any enterprise (there could be no subcontracting out of this responsibility) could only receive a ratio of the pay received by the worst paid? A chief executive could pay themselves whatever they wanted but would have to raise the pay of the poorest workers to achieve it. What we have here are ideas which could deal with the problems.

Why is this important? Well, for a number of reasons. The first reason why ideas are important is because they bring problems into focus. So long as we have cancer, people will die. As soon as we have an idea for curing cancer we no longer accept cancer as something inevitable and therefore to be endured. Simply having an idea for a solution to a problem starts to threaten that problem whether the idea works or not. Many of the ideas for curing cancer which have been put forward over the last 50 years have failed. Nevertheless, each of them reinforced the desire to find a cure, and many of them may not have worked in themselves but informed or inspired other ideas which did work. The first reason that an idea is important is the same as the reason it is important for an alcoholic to admit that he or she has a problem; by saying it we accept that something is wrong. So by putting forward proposals for ways to address the problem of wage inequality we bring a focus onto the problem. If we create solutions to the problem, the problem is dragged into the foreground. So just as the Victorians tolerated tuberculosis in a way we simply wouldn't, it is harder to tolerate poverty wages if there are real and workable ideas for how to prevent it. This is the power of ideas; they do not need to become anything more tangible than thoughts to begin to have an effect.

The second reason that ideas are important is that they force those who oppose change to engage with arguments about change. Many of the Victorian health reformers faced opposition to the reforms they proposed. Death will always be with us, some argued, and we cannot fight a force which is inevitable. This of course had a strong class bias which led people to argue that a high mortality rate among the poor was 'natural' and that to fight it was a waste of time. And yet when simple ideas were put forward which gave people hope that something could be done about health problems, those who opposed such measures were forced to engage with the debate. At one stage the response of a civic leader to a health problem in a slum part of their city would be to avoid it. But when someone came forward with a proposal to build better sanitation, for example, the civic leader is then forced to resist such a move. By forcing opponents to engage in this way they are drawn into the argument. They find themselves having to defend a policy which leads to the deaths of a lot of people against a policy which might help.

We have seen repeatedly in this book that one of the most important tools for preventing change is to make calls for change disappear. If you can force someone to engage with a debate, that first option of avoidance is lost. In Scotland we had a campaign in the Scottish Parliament to provide all school children with free school meals in a drive to improve diet and diet-related health. The governing parties didn't want to implement this policy, partly because it was reasonably expensive, but mainly because it was a policy which emerged from an opposition party. So they resisted the policy, but in so doing they were drawn into engaging with the issue and responded by instituting a series of healthy eating initiatives. The idea forced movement, and while that movement wasn't far enough, it is a start. Now if we see improvement from the healthy eating initiative we might find pressure to go further. Alternatively, if the initiatives fail to work there will be pressure to reconsider the issue of free school meals. Either way, the idea remains alive because all sides were forced to engage. Similarly, the ideas proposed to deal with wage inequality would, if taken up vigorously, force opponents to engage. There are plenty of arguments which can be deployed against the proposals but almost all of them require those opposing to implicitly or explicitly defend grotesque differences in the lives people can lead because of the money they earn. This is something that those opponents would rather not do.

The third reason that ideas are important is that they are not static. We saw the ways in which an idea for how to cure cancer relies on another previous idea, and how it in turn will influence another idea. In the previous chapter it was argued that alternatives to what we have will seldom fall out fully formed but rather that they emerge and develop. That process takes place through the interplay of ideas. Ideas are living things which alter each other. The concept of pay ratios would have been difficult to arrive at if it had not been for the idea of a minimum wage before it. Quite simply, without *lots* of ideas it is very much more difficult to generate ideas which are likely to work. It is important to have a lot of ideas because that is their natural state; ideas are a pack animal.

The fourth reason that ideas are important is the straightforward reason that when they work they make things better. If we don't imagine cures for cancer, we won't find them. If we don't imagine alternatives to poverty, poverty will never be eradicated. It is essential that we generate many more ideas about how to improve our world for the simple reason that our world needs improving.

And there is a final reason why ideas are important; that is that people need to be able to believe that things can be better. In a pre-Enlightenment world most people believed that change was the gift of God. They believed that only God could save them. In a post-Enlightenment world we recognise that change is in our own hands, but the belief is different. We do not believe so much that we can save ourselves, but that ideas can save us. There are plenty of people who are unhappy about the gross inequalities in our society, but as we have seen they have been led to believe that nothing can be done, that there are no alternatives, that what we have is the inevitable result of some cosmic law. If they can be shown that there are solutions to the inequality, solutions that work, they will start to believe in change again. Above all, ideas are the antidote to hopelessness.

Big change starts in small ways

It has been the aim of this book to lay bare the means through which hopelessness has been engendered. In doing this the aim has been to map out the dimensions and limits of hopelessness to show how much there is beyond those limits. It has been an attempt to show that the bars of our cage are not the end of our horizon and that we can imagine things greater than these limitations. There are many of us who wonder, not why haven't we achieved utopia, but more modestly where is our *Republic*, our *Com-*

munist Manifesto, our *Peaceful Path to Real Reform?* Where is our *plan* for a utopia?

Earlier it was argued that change never seems less possible than at the point just before it begins. When Rosa Parks refused to give up her seat to a white person on that bus it would have seemed a small and futile act. It of course sparked the final battles in the civil rights movement. The small groups of people who started the fight for a Scottish Parliament in the late 1960s seemed impotent and isolated at the time. Within 30 years it was a reality. Peaceful protest in India looked like an unlikely way to end imperial occupation. Nixon's crushing re-election in 1972 made him look untouchable. In fact, it is easy to create a very long list of things which happened because of small acts and because of small groups of people.

And so this is the final message of this book. Certainly it can be difficult to take on (never mind defeat) powerful interest groups. But throughout history big change has come in small ways. The impotence of progressives is often self imposed. Again and again throughout history a vibrant social imagination has changed the world for the better. We have to recapture such a social imagination in the early years of this new century. To do that we must liberate ourselves from the mindset that suffocates that social imagination, and to do that we must look dispassionately at the means of control which engenders that mindset.

Hope, ideas and the belief that things can be better have improved the lives of millions of people throughout history and they have changed the world. They will again.